I Am Mister Ed...

Allan "Rocky" Lane
Revealed

Linda Alexander

Published in the USA by:
BearManor Media
PO Box 1129
Duncan, Oklahoma 73534-1129
www.bearmanormedia.com

ISBN 978-1-59393-573-3

Printed in the United States of America.
Cover photo courtesy Emma Bushnell Private Collection.
Book design by Brian Pearce | Red Jacket Press.

Table of Contents

Allan "Rocky" Lane with his horse, Thunder, signed to his brother and sister-in-law, Tom and Jennie Costello. PHOTO COURTESY THE COSTELLO FAMILY COLLECTION

Allan, this one's for you. Thanks for all your help.

Acknowledgements and Gratitude

I thank God for giving me the ability to write to express, to tell a story, and to look into the past into the lives of people who have had an impact on the worlds of so many others.

My husband, *Tom Prevost*, is my rock and my love. I appreciate you in so many ways I can never fully express. Thank you for your always-there support.

Michael Napier and *Erik Napier*, always my boys no matter how old we all get, and *Kevin Prevost, Daniel Prevost, Richard Prevost* and your families, I'm a lucky lady to have all of you in my life.

This book would have never — I repeat, never — have happened without the assistance of Allan Lane's family. When I began the investigation needed to do justice to his life story, I was told by many people in-the-know for the "B" Western movie genre there were no living members of Allan Lane's family. In some ways, this proved to be borderline true but in the most important ways it could not have been further from the truth.

Allan Lane may not today have living family from his bloodline. Harry Albershart, however, has family who continue to claim him as their own, still lovingly calling him "Uncle Harry." When I found the Costello crew I found a group of people who had wanted for years to tell the truth about the man they knew as an uncle but had not yet figured out how to put his story together.

Allan — or Harry — was related to them by marriage. His mother married the Costello's grandfather and, in doing so, she became their beloved Gramanne. Harry became their larger-than-life uncle. These folks have generously shared memories and many personal effects, including photographs, documents, private family memories, and Allan's physical identification items to help this book offer a well-rounded and more accurate picture of Harry Albershart the man, also known as Allan "Rocky" Lane the actor, and Rocky Lane the horseman.

I can't thank *Pat Grayson-DeJong* enough. She has shared memories of life with her Uncle Harry and her grandmother, Gramanne, as well as professional insight and her friendship. I'm honored. *Tom Costello* shared his recollections, and he made sure photos and other Allan Lane personal effects were available to me. *Gerri Scharff* and her daughter, *Joeline Ojea*, were my first contacts with the Costello family. *John Costello* and *Judi Costello* each helped make it possible for the ball to start rolling. My deepest appreciation, Costello family.

Loretta "Lore" Kemsley kindly answered my query after I found her name and e-mail online via a *Mister Ed* website. Her insight into about twenty years of cowboy life as it related to Allan and others in his circle of acquaintances has given me a firsthand awareness I could not have found elsewhere. From there, we exchanged details, writing, and a shared interest in looking into the past. She has a wonderful website about her experiences growing up as the daughter of a horse trainer for early Hollywood, *http://ponymansdaughter.wordpress.com*. Happy to be able to call you a friend, Lore.

Bill "Pete" Peterson is a gem of a man. Pete knew Allan personally as a friend and confidante. His memories offered a look into Allan in his later years, allowing me a view of him which had never before been shared. Pete wrote Allan's eulogy — a beautiful tribute from the heart — and read it aloud at Allan's funeral. I'm grateful he allowed me to include it in this book.

Mac MacBride and *Dan Smith*, both involved with the horse racing industry, helped me find Pete Peterson, and for that I owe them a heaping dose of appreciation.

Rick Schneider gave me a great amount of insight into his aunt, Gladys Leslie [Schneider], Allan's first wife. His information on Gladys's family and career as well as his thoughts on her relationship with Allan, allowed me to dig deeper and close in on difficult-to-find minutiae. He was also a truly kind sounding board for my ideas. My deepest thanks, Rick.

Steve Morenberg was the son-in-law of Allan's last wife, Emma Raimondo Bushnell. He shared stories that gave me pertinent historical details. He also offered the use of documents and photos from Emma's personal collection. The cover photo of Allan Lane was owned by Emma and kept over the years since their divorce.

Larry Hilton shared memories of his uncle, Les Hilton, Mister Ed's trainer and friend to Allan Lane. His input, important to the final product, put to rest some unanswered questions!

My cousin in Los Angeles, *Annette Lockett*, was the perfect research partner. She went with me to cemeteries, libraries, church offices, interviews, house drive-bys, and any number of locations only a fellow genealogist and researcher would go. She and her husband, *Mike Lockett*, took me into their house, fed me, and made me feel at home. Love and thanks. Annette, there's another book waiting for us!

Richard Turner, Annette's son, thoughtfully checked with his personal contacts, of his own accord, to help me search for otherwise impossible-to-find details. Never underestimate the power of human kindness.

Cindy Walkov of Pinnacle Estate Properties in Los Angeles went out of her way to assist me — a stranger — as I dug even deeper. If you're moving to the San Fernando Valley, look her up!

Donna Gatti, excellent writer and friend and well-known in the world of angels, supported and encouraged me during the process of writing this book. Blessings, Donna.

Donna's writing critique group in Martinsburg, West Virginia, offered excellent suggestions and support whenever I dropped in to spend quality time with them. Their ideas added to the final product.

Karen Duffy gave me an enlightened perspective which really opened my eyes to issues connected with this story. I miss our lunches, Karen.

Lou Lettieri and *Sally Fraser* spoke about their experiences during filming of the failed *Red Ryder* TV pilot in which Allan Lane starred.

Alan Young gave me a phone interview and clarified issues which have remained murky over the years. I appreciate his kindness. In relation to this interview, I thank *Carol Summers* and *Rick Lertzman* for getting me in touch with Mr. Young.

Anita Stidham and her daughter, *Cyndi Nistal*, and her son, *Michael Stidham*, helped me learn about the California horse racing world of the 1960s and 1970s. They aided my research tremendously.

Peter McKay, son of actor Scott McKay, shared details about his father's career and what went on in his life after the airing of what is now widely known as the initial Mister Ed pilot, *The Wonderful World of Wilbur Pope*. Peter helped fill in the blanks.

Nancy Nalven authored *The Famous Mister Ed, The Unbridled Truth About America's Favorite Talking Horse*, published by Warner Books in 1991, and via e-mail she shared thoughts based on her research.

Babbie Green, daughter of Betty Furness, offered information only a family member could know.

I'm grateful to *Chuck Thornton* for his kindness when I started my work with this difficult project. As co-writer of the first book on Allan, *Allan*

"Rocky" Lane, Republic's Action Ace, authored with *David Rothel*, Chuck was one of the pioneers. David shared his thoughts and experience with me from working on that book. Both men forged a road toward a complete truth about Allan Lane.

Chuck Anderson owns, operates, and puts an extraordinary amount of time into an excellent website titled "The Old Corral" at: *http://www.b-westerns.com*. Chuck was instrumental in giving me a quick education in early Western entertainment history when I first began. He was always willing to offer answers to questions, and opinions when I had a theory, and he took time to go over the manuscript to check for historical errors from Allan's Western serial days. Thank you, Chuck.

Bobby Copeland, author of *Allan "Rocky" Lane, The Mystery Cowboy*, shared thoughts on what he knew and suspected of Allan's history…even though he was working on his book at the same time.

Rick Freudenthal thoughtfully sent me archived photos of Allan after nothing more than a voicemail from me. He and his wife have my gratitude for their generosity.

Bill Sasser, involved with the popular Williamsburg Film Festival, thoughtfully contacted me for author *Tinsley Yarbrough*. Tinsley offered photos and information very important to Allan's story, details I had not been able to find. My thanks to both men.

Many others jumped in to help after nothing more than a blind request from a stranger. I hope I mention everyone. If I missed you, my deepest apologies. These people were:

Fr. Denis P. Ahern, S.J. with Cincinnati's St. Xavier High School; John Bergeron; The family of Pat Buttram and Sheila Ryan Buttram; Bill Cappello; Mike Cline; Candice Curtis with Horse Racing Nation; Carolyn Daitch; James D'Arc, curator of Brigham Young University's Arts & Communications Archives; Rob DeCleene, *http://www.visit-southbend.com*; Pat Doyle, *http://www.baseball-almanac.com*; T. W. "Wally" Dunn; Tad Dunn; Gary Ewing, son of Gladys Leslie Ewing; Sue Forshey, http://www.bonanza.com/booths/Yesterdayswhisper; Joan R. Francis with Inglewood Cemetery; Russell "Cappy" Gagnon; Sandra Garcia-Myers, Ph.D at USC Cinematic Arts Library; Roger M. Grace, Editor/Co-Publisher of Metropolitan News-Enterprise; Tony Guzman with The Academy of Motion Picture Arts and Sciences; Doug Hegar; Mark G. Heike with AC Comics; Kathi Hill; Linda A. Hutchings, Brigham Young University; Lori Jackson of the Albershart Family; Kristine Krueger with National Film Information Service, The Margaret Herrick Library; actress Zohra Lampert; Wil Langford writing as Bill Peterson;

Dennis Lieberson, son of Will Lieberson of Fawcett Comics; Stephen Lodge; Susan Lowery of the Heritage Center of the Mishawaka [IN] Public Library; Claudia Luther with UCLA; Carlton Maese; Tod Maher; Boyd Majers; Vivian Montoya and others with the California Thoroughbred Breeders Association; Yvonne Ng, Reference Librarian for Arcadia [CA] Public Library; Gordon Olson; Chandra Powell with Texas Christian University; Dorothy and staff members with St. Mary's Catholic Church in Grand Rapids, Michigan; Camille Soriano, Pam Copeland, Teri Eve, and Debbie Felt of The Sandpipers Organization, http://www.sandpipers.org; Kathleen Schmitt with Cincinnati's Christ Hospital; Becky Schulte with Cincinnati's St. Xavier High School; Doug Senior, *http://www.boomerhead.com;* Fred Trueblood; Barbara Vander Mark, *http://mygrandrapids.info;* Marc Wanamaker of Bison Archives; and Denise Zigler with South Bend's [IN] Morris Performing Arts Center.

Foreword by Pat Grayson-DeJong, M.Ed.

Allan "Rocky" Lane was my uncle through my grandmother's marriage to my grandfather, Will Costello. We knew him as Uncle Harry. While we did not see our famous uncle nearly as often as we would have wished, when he did come to our family functions, he was the center of our attention. He was the uncle who always spent time entertaining and clowning around with us children while the other grown-ups talked in another room. Uncle Harry had no children of his own so I think he genuinely enjoyed being in our company.

One thing I remember most about my uncle was his loyalty to his family. His mother, Anne Costello, the grandmother I adored, had a very hard life trying to raise two children (Harry and Helen) on her own. Harry's father, William Albershart, left my grandmother and their two children early in their marriage. My grandmother was forced to cobble together a living with an eighth grade education and little else. What she did have was a great love for her children and a desire to keep them together no matter what the cost. Harry learned early on that in order to help his family survive he was going to have to work to help support his mother and his sister Helen. His loyalty to his mother and his sister continued throughout his entire lifetime.

To me, Uncle Harry was bigger than life. When he walked into a room, he was not only the tallest man I had ever seen (most likely 6'3" or more) but also the most handsome. I never saw him without his cowboy regalia and I would look in awe to this larger than life human specimen and think, "This is the kind of man I want someday." When he spoke, his voice was deep and resonant and commanded everyone's attention. It is not at all surprising that when he hit Hollywood, producers and directors were anxious to sign him up on his good looks and remarkable voice alone.

However, in this book, Linda Alexander begins to peel away the many layers that were my uncle and also show that Hollywood is fickle. In those days, you had to fit a particular mold to be successful. Allan Lane did not fit the typical Hollywood matinee idol of the day. He could be rude, abrupt, angry, and sometimes unpredictable. He was inflexible in his thinking and according to some, had no sense of humor. While his acting talent was impeccable, he had little tolerance for stupidity or for people who did not take the job of acting seriously. He had an incredible work ethic and didn't do well with those in the industry who did not. His anti-social behavior got him into many scrapes with the elite of Hollywood and he often found himself without work in his beloved field of acting.

This behavior spilled over into his personal life and his relationships with women. I only remember meeting one of my Uncle Harry's four wives and her name was Emma. She was as nice as she was beautiful. I was so disappointed when I learned that just months later they had divorced. Sadly, none of his marriages lasted more than a year. This says something about his unyielding personality. It is clear that my uncle desired a close and enduring relationship with a woman as evidenced by his many marriages. However he lacked the requisite tools to maintain a long-term relationship with anyone.

As a person who has spent most of my adult life studying, teaching and lecturing on the subject of autism spectrum disorders, it occurs to me that my uncle exhibited many of the same characteristics as a person with Asperger Syndrome. While it is impossible to know for sure since he is no longer here to observe or to interview, people who have this disorder tell us that their lives are very difficult because they do not understand the social rules and nuances of relationships. They spend their entire lives seeking companionship, yet are often unsuccessful in maintaining those relationships. Through no fault of their own, they are born with an inability to understand sarcasm or irony in conversations, facial expressions and body language, understanding others emotions, and understanding the give and take in conversations and in relationships. People with Asperger Syndrome must train themselves to mimic other people's responses. This is not an easy task but it is one that many people with this disorder can perfect to the point that you may not know they are any different from you and I until a situation occurs to which they have not perfected an appropriate response.

Perhaps Allan Lane spent his lifetime perfecting himself to look and act like any other guy when he was in the public sector. It is well known that Allan Lane was a wonderful actor. Could that have been the result of years of perfecting his ability to mimic others in order to fit in?? Perhaps the persona that he eventually became was of his own creation. Only God knows and we can only speculate at this point in time. It is important to note here that many famous and talented people have been diagnosed with Asperger. Of note is Susan Boyle, the *Britian's Got Talent* sensation who wowed the world with her magnificent voice. Other such notables are James Durbin, Dan Aykroyd, Daryl Hannah, Heather Kuzmich, and Temple Grandin.

Much has been written about Allan "Rocky" Lane that is not true. In this book, Linda Alexander has painstakingly uncovered another side of my uncle…a truer picture of the real person behind the persona of Allan "Rocky" Lane. Over the past year, she has shared many stories with me of how Allan himself helped her uncover never before revealed details about his life and his relationships. My family and I want to thank Linda for giving the kind and loving uncle we knew, a new voice. The voice that reveals the heart of who Allan "Rocky" Lane was.

Kindly submitted by:
Pat Grayson-DeJong, M.Ed., Rocky Allan Lane's niece
Autism Education Consultant and Lecturer
Granada Hills, California
http://www.autismdefender.com
2013

Preface

That is, of course, unless the horse is the famous...Allan "Rocky" Lane, the man behind the instantly recognizable voice of TV's now-iconic *Mister Ed.* Many have asked me why I chose Allan Lane as the subject for my book. My simple, though maybe odd, answer...Allan asked me to write his story.

Wrongly paraphrasing on purpose the TV show's theme song lyrics, I will say the generally accepted belief is that no one can talk to an individual who has passed on. Call me crazy — you won't be the first and you definitely won't be the last — but my truth is as it is. I did not choose to write about Allan Lane. Seems Allan needed to have his story told in more than simple sound bites, which is how it's been told to this date, and I happened to be the right biographer at the right time.

Things came about this way — as I got ready for work one morning, I turned on the TV at 6:30 and started flipping channels. For no reason of which I was consciously aware, I settled on *Mister Ed.* I had never watched the show as an adult and didn't recall seeing it as a child. As I looked up every now and then, but more importantly listened, I wondered, "Who was the voice for that horse?" I quickly realized there weren't any show credits to answer my question, so I began to search. And my curiosity heightened. Western entertainment historians would say I came late to this party and they would be correct, but by the time I discovered the answer to my initial question, slow on the uptake or otherwise, I already had dozens more lined up.

The more I dug into his background, the more Allan Lane proved to be overwhelmingly and irresistibly intriguing. He would not get out of my head. I learned he had a film resumé many A-list actors would have given their Screen Actors Guild card to be able to claim as their own. His story was full of flavor; had many ups and just as many downs; and had an admirable number of loves and more than his share of hates.

He had it all. He did it all. He lost it all.

Allan was well-known in his day and yet he was forgotten nearly as fast as one could say, "Mister Ed who?" In recent years, a slowly resurging awareness of how much he contributed to the entertainment industry has brought him back into an enlarging spotlight. Obviously, I didn't know who he was until I became curious about the voice of that funny talking horse. Yet the reality that Allan Lane, and Mister Ed, has his own sizeable following in the here-and-now is documented fact.

My process into the Allan Lane mystery began nearly two years ago. My research since then has taken me on a journey that has enlightened me about a man who was an enigma; a man difficult-to-know — as well as, in many ways, just plain difficult; and a man who has been, in my opinion, a sorely misunderstood public persona.

Truth is, he wasn't well-liked by the majority of his costars, and he knew this. He couldn't hold down a marriage — a fact that was certainly obvious to him. And if one is to believe — if is the word to pay attention to here — what has been publicly disseminated about him to date, he died without friends. This would be a sad commentary if it was all that was left of a man's legacy. I wanted to find out how much of what has been written about him to-date is fact. I wanted to learn why someone who had at one point been at the top of the entertainment heap had left this earth in such apparently unhappy circumstances.

He is no longer with us on this earth, so my book's intent is to offer an accurate and fair portrayal of Allan Lane. I hope I have made a respectable effort to show the how, why, and when of all those quirky bits of information that have previously been so widely circulated about him.

And Allan seemed willing to help me dig up the missing pieces of his story, of which there are layers upon layers. The deeper I got, the more I felt he was ready to give up his secrets. This was a monumental task which, at times, I thought I'd be unable to complete for a lack of verifiable information. But each time I was ready to surrender, details would somehow drop into my lap in ways I still cannot logically explain.

I took great pains to find people who had known Allan in his later years, particularly folks who were friends and acquaintances during his horse-racing period after *Mister Ed* left the screen. I interviewed a few actors who worked with him in his more undocumented roles. I admittedly did not do much in the way of interviewing anyone who worked with Allan during his *Red Ryder* or his *Rocky Lane* days.

This was intentional. Many such interviews have already been done, and the results are well-documented elsewhere by biographers such as Chuck Thornton, David Rothel, Bobby Copeland, and others. I do not question the truth of those interviews. No reason to reinvent that wheel. As well, a good many of those folks previously quoted are no longer with us to be inter-viewed again. I chose to instead focus on the to-date more hidden aspects of Allan Lane's life. I felt this would offer much more insight into the man he was by covering ground that has not yet been covered.

As written about that early poet, Juvenal, "The precise details of [his] life cannot be definitively reconstructed based on presently available evidence." I reference the mysterious Roman poet only because his life was so shrouded even in death, and his work is, for the most part, what stands for him after his passing. In his work has been found the core of the man himself. Juvenal, in some ways like Allan Lane, was caustic, difficult, and remains a mystery so many years beyond his lifetime. Yet still, people continue to try and figure him out.

There is much that *can* be definitively reconstructed about Allan Lane's life, and that is how this book came to be. I wanted to make every effort to put to rest, or offer background for, disparate details retold over the years in piece-meal about the actor and the man behind the actor…often two totally different people. Truth does not always equate to logic or to genuine understanding.

No one who could imbue a voiceless horse with such personality and even more, humanity and affection, could be all bad. The show, *Mister Ed*, was not the resounding success it has become for generations simply because of excellent writing, one good comedic actor, Alan Young, and a well-trained horse. There was another talented individual, a man on the scene from beginning to end, who was heavily involved in the achievements of the final equation. That man, Allan Lane, poured his personality into the figure of that talking animal through his unique voice and acting ability.

This is the personal story of Allan "Rocky" Lane…these days most widely known as either *Red Ryder* or *Rocky Lane* — both comic book heroes who came to life because of the actor who played them. Also, for my generation, this stands as an official and extensive public crediting of Allan Lane as the voice behind TV's talking horse, *Mister Ed*.

Allan Lane's Screen Actors Guild card. PHOTO COURTESY THE
COSTELLO FAMILY COLLECTION

Introduction

As of May 7, 1972, Allan Lane's Screen Actors Guild membership, stamped with that specific date, was to be renewed on the first of November of the following year. Allan was a member in good standing with the organization as well as a member of the California Thoroughbred Breeders Association and other official horse-related groups. He had a season pass for the grandstand box at Santa Anita, and he fully expected to play out the year, and many more, enjoying every minute he could at the track. Maybe there would be occasional work thrown in, if he could secure the jobs. But the track, going to the track, betting on the horses, and being amongst others who loved and understood the kind of horse-related life he loved, that was his happiness. That got him up in the morning. No one, least of all Allan himself, expected anything otherwise.

But life is what happens after plans are made. In September, Allan fell seriously ill, quite suddenly. He was in the hospital for six weeks, and he died at the end of October. His burial at the expansive and beautiful Inglewood Cemetery, right underneath a flight plan in and out of Los Angeles, took place on Halloween Day in 1973. The man born in Indiana as Harry Leonard Albershart, and known worldwide as *Red Ryder*, *Rocky Lane*, and the voice of TV's famous talking horse, *Mister Ed*, had died of a blood cancer called Myelofibrosis. Allan was sixty-four years old.

He had long been professionally known as Allan Lane during all those years of his Guild membership and even for years before. In his middle years, little boys and girls had known him first as the comic book hero *Red Ryder*, and then as *Rocky Lane* — a character created exclusively for him. Those personas were put to celluloid, and for a long time, kids delighted in seeing him on the big screen at the Saturday afternoon matinee picture show, saving damsels and children in distress, riding his horse far and wide over the Wild West, and making sure the bad guys always, always got their due — but never without a good gun battle and at least a few fistfights in the process. And justice always prevailed.

Yet that was only one of multiple generations to have seen this man's work on the silver screen. In his earliest days in Hollywood, his main audience had been adults. He was part of such films as the comedy *Maid's Night Out* (1938), the action-filled *King of the Royal Mounted* (1940), and many others. He made women swoon as he graced drawing rooms in some stories, and men cheered as he saved the world in other stories. He played opposite the likes of Loretta Young, Joan Fontaine, Lucille Ball, Shirley Temple, and Linda Stirling who was *The Tiger Woman* (1944)... many of the most beautiful, or well-known, or beautiful and well-known ladies in Hollywood.

In his more recent years, he had not often been seen but certainly had been heard, imbuing an otherwise-voiceless horse, *Mister Ed*, with not only the right tones to bring forth laughs from a well-written script but also to infuse heart, soul, and humanity into an animal he honestly felt he understood. Allan knew Mister Ed personally, and he represented him in a believable way so audiences would never question the horse's human side. And audiences never did question that horse's human side. *Mister Ed* was simply Mister Ed, a talking horse, real and authentic, with a voice that deserved to be heard...in great part thanks to Allan "Rocky" Lane.

Allan's entertainment career spanned over forty years on the large and small screens, in comic books, and in a vast array of product placements. Yet, when the cameras were turned off and publicity machines ceased to run on his behalf, his closest friends, most at the racetrack, knew him as Rocky. To his beloved mother and family he was always, and until the day he died, simply known as Harry. He had never officially changed his name.

Soon after he passed away, family members went to his apartment to clean it out. "It was a mess," his nephew Tom Costello explained, shaking his head. Tom's father, Allan's stepbrother, had been amongst those in the cleaning crew and related to his son what he saw. "Not a dirty mess but papers everywhere...racing sheets and horse rosters. Papers were everywhere."

Loretta Kemsley, as a teenager, lived next door to a man named Les Hilton. Les, a famous horse and animal trainer for the entertainment industry, was Mister Ed's trainer, and he and Allan were good friends. Loretta, known as Lore, met Allan at Les's home and spent time with him and Les's other cowboy friends. She knew these men as a young teenager would know neighbors and casual friends, and she believed Allan was without question "a horse person." As she pointed out, "Horse people are different. They don't relate in the same way as other people do."

Lore could say this with authority because she counted herself in the same category. She grew up around horses. Her father had trained animals for the Selig Zoo, an amazing establishment in its time, which grew out of the original Selig Polyscope Company, Southern California's first permanent movie studio. Lore's background gave her a deep love and awareness of horses, and she felt she understood them and they understood her much better than any human ever could. This is also how she saw Allan.

"He was always nice to us kids," she said. "Never a harsh word."

So what if this was Allan's truth? What if Allan Lane, the horse person, was a man who didn't know how to relate well to adults? What if, for reasons unknown then, his social and communication skills amongst adults were severely lacking? Yet, in the next breath, what if he was effortlessly able to engage four-legged creatures, young children, and teenagers?

What was the *real* story of Allan "Rocky" Lane?

CHAPTER ONE

The Beginning

According to a notice in the *South Bend Weekly Tribune*, "A son was born Tuesday to Mr. and Mrs. Albershart, of 224 East Joseph Street." The date was September 22, 1909, and the location was Mishawaka, Indiana. The child was beloved by his parents, particularly his mother. Getting a son into *this* family — a son who might thrive to adulthood — had been a hard-won battle.

Harry *Leonard* Albershart was to be the only living son of William Herbert and Linnie Anne Dayhuff Albershart. There was already a daughter, and there had been two other male children born to this couple. Both of those baby boys had been named Harry. Harry *Herman* Albershart came at the end of September in 1905 and died on a Sunday evening in early December of the same year. His mother and father buried him in the Mishawaka Cemetery. Another Harry, with "W" as his middle initial, likely William, arrived a few years before Harry Leonard, and Harry W. lived for only three years.

When Harry Leonard was born, there was cautious celebration in the Albershart household. His mother poured her every breath into this child, praying he would survive, thrive, and live a long life. A big baby, he weighed in at ten pounds at birth. Anne doted on him. When he got his first haircut, she saved a few of the original soft blond locks. She kept a meticulous baby book, noting how he offered the world his first laugh when he was only a month; gained nine pounds by the time he was three months old; and had added six more pounds in the next three months.

With each new day that dawned, a healthy one for Baby Harry Leonard, his mother's hopes for him grew stronger. More, never less, attention was heaped on her son, and nothing he did was too small to note in that baby book or to share with anyone who would listen.

Harry wore his first short clothes when he was but six months old and got his first pair of shoes only a little while later. He was an early talker, too. His first words were the usual, "Papa," "Mamma," and "Dada," but his mother considered him amazing, of course, since all these endearments were spoken before he was one year old. She was positively enamored that he took his first steps when he was barely a month shy of his original golden year.

Over the years, in any number of records and family details, Harry's mom was called Anne, Linnie Anne, Annie, and sometimes Anna. Her family said she "hated" the name of Annie and didn't care for Linnie. This book calls her Anne since that was the name she most often officially used and the one she preferred. Harry's father is addressed as Bill.

Anne had also been born in Mishawaka, in 1887. She was barely a child herself when, just shy of sixteen, she married Bill Albershart on July 11, 1903. In total, she bore him five children, based on detail listed for her in the United States census of 1940. Their marriage officially lasted eight years.

Helen Mae, their only daughter, entered the world in Mishawaka in 1907, a few years before Harry Leonard. The fifth child indicated in the census — one more in addition to Helen and Harry Leonard and the boys who passed on early — is known of only because of that official data. No detail has survived, except that the child was born after Harry Leonard. It is surmised the baby may have died at childbirth, since this is the only one who seemed to not have been given a proper birth name.

All of these children, including Harry Leonard, were born to a woman who thought there was nothing more important in life than the wellbeing of her offspring. From his earliest days, Harry favored her over his father. Exactly why is unknown. The troubled dynamics of the overall family, immediate and extended, ultimately reveal stories he and Helen would have lived through, offering insight into how his personal history was formed.

A number of odd, disturbing situations arose during Harry's adolescence. These instances help paint a picture of a background which, at very least, was unstable and volatile.

One of Anne's brothers was William "Bill" Dayhuff. When Harry was a small boy, Bill and his wife, Emma, owned a general store in Fairland, Michigan, about forty miles from Mishawaka. Harry and Helen were regular visitors, roaming the aisles and warming their hands on cold winter days over the big stove in the middle of the old building. At five and seven years of age, they would consume penny candy given to them by their aunt and uncle. Uncle Bill married Aunt Emma long before Harry and Helen came into the world, so the kids grew up knowing both of them as family.

On a cold February day in 1914, a local boy, nearly eighteen-year-old Harold Ullery, visited the store and struck up a friendly conversation with Aunt Emma. Local chatter said they were on cordial terms and he had done this many times before.

Yet on this particular Tuesday afternoon, as Emma stood near the stove looking out the window during one of her chats with Harold, something

Left: *Anne Dayhuff and William Albershart wedding photo; she was sixteen and he was twenty-seven.* Right: *Anne Dayhuff Albershart.* PHOTOS COURTESY THE COSTELLO FAMILY COLLECTION

went dreadfully wrong. For reasons he never truly explained, he unflinchingly took a revolver from his pocket and shot Emma in the head. Then, according to police reports, he calmly walked past her dead body, took all the store money she kept in a cigar box behind the counter and stuffed it in his pockets, along with candy and gum he grabbed on his way out the door.

Initially, Harold admitted only to visiting the store that day and returning later with a number of locals after hearing Mrs. Dayhuff was dead. Earliest reports said she had passed away from natural causes. However, it wasn't long before law officials had reason to be suspicious and the boy became the subject of an intense public investigation that was publicized not only locally but throughout the region.

The scandal did not go away quickly and was news report fodder for months, repeatedly making the front page of the local papers. As the plot thickened, official investigators were called in. Once it was obvious Emma Dayhuff's death did not result from natural causes, her body was more closely examined. A bullet was discovered and dug out of her head, with careful attention paid to the trajectory of the shot that put it there.

Emma Dayhuff's death certificate. Cause of death: Gunshot, murdered.

A potential scenario was established, and all it took from there was to get Harold to talk. He easily cracked under pressure and admitted to ending Mrs. Dayhuff's life but said it had been "an accident." He explained simply, "I just shot for the fun of it. Of course I didn't mean to kill her."

Emma's funeral drew folks from far and near. As a newspaper article read, "…practically the entire countryside turned out." There were many Dayhuff family members in the surrounding areas and not only the large extended family but great numbers of friends, as well as the plainly curious, showed up to learn of the young man's fate. The public wanted justice. A trial ensued and Harold Ullery was ultimately convicted of Emma Dayhuff's cold-blooded killing. "Impulsive murder without a motive," was the sheriff's determination, and a jury agreed.

Emma had been well-liked. The store had been a local gathering place for a long time. On the other side of this high-profile tragedy, Harold's parents were well-respected local farmers who also held a visible profile in the community. From the extraordinary amount of press that followed from beginning to end, an overall manic mood was shown to grip the community.

Anne Dayhuff Albershart, her siblings and her husband as well as their children, lived amidst the hysteria that accompanied this tragic and sense-less death. Anne attended Emma's funeral as well as Harold Ullery's trial. Helen was seven, and Harry Leonard was four-and-a-half. The family rented a two-story house situated a block off the railroad tracks that cut through Mishawaka, about three blocks and then some from where Bill usually worked at the Mishawaka Woolen Manufacturing Company. Since Bill and Anne had started their family, they moved from one small rented home to another, moving on every few years, and sometimes even yearly.

The murderer, eighteen-year-old Harold Ullery, was sentenced to prison for life. Two years later, he died there; the official cause was "inter-nal hemorrhage of long-standing." There was no physician on record, and a coroner's signature indicated he had verified the death but had not attended to the deceased prior to his passing. Did Harold commit suicide? There was no indication of it, but this brought the horrific situation back to the forefront for the community as well as the Albershart and Dayhuff families, and all their relatives.

Bill and Anne divorced the same year Harold Ullery died. On the sur-face, available information appears to show Bill did his part to support his wife and children. They were not dirt poor but didn't have a lot of money either. He worked various jobs throughout his time as a family man — laborer, salesman, machine operator.

It was June of 1916, a few months before Harry's seventh birthday, in an era when divorce was not well-accepted. If at all possible, a woman would usually stick with the marriage for financial reasons, the sake of the children, or both. Anne would not have been able to take care of herself, let alone herself and her children. Yet according to her granddaughter, Pat Grayson-DeJong, she was a strong and steely woman. Anne could be hard and difficult but in the next turn, deeply loving. Always the ultimate caretaker. Her children were her world.

So what caused her to move out of the family unit in which she had borne her children, away from a situation, dire or otherwise, where she had the certainty of a roof over their heads and food in their mouths? According to school documents, Bill was the caretaker on record for the children prior to the divorce, seemingly logical since he would have been considered the head of the household. The first full year after he and

Bill Albershart in an undated photo, probably taken in Mishawaka in the early days. PHOTO COURTESY THE COSTELLO FAMILY COLLECTION

Anne split, he was still named as their "parent, guardian, head of family, or person having charge of child or children."

What would have made Anne leave her children in the care of their father and go out on her own? Reading between the lines, other information potentially shows how the situation wasn't that simple.

Years later, official studio biographies and newspaper articles for Allan Lane, the Hollywood actor, state that when he was about seven, and during many summers afterward, he visited his "aunt and uncle's vast cattle ranch near Clovis, New Mexico." He did have paternal family connections in New Mexico, so this ranch appears to have been owned and/or operated by one of his dad's brothers or cousins. Harry may have been sent to a relative's home during this tumultuous time to give him a place to live while his parents sorted out more permanent arrangements. The specific "aunt and uncle," however, has never been definitively identified.

That same year, at the tender age of seven, "Harry Albershart" was listed in the city directory as working for the Mishawaka Woolen Manufacturing Company. He wasn't living with any member of his family. Instead, his home address was that of a Mrs. Josephine Eminger, a sixty-year-old widow who had run a boarding house for five years, since her husband's death. Harry's dad was not publicly listed, and his mother was also missing from major local records.

Yet their little boy was well-represented in the town directory. This was a clear-cut indication of how splintered Harry's family life had become. Other official early records show how he went to work early in life to help out with the family's financial woes. He was, in essence, on his own. This proved to be the start of him making his way. Far beyond his chronological years, Harry was forced to develop his own lifestyle, apart from his broken family. He also had to learn how to protect himself, both physically and emotionally. All of this would eventually become something of his trademark in years to come. At first as Harry Albershart, and then as Allan Lane, but no matter the name, he realized he could depend on few people beside himself.

This was backed up in a snippet Allan related in a May 1931 interview. He told a reporter he began "supporting himself" when he was seven, "first by selling papers, then by shining shoes after school hours." As an adult, he proved to have a stellar work ethic, one that people often remarked about. In his earliest years, doing the job right made the difference between having a place to sleep and food to eat. As he got older, this was ingrained into him as his way of life, of utmost importance even if the decisions he made cost him personal relationships. The man who would become Allan Lane learned, as a young boy named Harry Albershart, what it meant to see to his own well-being and earn an honest dollar.

On one hand, Harry was trying to find out where he belonged in the world. On the other, he was simply trying to survive. The following year, he experienced another personal upheaval directly at the hands of his mother. This new event explained why he had been without either parent during the later part of the year before.

On January 2, 1917, about six-and-a-half months after her divorce, Anne remarried. Her new husband was Dean Richard Null, and the wedding took place in Indianapolis. Being a divorced woman was nothing of which to be proud, and trying to keep herself and two children above water on her own would have been a lot to handle, if not impossible. Anne only had an eighth grade education and she lived by her wits. The new union explained why she had left Harry and Helen behind with their dad.

This was heartbreaking for both mother and kids but seemingly a choice made with the children's well-being in mind.

By June of 1919, when Harry was ten years old and Helen was twelve, official guardianship had been transferred to Anne. She once again had her children with her. Bill had remarried a few months earlier, on April 21. His second wedding was performed by the Reverend Ulysses S. Davis at the First Baptist Church in Mishawaka. Seemingly, Bill had a predisposition for women of a similar name. His new wife was Anna Thomas Easterday, a widow whose first husband had passed away about three years earlier.

Harry, his sister, mother, and stepfather started out their new life together in Mishawaka but it appeared not all was wonderful in their household. When the City Directory was printed for that year, Anne's new husband was physically in South Bend with another woman. Anne was in Mishawaka, working as a stenographer for the Mishawaka Woolen Manufacturing Company. Within days after the New Year of 1920, Anne and Dean had moved together to Grand Rapids, Michigan. If the United States census is to be believed, they had no children with them in their household.

Young Harry Albershart, barefoot and reading a book. PHOTO COURTESY THE COSTELLO FAMILY COLLECTION

By this time, Harry and his sister — nine and eleven — had already experienced a tumultuous life. They had a mother and a father, a stepfather and a stepmother, a local caretaker, and any number of aunts, uncles, and cousins, both local and out of state. Back again with their father, now with their new stepmother, they were expending all their childhood energies trying to navigate the landscape of life in Indiana after their mother's move to Michigan.

Family continued to offer colorful background for these growing-up years. John Burton "Bert" Dayhuff, a saloon owner, was one of Anne's many brothers. As early as 1910, regular articles on him and his business started appearing in Elkhart, Indiana, newspapers. Bert went up against the townspeople many times in attempts to acquire or renew his liquor license. He usually won. Another article told of when someone broke into his saloon; along with the police, Bert helped to apprehend the criminal.

Later in the year, Bert was once again in the news, but this time, he stood on the wrong side of the law. Arrested one evening in Mishawaka,

Left: *Brother and sister, Harry and Helen Albershart clowning around in Mishawaka, Indiana.* Right: *Harry in his early teens.* PHOTOS COURTESY THE COSTELLO FAMILY COLLECTION

he was charged with driving an automobile while intoxicated and colliding with "a machine" at ten o'clock. The report said no one was "badly injured" but both automobiles were heavily impacted, and property damage was extensive.

He behaved for a number of months, but that wasn't to last. In February of 1921, Uncle Bert was again arrested for drunk driving. Unlike a few years before, this time the other individuals unwittingly involved were not as fortunate. A newspaper headline read, "Runs Down Mishawaka Children." Bert Dayhuff had jumped a curb and "seriously injured" an eight-year-old boy and "less seriously hurt" his five-year-old sister. "Dayhuff had been drinking and was not in a fit condition to drive his car," the article finished.

Harry was twelve years old when his Uncle Bert ran over these children, and he was only four years older than the injured boy. Mishawaka was a tight community. Most everyone knew everyone else. The stain of such a near-tragedy may have left a shadow hanging over the family as Harry and his sister lived within this environment.

Anne remained married to Dean Null, still living in Grand Rapids in 1921. Harry may have gone back and forth between his parents but likely stayed for the longest periods with his father. In October of 1923, when he was only fourteen, he received commentary in the *Indianapolis Star* for his bowling prowess. He was a member of the Capitol No. 2 League in a team called The Capitol Alleys. This, along with the Mishawaka School District records, shows he was in Indiana with his father. Though somewhere in here Helen had gone to be with her mother and stepfather, these records indicate Harry had not yet joined them in Michigan — at least not permanently.

Dean Null passed away on June 28, 1924. Anne, living under the name of Anna Null, found herself single once more. Helen, now a young single student, lived with her at 843 Broadway Ave NW, creating a two-person household that required income to make it viable. Anne took in laundry, in no way a high-paying position. Harry was fifteen and still working at odd jobs. How much of his income went to support himself, his dad, or maybe was sent to his mother and sister, is unknown.

This period marked a transition for both Helen and Harry. His home life had thus far been beyond the pale, and even though the facts as to when he left home, and exactly why he left home, aren't set in stone, he appears to have finally decided there was little benefit in staying in his father's house, or in any attempt to live with his financially struggling mother. Instead, he once more went out on his own.

No one in the family could have known it at the time but life was to change forever for them when, on November 25, 1924, Anna Dayhuff Albershart Null became Mrs. William Costello in Grand Rapids. The marriage was performed at St. Mary's Catholic Church by the Reverend Joannes J. Riess.

Getting married in the Catholic Church was no easy task for a non-Catholic. The Church required that each individual be baptized as a Catholic before the ceremony would be performed. The process wasn't a quick one. Despite only five months between her previous husband's death and her next wedding, Anne did what she had to do to become Mrs.

Costello. She was accepted into the Church with an "absolute baptism" performed a few days before the wedding on November 22. Daughter Helen also received the sacrament, about a week earlier, though hers came with conditions.

How Anne met William Costello is unknown. How she came to be enveloped in the Church despite her previously divorced status is also in question. Her marriage to Bill Albershart had been performed in the Baptist Church. That ceremony would not have been recognized by the Catholic Church despite the children born of the union. Her last marriage had ended in her spouse's death but that one wouldn't have been recognized, either, due to her previous divorce. However the situation came to be, Anne and her daughter became part of a newly minted, sincere Catholic family.

Marriage certificate for Anne Albershart Null and William Costello.

Anne's husband was a factory worker in the airplane parts industry and a widower four years her senior. Will Costello owned his own home and had three young children when they united, the oldest only ten, just five years younger than Harry. The youngest was four. With one spoken "I do," Anne became a mother figure for three additional children, all of whom lived in her physical household while Harry did not.

Was Harry upset that his mother now took care of other children as if they were her own? He had initially moved from his father's home in Indiana to Kent County, Michigan, most likely to live with her. Records show Anne's new family included Will Costello, his children, and Helen. No sign of Harry. It's logical to believe he probably stayed there whenever he didn't live elsewhere, though census records and other documents do not show him as a member of the household at any time.

All of fifteen years old, he appears to have gone on to do his own thing. This is documented by newspaper tidbits that name him as a member of the Bay City Baseball Club in Bay City, Michigan, part of the

Michigan-Ontario League. This all played out about two hours away from where his mother resided. The Michigan-Ontario League represented a number of cities in the state, including Kent County, Bay City, and Grand Rapids. Harry would have been able to play for this bunch, periodically leaving his mother's home and going back and forth between where she lived, and wherever he was playing at the time.

CHAPTER TWO

A Brush
With The Spotlights

Harry was simply trying to find his way. The young man who began life as Harry Albershart had his first brush with the actor's spotlight roundabout the spring of 1925 after a return trip to the South Bend area from Michigan. A local production of a play called *The Patsy* opened. Harry received a part, possibly as a result of a favor he was finally able to call in from Arnold Bertram, a man whose shoes he had shined years before as a seven-year-old boy.

In those earlier days, one of Harry's more notable customers was Bertram, called by some "the dramatic impresario of South Bend." Mishawaka and South Bend, being all of about seven miles apart, were basically interchangeable at the time. The Mishawaka phone directory was, for example, a subset of the South Bend directory.

Harry's official history states he boldly asked the experienced theater man for an acting job. Bertram "promised to remember him," not the exact response Harry was looking for as he tried to find solid work. Bertram was part of a vaudeville duo called "Bertram and Andres," and his musical shows played out on the road. This was now about eight years later, and Bertram had remembered young Harry, making good on his promise.

Harry Albershart found the stage.

Official stories tell how Harry was in his second year at Notre Dame at this time. All such stories of him playing football for Notre Dame have proved to be untrue. He would have only been sixteen so regardless of any truth about his prowess on the football field, Harry Albershart would have simply been too young. He was, instead, scrapping around here and there, ultimately finding his way to a bit part in *The Patsy*. There is reason to believe he may have used the name Harry Albers for his initial foray under the spotlight.

The earliest known official bio for him, written in 1931 under the name of Allan Lane, was from the Mack Sennett Studios. It read that in 1925 he had "come to Los Angeles to play in *The Patsy* at Mayan." The Mayan, in those days a legitimate theater house, did not officially open until the summer of 1927. If the building didn't exist in 1925, clearly Harry didn't arrive in Los Angeles in 1925 for that purpose. The Mayan tradition-

Harry Albershart ready for his close-up.

ally featured stage productions including vaudeville revues, silent films, and even a few "talking pictures" later that year. *The Patsy* did go on to become a silent film starring Marion Davies but there is no record showing a Harry Albers, or Allan Lane, or any similar name as part of that production.

Newspaper reports after-the-fact told that while Harry was still in school he had "an amateur appearance" with a stock company for a "week's engagement," and "other similar experiences followed." This suggests what likely happened — he began in *The Patsy* in 1925 in South Bend. There were a number of ongoing school and civic organization productions of this large and complicated operation. Newspaper articles outlined how there were "so few theatres outside of the larger cities" with stages "large enough to properly handle this enormous production..."

Since the offering was too sizable to be moved to most cities, *The Patsy* (1927) went only to those theaters large enough and with proper accommodations. The Chicago troupe, identified as "the Midwest," had its own traveling professional cast. New York also had a professional cast. This would have limited locations where Harry could have been involved. The production ultimately became known as *If I Were King*, and Harry did end up in California with a bit part in a 1927 version at the Mayan.

In the midst of this, he did another play called *Young Woodley* (1928), the story of a "schoolboy" who fell in love with the headmaster's wife and was ultimately expelled. The subject matter was controversial and more than explicit enough for a sixteen-year-old kid. Written information claims he had a "bit part," which could have been something as innocuous as one of the students in a background scene. Little is known of the details, but timing would suggest he again went by the name of Harry Albers in any theatrical capacity.

The play did run on Broadway at the Belasco Theater but there is nothing to show Harry was involved there. Since he now periodically lived on the West Coast with Aunt Eva and Uncle Billy, and at other times in the Midwest, in addition to comings and goings elsewhere, he likely played in a road show version of the same production.

Harry bounced between Michigan, South Bend, Cincinnati, Los Angeles...and any number of other spots as he skipped around the country with road troupes and sports teams, offering "amateur appearances" in both venues. He was a good-looking young man who knew how to get work and keep it, and he was willing to do what was required to secure the paycheck. Other towns in which he played on stage were Detroit and Flint, Michigan, and cities in Upstate New York. He was sixteen to eighteen years old, and he had become quite the road warrior.

One article told of how his original determination to become a professional athlete "was shaken" by the call of the stage. There was no evidence of such in the summer of 1927 when Harry was in Traverse City,

Michigan. A July review of a game between the Traverse City Resorters and the Harbor Springs team applauded a "new lad" named Albershart, a "young player" in center field for the Resorters.

"Albershart doubled to right center," the piece applauded. His "single was the only legitimate measure taken by locals in the seventh" and he was credited with pulling off a two-base hit. The article added one of the "afternoon's greatest features" was "Albershart's grass blade circus catch" of a fly ball in the second inning.

The Resorters ended their season in late October. A team meeting was held at the local gathering place, Pete's Café, and the headline read, "Traverse Baseballers Wind Up Good Season." The highlights of the team's efforts were offered in great detail, and Harry was recorded as a part of this group.

Logistics suggest Harry played in Traverse City during the summer, living there with a team member or a sponsor or at a boarding house, while his mother and sister lived nearly three hours away. Massive Lake Michigan was common to both areas of the state. The team was called The Resorters in honor of the many people who summered there, and went home to more temperate climates in winter months.

Harry already had something of a split personality. He was a potentially rising young sports figure. He was also an engaging persona in the traveling theater. He had a place to stay with his Aunt Eva when he was in Los Angeles. This was where the actor in him took root and began to flourish. Elsewhere, he found his way by bunking with extended family members or being on his own, depending on his needs and where he had to be at any given time. He was eighteen, already a veteran paid worker for a number of years, and he knew how to take care of himself.

A combination of factors falls together as the overall basis of Harry's young teen years. He was in Grand Rapids with his mother and sister when he wasn't playing baseball in the summer months in Traverse City, and he was in Los Angeles with Aunt Eva and Uncle Billy when the theater, and Hollywood, began calling. These were the early days of his love affair with baseball as well as the time that triggered a forever-after lifelong love/hate relationship for him with the entertainment industry.

Helen stayed in Michigan and married a man named Clarence Wolven on December 4, 1926. She had become a nurse, an occupation in which she received two years of education. This lent credence to the controversy surrounding Harry's time in and out of various higher learning institutions. If his sister managed to get instruction beyond high school, living amidst such an untraditional family life and with a mother who took in laundry to get by, it wasn't impossible her brother also received a similar opportunity. There simply are no verifiable records of where he might have received that education…if he ever did.

Records in Kent County, Michigan, indicate both Helen and her mother married within two years of each other. Might it have been odd for Helen to become a newlywed only a few years after her mother said, "I do?" They married into the same family. Witnesses on Anne's marriage certificate were Edward and Elizabeth Finn. Witnesses for Helen's marriage to Clarence were George Needham and Mary Finn.

But who were the Finns? Mary was the daughter of Edward and Elizabeth. And Elizabeth? She was the sister of…William Costello, Anne's new husband. A family affair all around. The only one left out was Harry.

Harry's official biographies, and he himself, claimed he played for a team called the Cincinnati Reds in the early days. This would have been somewhere around 1926. While there has yet to be any discovery of this as fact, there was a Harry Albers who went to college at Cincinnati's St. Xavier that year, becoming a "star second baseman on the St. Xavier college team." This same young man was drafted to the Cincinnati Reds. St. Xavier's was then a preparatory school and had youngsters from early grades through college age.

Since Harry Albershart's past few years had been spent moving from one family member to another, and sometimes living on his own, and he did use the Harry Albers name on the stage, it was possible he also used the name in private life. Unlikely but not impossible.

Harry's father was born in Cincinnati, and he had an extensive family network there as well as across the Ohio River in Newport, Kentucky. Bill Albershart's father, and his brother Fred, owned the Johnson-Albershart Paper Company in Cincinnati, though Fred and the majority of the family lived in Kentucky. The Mack Sennett studio biography mentioned that Allan Lane's "grandfather has the largest paper whse mfg co in the U.S." This was at least one official fact that came very close to the real truth.

So the idea that Harry, under any name, would have lived in this area made complete sense. Yet the Harry Albers who went to St. Xavier went on to, shortly thereafter, play *baseball* with a team called the Cincinnati Reds. Publicity stories circulated about the young actor who was first Harry Albershart, then Harry Albers, and then Allan Lane, concentrated on a team of the same name but told of his participation with the Cincinnati Reds *football* team.

There is one plausible explanation. When the sports hero persona was being built for Allan Lane by movie studios, his unquestionable ability in a variety of sports, coupled with his real history in the various areas where these teams existed, may have intentionally intertwined fiction with fact, though a fact that belonged to someone else of one of those same names.

LEFT TO RIGHT—JIM BOYLE AND HARRY ALBERS

TWO ST. XAVIER BALL PLAYERS ARE SIGNED BY MAJOR CLUBS

Jim Boyle and Harry Albers, Graduated Today, to Join Giants and Reds, Respectively, Within a Week

Harry Albers from St. Xavier's.

Or there is the outside chance it *could* have been him playing for St. Xavier's as Harry Albers, and the intermingling of his sports abilities was intentional on the part of the publicity departments, him, or both. Extensive research by many who have tried to unravel this mystery has come up with no definitive answer. A photo of the Harry Albers from St.

Xavier's, compared to teen, as well as adult images of the actor, makes the story unlikely. Yet there are no comparable photos of Harry Albershart at that time in his life, so an absolute comparison is not possible.

Studio biographies usually took a kernel of truth from the individual's history and grew that seed into an entirely new tree of life, sometimes mixing fantasy with fact so well the bottom line became whatever was originally made up. Most of the details of truth were forever-after lost. On purpose.

One thing is fact; Harry Albershart *was* in Cincinnati during this time. And he had gone there from Traverse City, Michigan.

This was about the same period where the Notre Dame football hero story would have fit in, had it actually happened. By all public accounts, but listed during differing timeframes — early pre-high school to just after graduation age — Harry Albershart was said to have attended Notre Dame University. Almost since the initial claim was made, and at any time since when anyone wrote or spoke of Allan Lane the actor, there has been serious question as to the story's validity. Not a single official record ever surfaced to prove he attended Notre Dame.

This is made even odder by the timing for this claimed schooling, which included him playing football for the university. He would have been one of the students coached by the legendary Knute Rockne. If this had been true, he would have certainly been noted in some record, at some time... especially since he was reportedly one heck of a player. The combination of his athletic prowess — which he had proved in other sports — and a coach named Knute Rockne would have undoubtedly put his name in a record book. At the very least he would have been found in the Notre Dame archives as a student.

One definitive bit of reinforcement against the claim came in a *South Bend Tribune* editorial commentary in the summer of 2012. Russell "Cappy" Gagnon, retired director of the Notre Dame Stadium ushers, did extensive research in the school's archives as well as the registrar's office. He found nothing to indicate a young man named Harry Albershart ever attended the university, nonetheless played football there. Mr. Gagnon has since personally verified his earlier comments. No one using any of Harry's working names has been found in any Notre Dame records.

So did a publicist study the young man one day after he had arrived on the studio doorstep? Noticing his athletic build and discovering he had legitimately played at many sports before coming to Hollywood — baseball, football, golf, bowling — did the publicist arbitrarily decide, "Heck, we ought to make him a football hero!" Maybe the next question was, "What team should we say he played for? He's from Indiana. Why not Notre Dame? That would be believable, wouldn't it?"

Such a scenario is as plausible as any, and since this story has been repeated ever since as solid fact, the idea must have been believable from the start. However, the unequivocal answer to the mystery came from Harry's family. His niece, Pat, said Harry's mother told her and her siblings her son never played football for Notre Dame. He never attended Notre Dame. She said outright that the football hero story was made up. Yet another falsehood apparently created at the hands of a now-faceless studio press writer.

Allan did play football, however. He just did not play for Notre Dame. Newspaper pieces from November of 1927 — he would've been about eighteen — detailed a football player named "Albershart" who substituted for "S. Fisher," both members of the Cincinnati National Guard outfit.

The Cincinnati National Guard Public Relations office has indicated that to play football for the Cincinnati National Guard, Harry would have had to have been a member of that outfit. This is the first, and so far, only indicator that he ever had any sort of military training.

"Albershart's punt was blocked," the *Kokomo Daily Tribune* wrote a few days before that Thanksgiving. And with this and other unfortunate moves, the Kokomo American Legion team "easily defeated the Cincinnati National Guard outfit…" The article continued, "One of the backfields that is coming down from South Bend is what Rockne calls his 'pony backs.' These horsemen are a light, fast combination he starts his big battles with before he throws in the regulars." There are records to indicate Harry played for the team at least through the end of the year.

Notre Dame had the Reserves, which played as an independent team but, as an article stated about them, were "not in the state semi-pro race." So there does appear to have been a grain of logic, if not truth, which began the rumor about Allan Lane's football career with Notre Dame. The Reserves regularly played teams with which he had been associated, including the Cincinnati National Guards. He could have been spotted and singled out at any one of those games. He just wasn't spotted and singled out as a member of the Notre Dame bunch. A minor detail? The movie world would much more out of that.

Harry ultimately made his way to Hollywood as the end result of a trip to visit Aunt Eva and Uncle Billy. No evidence has surfaced to show he ever represented himself onscreen at any time as Harry Albershart. He had already used the name of Harry Albers and continued to do so for a short time before he forever-after became known as Allan Lane. His first introduction to the film world happened in great part thanks to Uncle Billy via his connections to the studios.

Another anecdote, which was added as truth to Allan Lane's biography, came about through his mother after her marriage into the Costello family. Her first husband had most often worked as a laborer. Her second husband, Dean Null, was a leather worker. And her third husband, Will Costello, at least early on, was a farmer and a laborer.

Under these circumstances, as listed on her son's Mack Sennett biography as well as in other places, how and when did Anne become a "light opera singer?" Was it before, during, or after she washed other people's clothing for her bread and butter? Or was it after she married Will Costello and lived a modest life with him and his children? Anne never gained any fame as a singer. Yet in newspaper interviews even Harry occasionally claimed this as his mother's "occupation."

The closest attempt to explain how this came to be truth — again only supposition — arose out of RCA Victor's stable of singers. They performed on records and sold in large numbers for their "Victor Light Opera Company." They did not showcase single-name, high-visibility stars, though a few performers, like Carlotta King, were taken from radio to screen when it was discovered the quality of their appearance matched the quality of their singing voice. Many women did this sort of work behind scenes for extra income. Few ever found fame, or even the slightest bit of recognition, even though their voices may have lived on into anonymous eternity.

This scenario is as plausible as any to explain how Anne Costello's professional claim to entertainment fame may have come about *if* it were fact. It's more likely it was something concocted to make Harry's background more engaging for the benefit of his official, though slightly skewered, history. His niece Pat, who knew Gramanne all her life, said Anne never sang…for a living or otherwise.

While exact details are fuzzy as to how and when Harry officially arrived in Hollywood, that he went to Hollywood at a young age is not in question. Shortly before the fateful move, he was still in Traverse City, Michigan, playing baseball with the Traverse City Resorters. By the fall, he had moved on to Cincinnati to play for the Cincinnati National Guards. Somewhere in there, he was finishing school, probably in Cincinnati and possibly while staying with his paternal grandfather and family.

In the midst of all this, the young man found the stage.

During this convoluted timeframe, Harry — likely using the name Harry Albers — got a part in another traveling production. This one was called *Hit The Deck* (1927), classified in a newspaper piece as a tale that carried "a bit of a plot, all about love." The official story of how he got the job related that a theater stock company manager happened to see him playing ball and thought so much of his physical appearance he offered

Harry at the age of seventeen in a professional photo. PHOTO COURTESY THE COSTELLO FAMILY COLLECTION

the young man a role in a stage production. One article said about this play, "Spice it all up with merry music, a big chorus of boys in navy suits and a flock of pretty girls — aboard ship and ashore in a charming Chinese setting…"

Harry reportedly finished out the season with that road show. A picture can tell a story where words have been left out. A professional photograph kept over the years by his family showed a well-dressed teenaged Harry in what looked to be a studio portrait. He posed in a spotless white shirt and pressed pants, his hair perfectly coiffed, looking as if he were ready to go onstage at any moment. His mother's handwriting on the back dates it to this period: "Just my boy at 17," is all it read, telling the "when" if not the "why."

A few articles say he was given the lead role in *Hit The Deck* as it went from town to town. An agent reportedly saw his work and, as Allan put it years later, "tried to sell me to the casting directors." As they traveled through Buffalo, New York, Winifred "Winnie" Sheehan, an executive for Fox Studios, was said to have seen Harry perform, and he was given a moving pictures screen test.

While the chain of events may, or may not, have happened exactly that way, nothing happened immediately. Harry's name, in any form, is not listed in the official Belasco Theatre playbook for *Hit The Deck*, so he clearly wasn't in the New York City cast. One newspaper piece, written by Charles G. Sampas in his "Hollywood" column, said the young man was in a play called *Murder With Music* between 1927–1928, "in Gotham." This indicates Harry did go to New York City during this period and he did work on the stage. There appears to be little about this play on record, though it went on to become a movie in 1941 with an entirely African American cast.

CHAPTER THREE

The Start, The Stop…and Start & Stop…and Stop & Start…

Somewhere in October of 1928, Harry unknowingly changed his life forever when he left New York to again visit Los Angeles, as one article put it, "for a rest." Aunt Eva and Uncle Billy always encouraged his visits to their Fourth Avenue home, and they were supportive of his efforts to make it as an actor.

This period is what most current Western historians refer to as Allan Lane's initial try at stardom. His stay in California proved to be fruitful. An article indicated he needed money, so while he bunked with his relatives, he "tried the movies." Uncle Billy worked as a studio electrician, and he had industry contacts. Between this, and recent work on stage in New York and elsewhere in the country, the now-officially-named Allan Lane found his way into the movie world.

The accepted line as to how Harry-turned-Allan — a good-looking new boy" — got his break, goes back to the Winnie Sheehan story. The young man's athletic appearance had come to Sheehan's attention. He was an executive in charge of production under William Fox at Fox Studios, and he saw something marketable in Allan.

Sheehan was involved with what was copyrighted as *William Fox Movietone Follies of 1929.* This was on the cusp of the talking picture era, and studios rushed to put out all sorts of productions showcasing sound along with beautiful people from the silent period whose voices made the cut.

The initial idea for this one was rather simple, planned as little more than a "plotless revue" and the first in a series. Studio executives intended it as an experiment and shrouded the entire effort in mystery, giving different

scenes to different directors who would then come up with a loose storyline as well as gags for every scene. Each director was also required to
select his players from the company's list of contract performers. The
entire set of scenes was expected to be put into one cohesive production.

Here is where Allan came in. Sheehan decided Allan had the right
face and build to be in the movies. He added him to the Fox roster, and
Movietone Follies of 1929 was just
the place for such a handsome
young man who well knew his way
around a dance floor.

Fox's Movietone Follies of 1929.

Some reports state he still
used the name of Harry Albers.
Elsewhere he was being called
Allan Lane. Either way, at this
point he was nothing more than
background scenery, but he still
snagged this part. He had been in
the right place at the right time,
and as a result of his good looks
and athletic build, he was now in
the movies.

The intended initial way of
doing business for *Movietone
Follies of 1929* eventually proved to
be too cumbersome. By March, the
effort was way over budget, and one managing director was hired to over-
see the original group of individual directors. Extensive and expensive lab
research had gone into an innovative type of 70-millimeter film which
William Fox called the "Grandeur" process, expected to offer better sound
recording. *Movietone Follies of 1929* was planned to soar to new heights
in the recently-minted sound picture industry. Instead, it was effectively
lost to history.

Allan was a movie ingénue but he was finding work. Somewhat con-
currently to the role he snagged in *Movietone Follies of 1929*, which proved
to be his first try at being an actor, he also had an uncredited bit in *Dream
of Love* (1928), a Joan Crawford and Nils Asther silent film for MGM
with an original title of *Adrienne Lecouvreur*. Directed by Fred Niblo, this
picture debuted in December of 1928. Allan's work in Hollywood had
started with Fox in the *Movietone Follies of 1929* effort a few months earlier, but that came out in theaters after *Dream of Love*.

By early the next year, *Film Daily* reported a list of Fox's contract play-ers, and Harry's name had been publicly changed to Allan Lane. No more Harry Albers. A photograph accompanied this report, verifying the con-nection between these two different-but-same identities.

In early 1929, it was clear this young man planned to get serious about an acting career. He had a professional portrait done by Peralta, also

Dream of Love *advertisement.*

known as Peralta Studios. A few years earlier, Peralta had been connected to Robert Brunton Studios, part of a working movie operation that ulti-mately became Paramount Pictures. A photography studio evolved, with locations in Los Angeles and San Francisco as well as Covina, California. By the time Allan crossed paths with Peralta's cameras, they were touted as "American's Best Known Studio of Photography," lauded for taking head shots of up-and-coming stars.

His Peralta portrait showed a handsome and well-heeled man-boy. Allan was twenty years old, and he had already played baseball and football on the road as well as acted with stage troupes from the Midwest to New York City. He'd even done a stint on Broadway, though without receiving any notable name recognition. He was an old soul in a young man's body. By the end of June of 1929, he was solidly in Hollywood, and suddenly he was playing with the big guys.

The previously first official credited film appearance for the actor named Allan Lane was in "a sound picture" titled *Not Quite Decent* starring Marie Dressler. Since talking pictures were quite novel and all the rage, many newspaper advertisements made a point to ensure their readers were aware all actors on this picture were "speaking their parts." Later in life, Allan laughed about the title, somewhat embarrassed at potential connotations.

Now known as Allan Lane, photo taken by Peralta Studio. PHOTO COURTESY THE COSTELLO FAMILY COLLECTION

Allan's other roles that year ranged from an unnamed juvenile in *Pleasure Craze* (1929) — which in the years since has also become known as *Pleasure Crazed* — a well-received early talkie starring Marguerite Churchill and Kenneth MacKenna; to a young football player in a Loretta Young feature titled *The Forward Pass* (1929). In one he wasn't listed in the credits, and in the other he was a mid-cast player with a character name.

Left: *Press ad for* The Forward Pass. Right: *Allan in* The Forward Pass.
PHOTO COURTESY THE COSTELLO FAMILY COLLECTION

Pleasure Craze was called "the all-taking hit" and "all dialogue talkie of the future." Other reports claimed it represented the "typical talking picture," while "...the speaking screen is still in what may be called the transition period." Producers were trying to "ascertain the public's reaction to this new medium." Allan had his start in an industry that itself was in its infancy, yet already enveloped in an evolution.

His part in the other picture that year was not a talkie. *The Forward Pass* was one of the silent films trying to hold on during the changing face of movies, and earned him his first real press recognition in assorted movie ads and articles. He was said to have a "sinister part which is ultimately redeemed." Allan played against Douglas Fairbanks, Jr., with Loretta Young in the middle of them as the romantic lead.

Allan made a friend while on the set of *The Forward Pass*, an actor named Guinn Williams, known widely by the nickname, "Big Boy." Ten years older than Allan, the nickname was a testament to his size given to him by Will Rogers. Big Boy and Allan did what many young hopefuls did while working to secure their big break; they exchanged signed head-shots, including sentiments they hoped would predict their futures.

Allan steadily began collecting movie credits. He had secured a theatrical agent, Ruth Collier of Collier, Inc. A few years later, she would partner with Minna Wallis and the business name would change to Collier-Wallis.

Guin "Big Boy" Williams, in a photo personally signed to Allan. PHOTO COURTESY THE COSTELLO FAMILY COLLECTION

At the time, though, Minna, producer Hal Wallis's sister, was Ruth's associate, and Ruth was earning her percentage peddling Allan Lane around town, along with many other gorgeous and promising young men and women hopefuls.

Between *Not Quite Decent* (1929) and *Pleasure Craze*, Allan was given the title role in a short named *Nighty Nighties* (1929). It would've been

Theater card for Words and Music.

nice if this quickie film had made a splash since Allan was considered "the star," but for whatever reason, it never took off and, in fact, received little-to-no publicity. Another short, *Knights Out* (1929), was made as Number Thirteen of a Fox series of three-reel "all-talking" comedies starring the well-known vaudeville team of Bobby Clark and Paul McCullough. One of Allan's costars was a young lady named Dixie Lee, who ultimately gave up acting to become Mrs. Bing Crosby.

Allan was also in the fourteenth of the same series, this one called *Two Detectives Wanted* (1929). In other records, the title is *Detectives Wanted.* This was already August, and Allan was adding movie titles to his resumé one after another. It didn't hurt that these films took little time to produce and bring to market, allowing him, and others in the casts the time to move quickly from project to project.

While he began to garner credits as Allan Lane, a few of his efforts as Harry Albers still showed up on the screen. He had one such appearance with an uncredited role in *Words and Music* (1929), a Fox film also out in August. He was under contract to Fox. This was one of two films in which Allan shared a bill for a brief moment with an actor who went on to make movie history. John Wayne, born as Marion Morrison, was also a new kid on the lot, going by the name of Duke Morrison. The other movie they had appeared in together had been *The Forward Pass.*

Allan's looks had put him on the fast track, and he was suddenly associating with the likes of Fanny Brice, her then-husband Billy Rose, and silent movie actresses/models Ann Pennington and Vivienne Segal. These people were almost exclusively New York-to-Hollywood, stage-turned-movie writers and actors. It made sense Allan would run with such a crowd since, in varying degrees, they all had the bright lights of the stage in common.

The one other solid thing they had in common was baseball. The ladies loved to watch, and the men loved to play. Not all were good, admittedly, but they adored the sport, and pick-up games were part of their regular recreation. Stories circulated about these games where any number of the guys would get together when the mood struck them to play, wherever and whenever they could find the time and space.

One report told of how Harry Ruby, George Bancroft, Billy Rose, Walter Catlett, Gene Towne, and Allan started one day socializing at Fanny Brice's home. They decided they wanted to play and went looking for a baseball diamond, roaming around from one school to another and then to another. At some point, they dispatched a telegram to Buster Keaton to join them, and then they went on playing. Keaton got to the location where they had been last, but not until they'd already left to go on to the next diamond. He was a bit miffed yet ended the day at Fanny Brice's home with everyone else, playing in her backyard with a "grandstand" of cheering spectators…most of whom were the lady friends of the men in the game.

Allan was fifteen or more years younger than most of these people, and being a part of their group and partaking of shared activities was an eccentric association. The love of the sport was just enough to bring them together. He wanted to be in the entertainment business, and they wanted to associate with a young, vibrant baseball player who understood their theatrical quirks.

The solid shared denominator was Harry Ruby, a baseball fanatic who eventually became officially known as the World's Greatest Baseball Fan. When Harry's earliest ambitions as a young man to play the game were foiled, he turned to vaudeville and became a pianist. Being a musician and songwriter stuck, and his future was well secured. Still, he never lost his love for baseball and he played the game, coached other teams, and effervescently supported young players whenever he got the chance. Allan had come to Hollywood from New York, also in 1929, and Harry appears as the major reason Allan was accepted into this early entertainment crowd.

Harry Ruby participated in New York baseball clubs at the same time Allan was a player. He also managed the local fire department team in the city before he went to Los Angeles to work in the movies, and even afterward, when he would go back and forth between the coasts. If there ever was an entertainer in love with baseball, it was Harry Ruby. When he wasn't composing songs and working with his business partner, Bert Kalmar, Harry was keeping company with major league players, and obviously some minor league players as well.

Beginning with his grand debut and continuing throughout the summer, Allan received repeated press coverage. He was a fresh face — a

strikingly handsome fresh face in Hollywood at a time when talking pictures were gaining steam with the entertainment-hungry public. His voice was rich, clear, and everything he needed it to be to make an impression in the movies, not only as the cameras rolled but also as sound recordings were still a novel addition to the mix. Allan Lane was the complete package, and great things were expected of him.

Much was made about his humble beginnings in Indiana and his Midwest wholesomeness. The eyes of Hollywood's top brass watched him sharply. Allan had been getting work, a considerable amount of work. He was given a

Harry Ruby during his early songwriting days.

solid supporting role right out of the gate as well as some good worker-bee opportunities, and he was on his way...or so he thought.

There was evidence, even at this early point, of Allan's thriftiness and dedication to his family's well-being. Having known the value of a dollar from his earliest years, he held on to every possible penny to ensure not only him but also his folks were taken care of. Hubbard Keavy, Hollywood reporter, said in his "Screen Life In Hollywood" column, "Lane doesn't seem to care about making an impression any place except on the screen, for he drives a second-hand roadster of ancient vintage, which is unusual in this town."

Another reporter said the newcomer did this because "its low cost of operation enabled him to send more money home 'to the folks.'" This spoke to Allan's work ethic. He had toiled away for his every dollar for well over a decade, investing in his needs, not his wants. A great deal of his paychecks went back to the family.

Allan, even then, cared little about what people thought of him except for how his work in front of a camera was received by employers and audiences. He had a job to do and working to the best of his ability, whatever his occupation, was first and foremost. He had been an overtly responsible individual since his early childhood days. Now that he made a solid-if-not-extravagant living, Allan's earnings rarely went toward frivolity.

Even as an adolescent, Allan felt different from those around him in similar circumstances. During this earliest period in Hollywood, where almost all of the other budding leading men were jaunting around town in the latest fashions and automobiles, doing their darnedest to look like they were on top of the world in every way, and act as such, Allan Lane stood out. He was a loner. He didn't drink or smoke to excess, and his socializing was mostly with folks who understood sports, rather than those seen as part of Hollywood's "It" crowd.

He couldn't be bothered with what others thought of him and how he handled his life. He had no patience for frivolity and inane interactions, and he related to others in a patently no-nonsense manner. Some thought he was bristly and cold. Others considered him downright arrogant and unpleasant. He was not a people-pleaser even then, and the act of pretending to be one wasn't a personality trait he cared to cultivate. Even in those days in the movie world, he wasn't known to attempt to make nice-nice with others to move another step up the ladder.

Allan's personality seemed to indicate he simply didn't have such skills in his repertoire. On a day-to-day basis, he did the work that came his way and then he went home, with no apparent understanding of the art of human social interaction.

Though he went through no known medical diagnosis process, it has been suggested Allan exhibited signs of what is now known as high-functioning Asperger's. A deeply focused individual, he was known to dedicate his effort, time, and attention to anything that directly interested him, pleasantly interacting with others while doing so, especially those who shared his interests. Then he would switch on a moment's notice into someone with little-to-no empathy for anyone. A highly volatile and antagonistic personality. An angry, impatient man few cared to be around. This ongoing cycle limited his social circle.

Allan did have a few friends, as proven with the Harry Ruby theater bunch. These were people who understood his nonconformity and seemed to look beyond the façade, underneath his initial pretense of bravado and devil-may-care. They were also flamboyant and sometimes over-the-top themselves. Allan Lane's companions knew that how he handled life wasn't necessarily a slight to them or to others.

One of Allan's newest friends was actress Mary Brian. She was a few years older than he was, which seemed to be the norm for him when it came to his more personal associations with industry people. By known accounts she was an all-round nice young lady, ultimately dubbed, "The Sweetest Girl in Pictures." Pretty, too. Mary would "drive around Hollywood with Allan in his ancient 'second-hand roadster,' and did so, as Allan once said, "with no concerns."

He commented in one article, "I like to get in my car and drive for miles and miles — alone." Yet when he had a chance to take along a friend, Mary was one of his favorites. Allan told a reporter of a time when the two of them were on a ride in his clunker. "One night, we had a blow-out. I was awfully embarrassed, but Mary wasn't. She took it like a sport and joked about it." Allan was more than impressed with her. "Some stars might have been high-hat...but Mary's a regular."

Mary Brian, actress, and one of Allan's early Hollywood friends.

In a number of ways he used that car to help him weed out the insincere so he could be certain of his true friends. His sensitivities were always on high alert. It wasn't so much that he didn't care about how others saw him. He had an inability to filter his reactions alongside a limited ability to understand honestly-close relationships. Allan didn't have these perceptions in his interaction tool bag.

He had a few other acquaintances who he liked to be around, namely Delores Del Rio and Buddy Rogers. His formality with these people, though, people he liked but didn't know well, showed how tenuous he felt with most individuals. Evidence of this difficulty wasn't lost in one particular comment he made. "Miss Del Rio is a wonderful person. She has been more than kind to me." He considered her a casual friend yet addressed her — as opposed to Mary Brian — in a more formal manner.

Allan didn't easily warm up to anyone. "I always figured, about that old car," he said, "that if people liked me they wouldn't mind riding in the tincan. And if they liked me only for my car, then they could go hang anyway." Though he wanted to have friends and to socialize, Allan found it more comfortable to be alone. When he was by himself, he didn't have the burden of worrying about how he might, or might not, fit in.

There was other direct evidence of how much easier it was for him to be by himself with his thoughts, while only now-and-then having the freedom to interact with a precious few who seemed to "get him," mostly people who shared defined common interests. One of those people was an actor who ultimately became infamous for reasons far beyond what Allan knew of him in those days.

Ramon Novarro was an avowed, deeply faithful Roman Catholic. His faith had been ingrained in him from childhood as the son of a well-to-do and highly respected Mexican dentist. His father moved his family from Mexico to Los Angeles in 1913 to escape the Mexican Revolution. Born in 1899, Novarro's birth name was José Ramón Gil Samaniego.

Allan turned to Catholicism at some time after his mother converted so she could marry William Costello in 1924. By all family accounts, Anne, from that day forward, remained an utterly by-the-book Catholic. When it came to her religion, there was no nonsense allowed. She attended Mass every Sunday, and during the week she was in a pew praying whenever she could get there. She spent quiet evenings in her living room, sitting in a chair as she meditated and said her rosary. Cursing was not allowed around her. Prayer and frugal living were her mantras. She denounced alcohol and all its evils, though sadly she found herself in the midst of a marriage marred by her husband's alcoholism. She deeply loved Will Costello, and the marriage remained intact in one form or another throughout the rest of her husband's life.

These beliefs she instilled in her son as best she could, though he was already fifteen years old by the time she came to be a believer in absolute Catholicism. Still, she was a strong-willed woman and he was an overtly dedicated son, and her way of life reflected on him as he grew into adulthood. He was, by far, much closer to his mother than he would ever be to his father. By 1930, Allan was twenty-two, on his own for some time, still figuring out where he wanted to go in life. Yet he devoutly remained his mother's son.

Catholicism appears to have been the glue in a friendship between Allan and Ramon Novarro. How long their alliance lasted, where and how it began, and how strong their personal connection was, remains a mystery. In the summer of 1930, Allan attended a Catholic men's retreat with Novarro at a place called El Retiro San Inigo in Los Altos, California.

El Retiro San Inigo was then a five-year-old Jesuit Retreat Center where men went to "experience the quiet, a time of prayer, and the wisdom and counsel of talented retreat directors."

Novarro lived not far off of Hollywood Boulevard with his parents, five siblings, and no less than five servants. When he wasn't tending to his growing movie presence, he officially organized these retreats. His name

Ramon Novarro, Allan and others, Los Angeles Man's Retreat, El Retiro San Inigo, June 14, 1930. PHOTO COURTESY THE COSTELLO FAMILY COLLECTION

and professional stature brought together a variety of men who wanted such an experience in the beautiful, peaceful setting where their spirituality was at the forefront. The busyness of their everyday lives could be tucked away, if even for a short time. Novarro was known to do this on numerous occasions and at least for this particular time, Allan was one of the men who went on a religious adventure with him.

A photo survives showing Allan, along with Novarro, three priests, and twelve others in layman's clothes. Allan's Fox Studios movie contract had been signed the year before, and he looked to be one of the youngest, if not the youngest, in the bunch. Novarro was ten years older, and the rest of the participants were middle-aged or beyond.

Seated between two priests, Novarro and Allan were singled out by their placement as well as their clothing — some of the nicest. The men behind them — everyone else stood, another indication Allan and Novarro held a special place in this group — ranged from what looked to be businessmen to middle-class workers. Some were clearly Caucasian, while others appeared to be well-to-do Mexicans.

El Retiro has verified Ramon Novarro's formal association with the organization. They have pictures showing him on the property in other years, and documents tell of his generous donations and offerings, such as elaborate and expensive statues placed around the grounds. The back of the photo that showed Allan with him on one of these weekends is personally signed and addressed to Allan's mother...not to Allan. "Dear Mrs. Costello: Here is a little remembrance of three happy days at 'El Retiro' with God and my best friend Allan."

In later years, Novarro was publicly known to be gay, but there is no indication the friendship between these two men went beyond anything platonic and spiritually-based. Novarro, as an older man, may have had other aspirations, but Allan's intentions appeared to be of an ethereal nature. After this retreat, he was not known to closely associate with Ramon Novarro again.

CHAPTER FOUR

The Stage...Again

The job of studio publicity people was to make their newest potential future stars shine brightly. In many ways that wasn't hard to do with the likes of young Allan Lane, but in other ways it was the impossible task. He was intelligent, took direction well in front of a camera, easily stepped into any variety of fictional personas, and was without question handsome and photogenic. Yet he was also brutally blunt, as if he had no filter between his brain and his mouth. He soon made it clear to bosses and co-workers alike that he had no intention of following in any predetermined mold, no matter what Hollywood might expect of him in exchange for a promising new career.

As of April of 1930, he shared a two-bedroom apartment at 1825 Argyle Avenue in Los Angeles with Charles L. King, an unemployed vaudevillian and theater singer fourteen years Allan's senior. They lived in a neighborhood where many entertainment types resided. Charles was a vaudeville performer who just the year before had had enough clout to play himself in MGM's *The Hollywood Revue 1929* — one of that year's runners-up for the Academy Award's Best Picture.

He and Allan may have met a few years earlier on the set of *Hit The Deck*, where Charles had a mid-cast list role as Bilge. By 1930, as he and Allan roomed together, Charles had but a few credits to his name and added only one other major known movie part a few years later. He died in London in 1944 while entertaining the troops.

So while King was on his way down in the entertainment world, Allan was on his way up. He had an agent and a contract with Fox Studios, and he was on track to build a good livelihood in the movie business. Yet his way of doing business became a problem for this newly-created rising star, and his career visibly suffered the consequences.

By the fall, he had a few MGM films under his belt, which seemed to indicate Fox Studios had dropped him. His only two credits that year were with MGM, and neither were show-stoppers, for the movies or for him personally. In fact, only one part was credited. In *Love In The Rough* (1930), starring Robert Montgomery and Dorothy Jordan, Allan had a small noted role.

The other part had him playing little more than background fluff in Cecil B. DeMille's just-barely pre-Motion Picture Product Code extravaganza titled *Madam Satan* (1930). This was a "lavish drama" of the "silks and sex of society." Another overview said, "A true hybrid, it updated the plot of Johann Strauss's operatta *Die Fledermaus* without the Strauss melodies and set in a Lubitsch-like atmosphere of boudoirs, lingerie and high infidelity. Added to this was…a riotous costume party set to music, celebrated merrily inside a Zeppelin high over Paris."

Some have called this "DeMille's weirdest film," and Allan's presence on the screen provided little more than eye candy amidst an overdose of eye candy. If one cared to look for him, he might have been seen playing a majordomo in a mob-sized group during the wild costume party scene.

Vaudevillian–turned–movie-actor Charles King, Allan's one-time housemate.

By October, he was feeling as if Hollywood could not do much more for him. He was only twenty-two, but he'd been around the block a few times. He needed forward movement, all the time, or else he wasn't even remotely happy, so he decided to do what he seemed to do best. One article quoted him as saying he "became so disgusted" with himself he packed up "and beat it back to good old Broadway."

So he moved again, returning to New York and to what had become his acting roots: the live stage. The New York stage and stage people were different animals than those who consumed Hollywood. Allan needed a break.

For the remainder of 1930, Allan was on the East Coast, working the stage and, when he wasn't acting, he played baseball and made connections in the sports arena...and in the romance department. When it came down to interacting with others, he did much better in and around New York City. Requirements weren't as stringent for him to pretend to be someone he was not. He wasn't too serious about acting or about much of anything at that point. Allan was simply trying to make a few bucks while he figured out what he should do next.

Madam Satan, *Cecil B. DeMille's "weirdest" film in which Allan played an unnamed "majordomo" amidst a host of odd characters.*

Mack Sennett's bio of Allan, created a few years later, stated that in 1930, Allan had the "lead" in a play titled *Life Is Like That*. Curtains went up onstage on December 22 at the Little Theatre at 240 West Forty-Fourth Street in Midtown Manhattan. This one lasted all of a month, and the theater went dark on the production before the end of January. He had arrived in New York no earlier than mid-October, so timing proves he either secured the work before he left the West Coast, or quickly got the job after he arrived in New York.

There was an actor and stage production manager named Victor Morley who may have figured prominently in Allan's life at this point. Victor had been around for many years, having been born in England in the 1870s. Once he made his way to the United States and to the New York stage decades later, he did quite well. His unusual British accent gave him his initial break and served to connect him with the world of grease paint time and time again.

When Victor wasn't acting, he was staging Broadway and close-in productions. Many young actors and hopefuls crossed his path in a whole host of ways. While solid detail tying Victor to Allan isn't immediately evident, there is reason to believe he at least made Allan's acquaintance and may have helped bring Allan together with his first wife, Gladys Leslie Schneider.

Gladys was only sixteen in 1930. She was born in Baltimore, and in the latter part of that year she lived with her grandparents in the Bronx. Despite her tender age, she was a dancer professionally using the name of Gladys Leslie. Her older sister, Willye May, was known as Billie Mae or sometimes Mae. Willye was six years older, allowing for Gladys to follow in her footsteps whenever the occasion arose.

Vaudeville was all the rage. Stage shows were full of comedians, acrobats, singers, dancers, assorted musicians, elocutionists, and any other sort of entertainment one could imagine — some of which defied imagination. Victor Morley could pick and choose from the vast array of talent that crossed a stage on any given day, offering each hopeful a chance at the bright lights of Broadway. And that's what he did with Willye when she won a part in *The Wooden Soldier*, a play he staged on Broadway in mid-1931.

Allan was already known to run amid New York theater circles as well as have close association with vaudeville and other traveling entertainers. Since there is no exact detail as to how this literally played out — but it is known for certain Allan Lane, aka Harry Albershart, and Gladys Leslie, aka Gladys Schneider, married — one has to look at the stages of Allan's life and where he was during those periods to piece together when he and Gladys met and became romantic.

Whether or not Victor Morley was a player in Allan's introduction to Gladys is not known for certain, but he did stage Gladys' sister's one-and-only excursion onto Broadway. Morley was also closely aligned with Helen Shipman and her to-be husband, Edward Pawley — seasoned actors who met as members of the cast of *Life Is Like That*, in which Allan had a part during this generally-same time period.

The official setting for *Life Is Like That* was, "The penthouse of William Courtney in the East Fifties in New York City." One of Allan's official early biographies claimed he had the lead. Since William Courtney was played by Edward Pawley, it is unclear how Allan could have had "the lead" in this play unless his official biographical detail listed that in error, or intentionally, when it was really the work he did in *Hit The Deck*, where some stories claimed Allan had stepped in for the ill leading man at a moment's notice.

Though he did appear in *Hit The Deck* prior to his first try in Hollywood, the timing may have been skewered in his subsequent press material. It seems more likely he would have taken on a lead at this point in his acting career, with a bit more experience under his belt. Pawley, also a Midwesterner, was eight years Allan's senior, tall and dark, and he had a similar career in those early years. He had not yet gone to Hollywood.

Playbill for Life Is Like That.

It is nearly certain that Allan and Gladys were introduced when they were both on the periphery of the Broadway stage. Gladys reportedly went to Hollywood to try her hand at acting, but the date of her trip is unknown. Though it is possible she met Allan in Los Angeles in late 1930 and he brought her back to New York, her nephew, Rick Schneider, believes she was too young then and hadn't yet left her family. The more believable scenario would have had Allan and Willye meeting first. Their careers were similar, and they circulated amongst many of the same people.

In February of 1931, Allan appeared in New York in *Zero Hour*, starring veteran actress Alice Brady. Some references called it *The Zero Hour*. There was a lot of hoopla on this effort listed after-the-fact in Allan's biographies, yet during real time it was dubious whether or not the production ever got far off the ground. On January 18, 1931, *The Milwaukee Sentinel* wrote, "They haven't found a leading man yet but they have Alice Brady as the star, so why worry about trivial details?" The piece went on to say *Zero Hour* would be seen on the evening of February 2 "in Newark." The playhouse was the Broad Street Theater.

Yet again, a studio publicity machine seems to have made more out of a tidbit on Allan's resumé than what the event actually deserved. The same article gave evidence of what was expected to come: "New York is promised a long engagement a fortnight after the neighbors across the river have ceased applauding." Within a scant few weeks, those "neighbors" appeared to have "ceased applauding" a bit too early for *Zero Hour* to make it all the way to Broadway.

There is nothing to indicate this play ever got there. Alice Brady's official resumé has a telling lack of activity during that time. *Zero Hour* looks to have had little more than a short run across the river, and that was the end of that. The play did serve an important purpose, though. Some newspaper articles listed Allan as a minor cast member. Others said he was Brady's leading man — unlikely since she was seventeen years older. Either way, he garnered another reputable theatrical experience.

This brief New York interlude offered him renewed credibility in the movie world, which was something he hadn't been actively seeking. Though he wasn't setting the world on fire, he was comfortable on the stage. Yet the added exposure made waves across the country and proved to be just enough attention for him to be noticed all over again. He was forced to make another career decision…and another move. That month, gossip columnist for the *Los Angeles Times*, Grace Kingsley, announced, "Allan Lane signs long-term Warner contract."

Fine print indicated he would be part of the Warner Bros. Studios stable for five years. An additional article announced, "Lane to Leave Stage — another young stage player has been signed for the screen. Allan Lane is the latest Broadway celebrity to cast his lot with the audible screen…He has been playing on the stage as Alice Brady's leading man in her current play, *The Zero Hour*."

As had already happened repeatedly for this young actor, the press ignored details that didn't serve him well and embellished those that did. That Allan, as "another young stage player" had previously been "signed for the screen" was not mentioned this time. That he had no more than a few years before already "cast his lot with the audible screen" was also omitted from this new effort to tell his story. And the truth that barely a few theater enthusiasts knew of his name on a marquee was a contradiction to the statement that he was "the latest Broadway celebrity…" to go Hollywood.

Still, the Hollywood machine renewed efforts to make a big deal out of him, and in his mind Allan had finally arrived. Once again he had arrived, but only one thing was certain. He was on the move yet again, so he departed from New York to go back to the West Coast. This trip had resulted from the direct Warner contract offer. In fact, one article said, "… several picture producers were bidding for his services." Either another exaggeration, or his voice and fine form had been remembered in a business that easily forgot so many young screen hopefuls.

Whatever the case, no sooner than he stepped foot in town, Warner Bros. began to carefully groom him. They started by sending him out to be seen at promotional events in and around Hollywood. He was asked to play nice-nice with the press, and for a time, he behaved like the perfect matinee idol. Newspaper articles helped promote his present attempt to set the movie world on fire. One piece titled, "Patient Years Bring Success for Allan Lane," made note of his efforts. "For years Allan Lane went from studio to studio playing small parts, hoping that some director or producer might recognize his talents and give him an opportunity..."

The concept of Allan Lane being patient had never before been mentioned in professional circles, and never would be again.

In April, soon after he had re-established himself, Allan was the Master of Ceremonies for the "Modes of Filmdom," an event held in the Blossom Room at the Roosevelt Hotel. The Roosevelt, only four years old, had been financed by Douglas Fairbanks, Mary Pickford, and Louis B. Mayer, and it was one of the hottest places to be seen. Allan officiated over a noon luncheon and high fashion show, cutting quite the classy figure and impressing all around him.

The month of May brought him even more visibility. An article said his current home base in Los Angeles marked "his second coming to Hollywood, a triumph for him, for he has been rediscovered by the films that let him go two years ago after a brief trial." The piece was written by Robbin Coons, a well-known movie critic.

As the summer rolled around, Allan found himself being used in a set of entertainment-based golf shorts created as vehicles to showcase golfer Bobby Jones. The string of quickie films was ongoing, and Allan, along with Loretta Young, was in *The Brassie* (1931) — Number Eight of the *How I Play Golf* series. The flimsy story had Allan and Loretta as a couple planning to elope. Bobby Jones entered the picture, proving to be an excellent ruse to divert Loretta's father from discovering their intent. Allan's real-life ability on the golf course was a factor in getting him the role, and though neither he nor Loretta Young received professional credit for their work, they had starring parts...if one didn't count Bobby Jones's name in the title.

Allan was supposed to have been in *Smart Money* (1931), a feature film that debuted in July with Edward G. Robinson as the star, and James Cagney beside him. Since there were "twenty-four well-defined characters" in this story, there were many actors in the cast to take on those parts and in different press commentary any or all of them were mentioned. Allan was one of those actors, even as reviews went to press. He did make the film but his part was ultimately deemed unnecessary to the final product, and he was cut out.

In a work-up to the film, a press piece in the gossip column, "Screen Life In Hollywood," compared Allan's career in ways to that of Robinson.

Allan playing golf for the camera. PHOTO COURTESY THE COSTELLO FAMILY COLLECTION

Warner Bros. may have been grooming Allan to walk in Robinson's shoes. Though they were two very different men, with vastly different looks and demeanors, they had similar personal storylines relating to their repeated attempts to make it in the movies.

"Allan Lane was in Hollywood, too, two years ago (referencing Robinson being turned down his first time in town), but didn't have much luck...Someone at the time suggested he be put under contract, but nothing was done about it. Now he has been 'discovered' anew." Obviously this was written, and published, before it was known Allan Lane was not featured in the Robinson film. The piece also neglected to reference Allan's earlier Fox contract.

Yet that was not the only "Edward G. Robinson-Allan Lane" attempted pairing. There was another which, seemingly through no fault of either actor, never made it to the screen. A film titled *The Idol* had been slated to go into production in February. Allan was to support Robinson in a story based on a play of the same name by Martin Brown. The tale told of a famous master of the Russian ballet, but the production apparently never got off the ground. As with other intended projects for Allan during that period, this one was another promise made to him by the studio that never saw the light of day.

Night Nurse (1931), with already-experienced actress, Barbara Stanwyck, arrived in theaters in August as the next in line to be added to Allan's growing resumé of uncredited parts. He was noticed, though, as newspaper reports singled him out as part of a solid supporting cast, billing him fourth behind Ben Lyon, Joan Blondell, and the to-become-famous Clark Gable. However, when the movie got to the theaters, Allan was seen as nothing more than an "intern," and he received no specific credit for his work.

Later in the month, he was in *The Star Witness* (1931). Movie ads mentioned his name, saying he and other actors were all "equally well known to screen fans...[and] are seen to advantage." But as had become almost the norm for him, his public press didn't equal the on-camera work he did. Allan's part was once more without a name. He played a "young deputy" and received no name recognition in the final count.

There was what appears to have been a mystery movie — an Oliver and Hardy film — slated for September. *Tattooed* was "a waterfront story, in which Stan and Oliver [Oliver and Hardy] have numerous misadventures in a sailor's boarding house." By recorded accounts, this film appears to never have made it out of the concept stage.

Allan had signed a contract with Warner Bros. believing, based on what he had been told by the executives who initially courted him, he would have great opportunities come his way. One of those opportunities, in addition to the Edward G. Robinson movies that proved to be a bust, was *The Reckless Hour* (1931), a film starring Dorothy Mackaill, already quite the leading lady for a half dozen or so years. This movie was indicated to be the reason Allan was "brought here [Hollywood] from New York to play the lead…" The storyline arose from an adaptation of a stage play titled *Ambush*.

Honor of the Family, *starring Bebe Daniels.*

The movie was made, but when it hit the screens, Allan Lane was not included. There is no official record to indicate why he wasn't ultimately in the cast. Mackaill was about six years older. She portrayed a high-fashion style model by day, going home to her quarreling family in the evenings. Her character fell in love with an artist who betrayed her trust and turned her into a cynic. The day was saved when another lover came in and set her world upright.

Allan was only twenty-two. He may have proven to be too young as Mackaill's costar. Every male actor involved in the final product, except one, was nearly decades older. Possibly the brass simply decided he wasn't right for the story. Or perhaps something more involved occurred to require a change in plans. However it came about, or didn't, this proved to be yet another disappointment for Allan.

He was seen on the screen four times in the month of October — the same month *The Reckless Hour* debuted. Two of these roles were titled characters and the other two went uncredited, turning out as nothing more than eye-candy for background effect. He was getting a good amount of press but little serious attention for his work.

His automobile situation had improved, though, and the press made note.

Delores Costello on her wedding day to John Barrymore.

One article mentioned what he had driven during his first stint around Hollywood, and it added, "This time, with a better contract and surer future, he still drives an unpretentious vehicle, although a new model." Allan had used a bit of the money he socked away as a contract actor to upgrade his wheels, and since the subject of his car had been a story which circulated a few years before, it received renewed attention. He may have been making more money but he still wasn't raking in the dollars, and this piece spoke to his thriftiness and how well he was able to manage his pocketbook.

Honor of the Family (1931), "a sprightly modernization of Balzac's famous play," was out on celluloid in October, managing to put together "melodrama, comedy and romance at the same time — a difficult feat achieved with admirable unity." Allan's name was listed in press for this production, though he was way down the cast list in a role supporting the stars, Bebe Daniels and Warren William, and their primary costars.

Allan crossed paths with many of early Hollywood's greats, near-greats, and relatives of these folks, if only on a film set. His movie credits looked like cast lists of the "Who's Who" of early talking films. *Expensive Women* (1931) was a good example of this. Dolores Costello was the female lead. This was her last Warner Bros. film and something of a first retirement for her. She left to become the wife of John Barrymore, and the mother of his famous children.

The movie did little, if anything, for Allan's career. He played an unnamed party boy. This, in an odd way, indicated acting ability on his part. Of all the possible negative labels that might have fit him, being a party type wasn't really one of them. Once again, his name was included as part of the cast in most of the official press circulating the country but proved to be nothing more than another blip on his acting resumé — a credit, a frustrating credit, that got him nowhere.

Hal Roach Studios got him next. He was put in a short starring the beautiful and successful comedienne Thelma Todd. Her story became a tragic one only four years later when she was found dead in her garage, reportedly the result of a suicide, which has since remained mired in controversy. Then, though, she was riding high, and *War Mamas* (1931) was but a quickie on her path to more substantial roles. Zasu Pitts was her costar and the two played unexpected spies in World War I whiling away an evening with a few German officers. Allan played the Number One "doughboy."

He rounded out 1931 with a few more forgettable roles. In one, Allan ran across the screen in *Local Boy Makes Good*, also known as *The Poor Nut* (1931). Literally, he ran across the screen. The storyline surrounded a college, a misguided love triangle, and a track meet. The track meet was where Allan came in…and went. The stars were Joe E. Brown and Dorothy Lee.

In another, which didn't hit the screens before January of 1932, he offered the romantic element in a Laurel and Hardy short comedy titled *Any Old Port*. The movie received high marks as "a laugh riot," and "a comedy sensation." Allan, however, was so forgettable his bit never made its way to his official list of movie appearances, even though newspaper tidbits stated the "love interest is handled by Allan Lane and Jacqueline Wells." Wells received no credit either, so there is the possibility that both were cut before the end result came out in theaters. Laurel and Hardy weren't often known for the romance in their films.

CHAPTER FIVE

The Ad Man
Who Played Football

An article written in the late 1920s had stated, "For years Allan Lane went from studio to studio playing small parts, hoping that some director or producer might recognize his talents and give him an opportunity." This was, again, an exaggeration. Allan had only been making movies for about a year. He had, at the time of the article, only a handful of credits to his name — absolutely nothing of great note — and he was by no means a seasoned veteran.

On the other hand, Allan was the sort who expected results would come to him fast, and always quicker than they ever did. He wanted to move up the chain and did not want to spend a lot of time cooling his heels in the background. Hollywood, to his chagrin, had not operated that way for him. One thing was true in the earlier gossip snippet: He *had* gone from "studio to studio," first with a contract and then as a free agent, not under obligation to any specific studio.

Now, with him as a contract player for a major movie entity, the press machine worked overtime to build an even more solid and glowing backstory for Allan. Twentieth Century-Fox is likely the operation that began the Allan Lane-Notre Dame football hero legend in 1929. The tale began circulating after his first film with them, and then it grew legs. By the start of 1932, official listings said he had been a "halfback on Notre Dame team."

The rest of his physical talents went on to read as if he were a king-of-sports, stating he had a history with "baseball, football, tennis, golf, riding, swimming." Since a good bit of the list was true, the idea he could have excelled at Notre Dame apparently seemed a logical path for a nameless studio publicity person. This untruth was never actively questioned in his lifetime.

From February of 1931 and through half of 1932, Allan was under contract to Warner Bros. Yet the originally planned "long term" solid association hadn't proved as fruitful as originally expected, on either end. In December of 1931, though he was still with Warner Bros., he was doing a picture for Mack Sennett, apparently as a loan-out. Sennett distributed an official biography on him, crediting Allan with all the by-now-usual promotional details. He had an address in Los Angeles, living in an apartment on a windy road in the hills above Hollywood. His address was 2425 Cheremoya.

His Mack Sennett appearance was in a fluffy comedy titled *Heavens! My Husband!* (1932). In this two-reel short, his character was officially categorized as a "juvenile" named Jimmy Benson. Starring Andy Clyde and Dorothy Granger, *Heavens! My Husband!* was released in March of 1932 with a tagline reading, "Andy's honeymoon at Niagara Falls is disrupted by a kibitzer." Press said it was "the funniest, cleanest comedy of the year" and "guaranteed to make you laugh till you cry!" This was the sort of laugh fest often added to the bill behind a variety of A-list movies.

Sennett Studios was facing financial difficulties. They may have utilized Allan in hopes his pretty face would bring them up in the ranks. Andy Clyde, one of those actors who looked old even when he was young, had been with Sennett for over six years. He was only forty when *Heavens! My Husband!* hit the screens, yet he already appeared on the early side of elderly. Though he was one of the studio's major players, shortly after this feature aired, his salary was cut — soon after, he moved to Columbia Pictures. Clyde's experiences with Sennett might have offered Allan visions of what might be in his future if he continued to associate with Mack Sennett. They were on the brink of falling by the wayside, and did so only a few years later. After one picture for them, Allan was returned to Warner Bros.

He did about a picture a month at this point. There are reports he was in a Douglas Fairbanks, Jr. movie that April. *It's Tough To Be Famous* (1932) told the story of a Navy war hero plucked from obscurity and thrown into the limelight, oftentimes in the face of his frustration over losing sight of what was important in his life. The movie's theme was rumored to be based on the Lindbergh story, before the baby scandal. Allan, if he was in this one, was never credited and so embedded in the background as to be invisible.

Press called *The Famous Ferguson Case* (1932), made early in the year and on movie screens in May, "the most realistic newspaper picture yet made" and "a screen presentation of a tragedy of real life." For Allan, as his next piece of work, this was nothing more than a barely-there credit, a no-name portrayal of a reporter — in a storyline filled with reporters.

Many others of a similar ilk followed suit. There was *The Tenderfoot* (1932) with Joe E. Brown and Ginger Rogers, also out in May. Allan Lane…uncredited. Since Allan and Ginger were supposedly stepping out on the town together just a few years later, this may have been where they met. Or, just as likely, the studios put them together for the flash of the camera's light bulbs.

Next, Loretta Young starred in *Week-End Marriage* (1932), which ultimately was renamed *Working Wives* — the title changing somewhere between inception and screen. Her male costar was Norman Foster. Foster was six years older than Allan but had a similar career path — theater, both on the road and on Broadway, and many smaller roles leading up to what appeared to now be a growing career.

Unlike Allan, however, Foster had managed to hold his ground. At the time he filmed *Week-End Marriage,* he was lined up with solid roles, one right after the other. He was married to Claudette Colbert but, interestingly, only a few years later, he divorced her and married Loretta Young's younger sister, Sally Blane. Foster ultimately became a director.

For Allan Lane this was yet again nothing more than an uncredited quickie, even though he was mentioned briefly in some of the movie's officially-circulated press.

A few months later, Allan was rubbing noses with Jimmy Cagney as well as a number of other screen notables. *Winner Takes All* (1932) starred Cagney, while featuring the likes of silent-turned-talkie actress Marian Nixon; Guy Kibbee, who'd already been around the block quite a few times; and Virginia Bruce. Bruce was a lovely young actress who, at about the same time as the movie hit the screens, was holding court with one of the newest A-list leading men: Robert Taylor. Virginia was close in age to Allan, and he played Monty, one of her friends. The bit, as had become his usual fare these days, went officially uncredited.

Hollywood was then, as in its earlier days and even more than at any time thereafter, a production mill, churning out pictures in an attempt to appease a crowd hungry for entertainment, something to remove them from a humdrum everyday life. Not only was the motion picture industry still something of a novelty but the world wanted to pull itself out of the Great Depression, causing an overwhelming need for distraction.

Between his contract work and occasional loan-outs, Allan was included in a total of ten films in 1932. There was also *Crooner; A Successful Calamity* with George Arliss and Mary Astor; *The Crash* starring Ruth

Chatterton and George Brent; and *One Way Passage* with William Powell and Kay Francis, a melodramatic sob story which was called "one of the screens best love stories in 1932." Allan once more played a platonic friend, this time for Kay Francis's character — and yes, he went uncredited.

A Successful Calamity, which came out in September, was notable for Allan only because he played a "polo player." As his first onscreen appearance to prove he was able to ride a horse as early as his early twenties, the part unknowingly foretold of what would be the basis of his future success. This was long before he was ever required to ride as the star of his own series, and even longer before he became the voice of a horse.

These movies rounded out Allan's year. All of the parts were as friends of the stars or folks in the crowd, and they went, for the most part, without any notice. For the experience alone, he took on just about every role offered him, "whether it gave him a chance to read a line or not."

When the role in a movie titled *Miss Pinkerton* (1932) came his way, Allan was excited and had high hopes. Finally, he was offered the chance to play a character, Herbert Wynn, who would be the central piece of the storyline. One article, after the fact, put it this way, "An important part in the Mary Roberts Rinehart thriller, *Miss Pinkerton*, is that of the corpus delicti."

Another reporter explained how Allan Lane, "an ambitious young actor," was initially delighted to find he was cast as Herbert Wynne. At the time he signed on, though, he didn't realize his "important part" would end up as nothing more than a body at the opening of the story. For the rest of the movie he remained "one ear buried in the carpet, quite dead." Once the filming was completed and the movie went into production, Allan found himself even more disappointed when he learned his appearance would be left on the cutting room floor. Somewhere along the way, an executive decided the story could be told quite well without benefit of a breathing actor in the title role. There was but small consolation when he got a paycheck for the work he did, which the movie-going public never saw.

Allan was disheartened. He wasn't happy with the parts he had been given, and it seemed Warner Bros. wasn't much thrilled with him, either. Not a single role had offered him the least opportunity to be seriously noticed. He was a young man who liked to be on the move as opposed to sitting around and forever cooling his heels under the heat of the cameras. He also preferred to play characters with life in them. Not an unreasonable expectation. He had signed a contract with Warner Bros. on the understanding he would star in at least one major film, and a few others with great promise would be offered to him. No such thing had come to pass.

Still, to be fair to the studio, Allan had known what he would be up against when he agreed to give Hollywood another go. Unfulfilled promises were made all the time in the movie industry, and despite his tender age, this wasn't his first time around the track. What he hadn't counted on was how difficult it would be for someone with his personality to be successful in an environment he felt was disingenuous.

Lobby card for One Way Passage.

Studios took a chance with every actor signed. Some of the talent worked, some didn't. Allan was blunt, outspoken, and often abrasive. According to Chester B. Hahn's column, "This, that, and t'other…" Allan Lane was released from his Warner Bros. contract in June of 1932, along with a handful of other actors, including Ruth Hall, Betty Gillette, and Gloria Shea.

Allan needed another break from Tinseltown. Tinseltown may have needed another break from Allan. He was a small part of no less than seven pictures that hit the screen during this period. Promises had been broken on both ends, and Allan had to live with the reality that when he signed with Warner Bros., he had been offered opportunities with other studios — offers he turned down. He made his own choices and they proved to not go as well as he had expected.

The studio choice had been his alone. Had he made the right decision? Had he selected the best studio for him? While his visible presence on

Allan Lane, in an early headshot. To Hollywood or not to Hollywood? PHOTO COURTESY THE COSTELLO FAMILY COLLECTION

film continued for a few more months as the movies he had already made hit the screens, his physical presence in town fell off the radar, seemingly overnight. When he had an opening to move one more time, he seized the opportunity.

Allan packed up and left Hollywood in mid-1932. What he did for the next nearly two years is not well-documented. What is known is that he found love — or at least he thought he was in love. While a line-up of pictures including Allan Lane's name in the cast list were hitting the theaters, one after another, word that his contract had been dropped was public knowledge by mid-June. He certainly knew he was out of work ahead of that date — probably the early part of the month — and he once again decided to leave town.

Gladys Leslie Schneider, one of a few known photos of her in younger years.
PHOTO COURTESY HER NEPHEW,
RICK SCHNEIDER

He was ticked off with Hollywood and wasted no time in leaving. He and the petite, pretty blonde dancer, Gladys Leslie Schneider, married just nine days later in Westchester County, New York. A look at Allan's professional timeline would support the likelihood he and Gladys Schneider met in New York City in early June of 1932. They couldn't have known each other more than a few days unless the couple had previously met through Willye, Gladys's sister.

Allan's residence on their marriage certificate was listed in Los Angeles. The address he gave was his apartment at 2425 Cheremoya, the same home base he had reported for his Mack Sennett bio. His departure from California had been quick, and he may not have known where he would end up. Or possibly he didn't yet have a local address. Where he lived with his new bride is unknown. They both added years to their real ages — Allan saying he was born in 1903 and Gladys in 1911 — so they may have run off to get married, without approval of her family.

However it began, his marriage soured after only a few months, and Allan appears to have left New York right after the ringing of wedding bells soured. On the road again. He had already proven to be something of a vagabond, rarely staying in one place for long. His official biographical material claimed that soon after, he was playing backfield for the Cincinnati Reds, a "professional football aggregation" with the Western Division of the National Football League. Quotes from Allan stated he "went back to professional football with my old team."

Gladys Leslie Schneider seated on the left, her mother in the middle, and her sister, Willye seated on the right, with other sister, Alphia standing on right.
PHOTO COURTESY HER NEPHEW, RICK SCHNEIDER

While no records have surfaced to prove he played for the Cincinnati Reds at any point in his life, the team's history was short-lived and little documentation has survived for their time in action, so it is possible he was with them for a while. He had family in Cincinnati, and when he was tired of Hollywood and New York, he tended to go back to his people when he needed a break. Yet the team was reportedly established on July 8, 1933, so the likelihood Allan "went back" is hard to figure out. Otherwise, the rest of the timing makes sense in relation to Allan's personal history.

Other records have proven Allan to be cagey in interviews when it came to that time in his life. He didn't want to verify for any press entities what name he used when he played football, making it more difficult to trace his actual whereabouts and define what he did, or did not do, when he was away from Hollywood. One article reported, "The mystery of 'Who is Allan Lane?' can keep right on being a mystery as far as he is concerned."

Rumors swirled about that he went under any number of names and played for any number of teams, all of which were exactly that — rumors. This crazy publicity was great for a young man who had already garnered a bit of attention in Hollywood, a town where visibility and public awareness were all-important. Allan knew how to play the game. The circulating stories, true or otherwise, allowed him to easily disappear whenever he chose to do so. An ongoing uncertainty surrounding his real name aided greatly in the effort.

Chuck Anderson, owner of the "Old Corral" website, wrote of a 1938 *Screen Book* magazine article, sent to him by a man named Gerald Griffore, which included a "lengthy" profile on Allan. Among other tidbits, this piece had Allan telling the reporter he had "shagged fly balls and trained with the Chicago Cubs and Chicago White Sox baseball teams." This may have been fact, a theory based on family photos. One showed Allan in a Chicago uniform with team members, and in another, he was alone as he offered himself up in a number of game poses. Another possibility is that whatever studio he had been with at the time put him out on the field. Either way, he looked the part and the information could easily fit into his official biography.

Official detail relates that Allan next played football in New Jersey. If the Cincinnati Reds period was true, and under whatever name he played for them during their 1933–1934 season — a time when all other information on him seems scant if not completely missing — then stories of how he came to play football in New Jersey could easily follow suit. He was trying to decide what to do next. He was disgusted with the Hollywood route, and felt he had gotten nowhere very fast. He returned to Cincinnati to visit family, and may have become a part of the fledgling, but not-too-successful, Cincinnati Reds.

From there, he could have made his way east yet again and played with the East Orange Tornadoes in New Jersey. At a later date, he said to a reporter, "Don't ask me whether my name really is Lane or not." He was recorded on the Tornadoes rosters in a month's worth of games from mid-September to about mid-October, under the name of Allan Lane. He reportedly left this team because they owed him $130. Since money was important to the success of whatever he might do in the future, it was crucial he be paid what he had honestly earned. He was not about to do a job without getting his due. Allan did not take kindly to unfulfilled obligations.

Soon after, he signed on with another team, the Paterson Panthers, again in New Jersey. Known dates for his association with them lasted about three months, from October to late December.

This is when the idea for a solid business venture gained traction. He

Allan in uniform with team members in Chicago. PHOTO COURTESY THE COSTELLO FAMILY COLLECTION

had been saving his money and formulating options. Allan needed to invest money to make his plan a reality. Going back to the stage would build up his bank account even more. This go-round he added modeling to his repertoire. He still had a considerable amount of positive press going for him thanks to his most recent small, but notable, film parts. Professional media commentary backed up that resumé and the ambiguity surrounding what he had done with his life in between stints in front of a camera added spice to the "Who is Allan Lane?" mystery.

Whether he called himself Harry Albers or Allan Lane, he had already acted alongside a bevy of big-time marquee names, including Edward G. Robinson, Clark Gable, Joan Crawford, and Barbara Stanwyck. This added credibility to his fledgling efforts, whatever they may be. Still, none of his onscreen appearances had caught fire with the movie-going public so he didn't see the movies as being the right place for him. At least not yet. If he had stayed in that arena, he felt in danger of falling into obscurity before he found his chance to shine.

He said of his initial movie-making period, "Pictures didn't appeal to me, nor did Hollywood itself, and I convinced myself that since I'd never be able to do well on the screen, I'd forget the whole business."

Allan ready to play ball in Chicago. PHOTO COURTESY THE COSTELLO FAMILY COLLECTION

He didn't exactly forget the business, though he did step away from the screen. Returning once more to New York and setting his sights on something new proved to be a growth opportunity. Allan was all about going forward and continuing to work, even if he repeatedly had to change course midstream to keep his motor running. Since he began in the entertainment world seven or so years earlier, he had been enamored with the magic a camera made, and how it could project an entire story with but one well-placed image. He decided to leverage his varied experience as well as his good looks and fine figure, and he moonlighted as a model in addition to the occasional stage work that came his way. Allan looked forward to a bright future.

CHAPTER SIX

The Ladies...Part Two

Modeling offered Allan an entirely new social circle, and he had no problem finding companionship after-hours. Being an available and handsome young man, surrounded by beautiful woman also trying to find their big break, gave him his pick of the ladies and then some. One in particular caught his eye, and she returned the feelings.

An artist's model known then as Elizabeth Miller, the young lady was born and raised in Pensacola, Florida. She acted in school plays, and her natural good looks didn't escape anyone's notice, particularly Allan's. Most of Elizabeth's friends called her Betty, but her family often called her Rosa. She had been encouraged to move to New York City from Florida to pursue an acting career, and she started with print ads for a variety of products, with hopes of making her way into the movie world. By the early 1930s, barely over twenty-one, Elizabeth had been seen in a variety of newspaper and magazine advertisements, including high-end courtier clothing.

Allan also posed in print ads for an assortment of products. His thick, wavy hair and classic face fit the bill perfectly. One job had him dressed in a spotless tuxedo as he classically represented Vaseline Hair Tonic.

One more showed Allan's profile as he smilingly exhibited his smooth shave, achieved thanks to the wonders of "Williams Glider," the new "brushless shave."

Yet another, this one for Rexall Milk of Magnesia toothpaste, featured the young Betty Miller with a handsome man at her side. That young man was Allan. Both had the required big smile and beautifully sparkling white teeth needed to sell toothpaste. They looked like a couple in love.

If they weren't in love right then, they thought they were soon after. A brief newspaper tidbit reported that the five-feet-five-inches "artist's model" Elizabeth Miller weighed in at barely over one hundred pounds. She first adopted the surname of Kathryn in most professional circles. At the time, she was Betty Miller, and she and Allan Lane — still privately known as Harry Albershart — wed about 1933. He was twenty-four and she was twenty-one.

Newly-married Allan continued to pose in front of the still camera but began to put in more time behind the lens. Ever since his first foray into Hollywood, he had looked for a chance to operate the camera and direct

 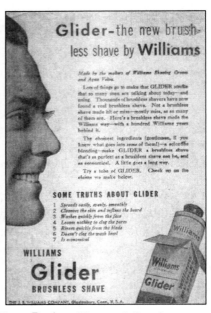

Left: *Allan modeling for Vaseline Hair Tonic.* Right: *Allan modeling for Williams Brushless Shave.* PHOTOS COURTESY THE COSTELLO FAMILY COLLECTION

the camera's action. He preferred working behind the camera as opposed to being the subject. He was fascinated by different forms of lighting and how light was able to catch the angles in his subject's faces as well as in and around inanimate objects.

Ultimately, Allan hoped to become a movie director, but he knew he had to make his way up the food chain. The story goes that when he got to New York City, he found a job in the mailing department of one of the big advertising agencies. This was a respectable job, but Allan didn't feel as if he would make great strides in such a position. He wanted to make his mark faster than he logically would if he climbed the ladder in the traditional way. He was impatient, feeling as if he had already spent a lot of time spinning his wheels.

"I discovered," he said in an interview, "that if I wanted to work my way up, it would take me many years to reach the executive offices located on the eleventh floor. That was too long for me."

So he went about it in another way. He diligently studied the trade magazines and discovered how most advertising was done predominantly with photographs. Yet again, it was the cameras that made the difference.

Allan modeling with Elizabeth "Betty" Miller for Rexall Milk of Magnesia toothpaste. PHOTO COURTESY THE COSTELLO FAMILY COLLECTION

Allan was methodical and not afraid of hard work if he felt it would get him where he wanted to go. He didn't necessarily have the schooling to put him at the head of the class, but he did have the street smarts. He went from the mailroom to a job as a commercial art salesman, and he intentionally made the right contacts in advertising agencies in and around New York City. It didn't take a full year before he was well-known by the folks he felt he needed to know.

By the fall of 1934, Allan had built a solid client list, and he started to call on them again — this time not as a salesman for someone else's company but as the front man for his own agency. He promised top-of-the-line work, showing them a portfolio he had built up on his off time, and they promised him the jobs. He played football behind the scenes, mostly to finance his agency efforts. He also borrowed money from a few family members and friends to make his dream come true.

Allan proved his mettle, becoming known as a topnotch ad man with a knack for pulling off just the right lighting to get the best shot, which, in turn, created successful print advertisements. Whether his focus was an inanimate object or a beautiful lady, he had an eye for seeing images in terms of dollar signs added to the pocketbooks of his clients. Allan Lane became known as able to figure out the most ideal placements for the highest profit.

Unfortunately, his marriage was already on the skids, and his union with Betty Miller was not to last. They made their way to divorce court between late 1934 and early 1935. Exactly what went wrong is unknown but what is public knowledge tells that Harry Cohn, who would soon became scion of Columbia Pictures and who was seriously smitten with Betty, was an instrumental factor in her split from Allan.

Cohn met her in New York at the Central Park Casino. She was still a model and was looking for a way into the movies. He promised her a contract, telling her he would take her places she had only dreamed of going. She stated in an article a few years later, "It is very hard to get started in the movies but I was most fortunate in making the right connections before I went and consequently I have made more rapid progress than most persons with ambition to become an actress."

Her "right connections," in the guise of Harry Cohn, convinced her to move to Los Angeles. He promised her a sweet deal with his Columbia Pictures. Betty had plans to move up in the industry, and the same article said as much. "Right now I am just getting to my goal as I took parts in Western roles for some time after going into the screen business." Her next choice of words seemed to indicate she felt those "Western roles" had been beneath her. "My last pictures were 'A' rated," she stressed.

And those "A" rated" pictures had come to her as a result of Harry Cohn being true to the offer he made to her. By the spring of 1936, the now-named actress, Joan Perry, under the "management of her aunt, Mrs. E.S. Lester," was being touted as one of Columbia's "new faces," with a bevy of charming ladies in the mix, including Florence Rice, Gloria Shea, Ann Sothern, and a few more. They were, an article said, "...all young, all lovely, all, when they came to Columbia, a decided novelty to screen audiences."

There was one major point in Betty-turned-Joan's favor, setting her apart from the other beauties: At the time she and the others were signed, Harry Cohn had also signed a gorgeous young lady named Rita Hayworth. He changed Betty's name to Joan Perry — Betty Miller was just too common — and made an audacious proclamation regarding the futures of both Hayworth and Perry. This public statement figured strongly into Perry's relationship with Allan.

Cohn was a bold, brash man known for his take-no-prisoners attitude. He was not often liked by the people who worked for him or worked around him. Many feared him. He was extraordinarily enamored of the dark-haired, beautiful young model from Florida, yet on the other hand, he knew what he had, in a business sense, in the form of Rita Hayworth.

Harry Cohn set his personal sights on Betty, aka Joan Perry, pursuing her for more than simply her screen persona. He refused to take no for an answer from her. Cohn usually got what he wanted, and he definitely got what he wanted with both of these women. The now-infamous line attributed to him, and directed at her at the time he secured Joan's signature on the studio contact's dotted line, was, "Hayworth will be a star and you will be my wife."

He was twenty years Joan's senior, but nothing could stop the intimidating, overbearing Harry Cohn. Cohn had big plans for her, which put Allan, as her husband, in the middle of this grand scheme. He was legally wed to the same woman who Harry Cohn publicly stated he would marry. The minor details — Cohn was already married, he had shown the ultimate disrespect for his wife, he was Jewish, and Joan was a church-going Catholic girl, and she was at the time Allan's wife — seemed to matter not in the least to Harry Cohn.

How much this may have emotionally affected Allan is speculation. However, Betty Miller, aka Joan Perry, aka Mrs. Harry Albershart, did leave New York. She also left Allan Lane. Soon after arriving in Los Angeles, in September of 1935, she signed a movie contract with Cohn's Columbia Pictures under the professional name of Joan Perry. If she and Allan were not yet divorced, they were soon after.

There were six years between when she signed her contract and when she officially became Harry Cohn's wife, and those years were put to good use toward her career. She was given a complete biographical makeover. Publicity amnesia helped to wipe her out of Allan's life, at least in the public's eye. Her entire film career amounted to less than twenty movies, so in many ways, Cohn's earlier prediction had been starkly prophetic and right on the mark. Rita Hayworth did become a star. Joan Perry did become Harry Cohn's wife.

Allan had, over the years of his short life, honed skills he learned working his way around all sorts of businesses from his earliest school days. One of those jobs came to him right after he left school, when he had taken a job as a photographic illustrator. As a thirsty student of the environment around him, he added various camera techniques to his growing repertoire, and developed new ones on his own. He realized he really enjoyed this sort of work and now that he finally had the chance to put his learning to practical use, he hung out a shingle under his own name, going to work as the owner of an ad agency.

The football money he had earned on the side was added to the pot, and Allan found a great location for his new business. With letterhead and cards that boldly read, "Allan Lane Inc. Photographic Illustrators," his business address was, "GRAND CENTRAL PALACE BUILDING. * 480 LEXINGTON AVE. * NEW YORK." A notation on December 6, 1932, in the *New York Times* indicated "Allan Lane, Inc." had rented office space. From then on, he got busy with the job of satisfying his growing clientele list.

Allan's second wife, Betty Miller, who became known in Hollywood first as Joan Perry and then, years after her divorce from Allan, as Mrs. Harry Cohn.

The Grand Central Palace Building was literally grand: a "beautiful and imposing structure built entirely of white granite" and New York's principal exhibition hall. Designed by the same team that had created the Grand Central Terminal, the Palace Building had a total of ten stories, including the ground level. The structure had a building-wide penthouse area. Movies filmed in New York City that required large spaces were known to film on the roof. The interior was utilized "exclusively for industrial and business exhibition conventions of all kinds." As part of the Grand Central District, people would come and go from this centralized point, utilizing the train station that tied the busy location together.

This was a perfect place for a venture such as Allan's. He was in the thick of a community that combined artistry and business. With trade shows and events continually going on all around him, he was centrally located to acquire new business day after day. A few of his highest-profile clients were Ford Motor Company, Camay Soap, Lucky Strike Cigarettes, and Wrigley's Chewing Gum. Word got around town that Allan Lane Inc. Photographic Illustrators would offer a unique take on a product — human or otherwise.

Allan wasn't putting all his talents into one section of the market, however. As always, he continued to have many interests. Whichever proved

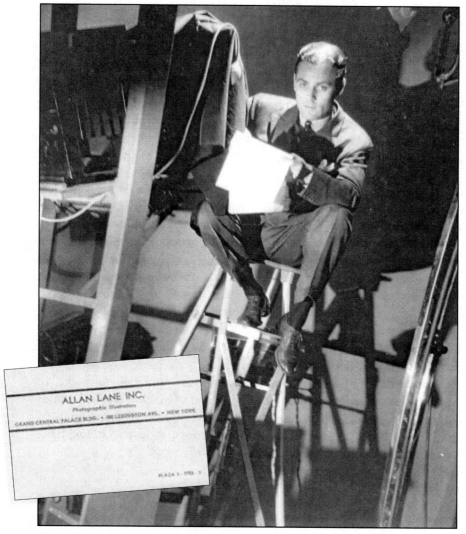

As the head of Allan Lane Inc. Photographic Illustrators, behind the camera and directing the action. PHOTOS COURTESY THE COSTELLO FAMILY COLLECTION

to be the standout at any given time became the direction in which he moved for the foreseeable future. Allan had been quite the athlete ever since his earliest days in Indiana, and his love of baseball and football kept him going when he wasn't taking photographs. This served him twofold. Not only did this give him an outlet for his physical side but it also helped fund his efforts as a businessman and pay his bills. He didn't just play the game to enjoy it. Allan ultimately played to put money in his pocket.

The years of 1935 and 1936 are assumed to have been productive business years for Allan with little-to-no-known personal activity in the theater or in the movies. Instead, he kept busy building a name for himself in the world of advertising, creating quality products with his camera work and industry acumen. He found a niche in the creation of photographic portfolios for young model hopefuls, keeping his professional hand active in Hollywood's pocket without having to deal directly with that environment. He became known in and around the movie business for his artistic and creative take on headshots and publicity shots of those looking to break into the movies.

In particular, he had quite a camera eye for females, and his particular ability to light a young woman's face and form caught the attention of many studio executives. He hired and used young ladies to model for product shots, and they, in turn, had their portfolios done by him. This was a symbiotic relationship. He reportedly gave more than one future actress her first job as a model. He made a screen test for an unnamed movie-struck model, which got her a job at Twentieth Century-Fox. The studio became as interested, if not more so, in the creator of her screen test as they had been interested in the actress. They were said to have been impressed by how it was "unusually lighted and staged."

It looked as if Allan Lane might find the great success he had hoped for early on, with behind-the-scenes production and camera work. He may have never, in fact, returned to Hollywood of his own accord to stand in front of a camera, if Tinseltown had not once again called on him to do so. He was like a cat with nine lives in the movie industry, coming back again, and again, and even yet again.

CHAPTER SEVEN

Hollywood Comes Calling...Again

Before the summer of 1936 hit its peak, Allan Lane had been cajoled into coming back to Hollywood one more time, not as a photographer or a producer but with yet another promise of a solid acting contract — this time with Twentieth Century-Fox. The studio backed up their promise with a listing of on-paper roles he would be given, allowing him to hope for the high visibility he had not yet achieved as an actor.

The carrot dangled in front of his face was substantial enough to make him believe in the offer, and he had high hopes this time for his future in movies. This contract appears to have been a variation on one of the offers made to him a few years earlier when he initially went to Hollywood and signed with Warner Bros. Allan decided to take the money he had earned so far and close the doors to his agency, going back to the West Coast.

Upon his return to Hollywood, one thing was for sure: he was not in need of work. Twentieth Century-Fox initially made good on their offer, and parts streamed his way. With two marriages behind him to account for his personal experience, and a solid business background added to his professional repertoire, Allan Lane proved this time to be nobody's fool. He wasn't easy to fit into a particular mold, and by this point, most movie executives knew this.

On the other side of the coin, Allan was required to submit to the studio's demands, and he was more than aware he was no longer the boss. Despite his agreement to play by the rules, whether or not he would hold up his end of the bargain with his new contract was anyone's guess. Everyone on both sides had gone into this agreement with awareness of the other's peccadilloes, and a promising outcome was expected.

Since fitting talent into preconceived molds was what Hollywood did best, Allan Lane being invited back into the fold said a lot about his skill set. This was a town that made its fortune on the backs of malleable hopefuls. Allan signed his new contract with Twentieth Century-Fox at the end of June. Newspapers reports said the signing came to him "at a steep salary," and the multi-experienced actor hoped "to work into test-

Lois Wilson, Jane Darwell, and Allan in Laughing At Trouble. PHOTO COURTESY THE COSTELLO FAMILY COLLECTION

ing and eventually directing." His ability to operate a camera may have been a part of the deal that had lured him once again into the center of the movie business.

Gossip columnists had been given early notice about his return. Articles began appearing which mentioned his name, taking note of his again giving acting a try yet mentioning nothing about his camera abilities. Pre-production articles said he would have "an important role" in a film which reportedly began filming on July 22. The film title was *Fifteen Maiden Lane* (1936), and actor Alan Dinehart was also scheduled as a pivotal supporting player. The stars were Claire Trevor and Cesar Romero. For whatever reason, neither man ended up in the final version. Shades of earlier experiences for Allan Lane were already showing up.

December of 1936 was a month of multiple movie releases for him. *Laughing at Trouble* (1936) was early on titled *Laughing at Death*. Filmed between August and September, the light fare was in theaters by mid-December. This was Allan's first solid supporting role since his latest return to Hollywood. It was also his first film on the screen in four years. He worked with, among others, Margaret Hamilton who had not yet made

Allan with Shirley Temple in Stowaway. PHOTO COURTESY THE COSTELLO FAMILY COLLECTION

her monumental mark on movie history with *The Wizard of Oz* (1939), still yet a few years away. She was only seven years older than Allan, but even then, she looked far beyond her years. Also in the cast was John Carradine.

On Christmas Day, *Stowaway* (1936) debuted across the country. The movie's star — eight-year-old Shirley Temple — had already churned out thirty-five performances, and a good majority of them vehicles that featured her in the lead. She was an old pro in a little girl's body. Allan was also an old pro, about twenty years her senior and without even a small slice of the starring successes she had.

This production was not without difficulty in getting to the screen. Numerous newspaper reports came out in the month prior to the film being unveiled, telling of illness attacking the set. "For the third time influenza has jinxed the new Shirley Temple picture at Twentieth-Century Fox," one article said. First Shirley fell victim to influenza, with her bout bad enough to completely halt the production. Then it was Alice Faye, one of Shirley's lead co-stars. No sooner had they recovered enough to get back on track with filming, Allan was forced into bed rest. There was a mass number of actors all across Hollywood getting sick, playing havoc with a host of films set to be unleashed on the American public.

Stowaway unintentionally proved to be a mirror of Allan's current life path. Though he could have had no way of knowing it then, the similarities followed him even into the future. In this story, he played "the other man." He had been the other man in his marriage to Joan Perry, and this was a role he would become accustomed to in future movies.

Allan's character, Richard Hope, was quite the Mama's Boy. Throughout most of the film, Mother Hope directed almost every aspect of her son's life. While Allan never gave his own mother carte blanche with his affairs — he was rather closed-mouth about much of what he did when he wasn't in her presence — he was extremely dedicated to her, and family members fondly remembered him as a Mama's Boy. He was known as a man who took great care of his mother's well-being, and he genuinely loved and appreciated all she did for him. He felt his attention to her was a returned favor, and he considered her to be his best friend.

In *Stowaway*, Allan's character, Richard, eventually got the flick about how his mother's busybody attitude negatively affected his life, but he learned this lesson too late to make the difference. His girl ended up with the playboy. Allan's wife, just a few years earlier, had ended up with the movie mogul.

Allan didn't like this "brand of movie," and he disliked the characterizations he was forced to play. Even though he was acting opposite any number of great stars, he resisted the image Hollywood wanted to make of him as their long-term goal for his future. In his earlier go-rounds, when he would have taken any sort of speaking part just to get the visibility, he found himself barely seen on the screen in the final product.

Now, when he was finally being played as a solid second-string character actor, with potential for something more solid in the near future, he discovered that wasn't what he wanted, either. He was despondent and felt painted into a corner. This was another unhappy period in Allan's life. The work he was receiving had no depth and didn't fulfill him, yet it did offer him a decent paycheck. At the time, he was not receiving any better offers and he had to play the game.

Romance took his mind off his professional dissatisfaction for a while. He had a busy dating schedule, and the press took notice, quite likely by design. Actress Betty Furness, already a known quantity in Hollywood prior to meeting Allan, supposedly became his steady girl throughout much of the second half of 1936. One tidbit announced, "If you believe her friends, Betty Furness likes Allan Lane *very* much."

Betty Furness in the early days.

They were seen together so often it became an entertaining guessing game for newspaper columnists whether or not she would become Mrs. Allan Lane and, if so, when the wedding bells would ring. She returned to Los Angeles that October from a trip east. Harrison Carroll, a King Features Syndicated columnist, said, "When Betty Furness hopped off the train from New York she had so many hat boxes it took her mother, two porters, and Allan Lane to carry them to the car. Since Hollywood saw her last, Betty has changed the color of her hair to a deep amber brown." Reporters had a thing for Betty's hats, for which she was known far and wide, and for the ever-changing color of her hair.

A month later, a "Hollywood Romance Chart" for the upcoming "1937-1938 Matrimonial Derby" came out, announcing Allan and Betty had just "patched up a quarrel." In November, they were seen happily dining together "at Harry Sugarman's Tropics."

Allan was also spotted the same month "rushing Anita Louise," apparently during his quarrel with Betty. He and Betty ultimately mended their rift since they were still noted together for awhile afterward. Into early 1937, there were rumors of an on-again, off-again Allan Lane-Betty Furness romance.

She was reportedly "getting many long distance calls" from him. She was in Los Angeles and he was, for a brief time, back in New York. He may have had business to clear up with his previous photography venture. It wasn't long, though, before he returned to California. He lived in a modest apartment building near Wilshire Boulevard — the perfect place for a bachelor who never stayed anywhere too long.

A newspaper piece about Allan and Betty began this way: "Certainly they had spats and this was taken as an indication that they might have been serious because true love never runs smoothly," and ended with, "However, such is not the case." In the final count, a union between the two was not meant to be. In fact, a union between them was probably never truly in the offing to any great degree. This bit of trivia proved to be the end of a newsworthy romance that lasted only long enough to ensure Allan's name was kept in the press.

Betty did marry the next year, to composer and musical arranger Johnny Green. Their daughter, Babbie Green, said her mother's scrapbooks, which she has carefully kept over the years, proved Allan and Betty as a couple were, for the most part, not much more than a publicist's creation.

The period following Allan's latest return to Hollywood was the most public to date in regards to his romantic life. The studio's publicity department worked overtime on his behalf. After Betty, a line-up of beautiful Hollywood ladies was seen on his arm. Mary Frances Gifford, known around town as Frances, was next. She had been signed to a contract by Samuel Goldwyn when she was only sixteen. The relationship, if it could be called such, was no more than the blink of an eye before gossips had him once again courting Anita Louise, taking her to a "swank premiere."

An article in the fall seemed to be written with Allan in mind, though his name wasn't mentioned a single time. The headline read, "Photographers Think Blondes In Ascendency," and it discussed how photographers, "contrary to the general opinion of the movie colony," believed blondes were set to dominate the screen. There was a list of the photographer's collective choices for women most likely to succeed in the movies that year. Out of the ten, seven were blondes. Nearly half of these ladies had been romantically connected to Allan, including Joan Perry, who within a short period of making her way to Hollywood had already become a brunette. Either Allan had extraordinarily good taste, which was possible, or the studio was making sure he was being seen with the loveliest of the lovelies, which was even more likely.

Ginger Rogers followed next in the Allan Lane dating parade. She and Allan were seen cozying up in various locales. Gossip lady Louella Parsons, said he was "the latest" to fall for her, "but probably not the last." She "was giving herself…to a chosen few — including her latest masculine companion, Allan Lane." Ginger had been in the movies for nearly a decade, and this was a slow professional year for her. Sheilah Graham whispered a month later, "The Allan Lane-Ginger Rogers romance continues to look serious." One piece went on to identify Allan not as an upcoming film star or anything else related to Hollywood but instead as a "T.C.U. football player." Allan never played for Texas Christian University, as officially verified by the school's Admissions department.

This period may have been when Allan first discovered his love for betting on the horses — an amusement that would take up much of his time in the future. He was part of a Hollywood crowd that celebrated the opening of The Dunes Club in Palm Springs. The club was owned by reported mob figure Al Wertheimer, and proved to be all the rage. Everyone from the most well-known of Hollywood's elite — the likes of Clark Gable and Errol Flynn and Humphrey Bogart — to Tinseltown's up-and-coming, like Allan, were regulars.

Former Palm Springs Mayor Frank Bogert stated, "There was gambling every night, beautiful women and more money than you could shake a stick at." Some local hotels had special phone lines hooked up to the tables at The Dunes so guests could place bets on the races at Santa Anita in Los Angeles and other tracks. Those race tracks eventually became Allan's second home.

He was a blip across the screen in many a gossip column, with reports of him sighted at this-or-that club...The Palomar and many others. One tidbit stated, "Johnnie Weismuller, Roger Converse, Allan Lane, Lee Bowman" and others were "staggering in at the nightspots." Depending on how much one would believe the veracity of the almost-countless Hollywood gossips of the day, such a comment, this one compliments of Charles Sampas, might indicate much partying was going on during this period of Allan's life.

Asked early the following year who of the opposite sex attracted him, Allan named Jean Harlow, Greta Garbo, and Marlene Dietrich. He gave them all-inclusive praise for their "'earthiness,' 'natural assets,' 'their everything,' and 'their nostalgic and beautiful languor.'" All were A-list actresses of his generation, his age or a bit older. This gave insight into what sort of woman attracted him. Classy and usually blonde. The article made him look good by having his name attached to each one of these top-of-the-line stars, if only in a press piece.

His studio was craftily using the media in an attempt to develop Allan into a leading man — a drawing-room-type of suave and debonair gentleman who ladies could not resist. While his photogenic appearance supported such an image, there was something lacking, something that never seemed to click. Readers of movie magazines found it difficult to see him as a solid screen idol. That lack of personal connection with his intended audience would keep him on the outside-looking-in. He continued to pick up regular film work yet nothing changed in his popularity ratings. He had difficulty making a splash with the movie-going public.

As the New Year came upon Allan, the specter of illness again plagued him, also taking down numerous film sets across town. One article blared, "The flu has invaded Hollywood, sent high-price stars to bed and jumbled picture schedules in the movie industry." Allan was noted to be again, or still, under the weather in mid-January, and he was put on the studio's "sick list," along with Loretta Young, Michael Whalen, Simone Simon, and Thomas Beck. Eventually Hollywood fully recovered, and the studio's infirmary thankfully received less business.

Back to good health, Allan was ready to once more feed the publicity machine. His next romantic go-round, according to Louella Parsons, was with Claire Trevor, with whom he was supposed to have made *Fifteen Maiden Lane* only a few years earlier. She was also a Twentieth Century-Fox

Advertisement for Fifty Roads to Town, *with Allan listed in supporting cast.*

actress, and having two of the studio's pretty people linked together romantically was good for the pair's image, singularly and together. The ensuing public chatter didn't hurt the studio any, either. They were touted as "a new combination" in March of 1937, though their togetherness was truly nothing more than a flash in the pan or, more likely, the flash of a few photographers' light bulbs.

A relationship with model and socialite Bobbie Molyneaux, though one that didn't last a whole lot longer than the others, was a bit more sincere. Louella Parsons said about her, "Ever see a dream walking? Well some of us did in the Beverly Hills Polo Room." Molyneaux wasn't directly connected to any studio or movie machine which would profit, either way, by being seen with him or him being seen with her. They were simply two beautiful people who came together, even for a short time.

The last three-quarters of 1937 picked up steam for Allan in the movie-making department. His private life took a backseat, though it never fully disappeared from the radar. He was seen romancing a number of suitable and beautiful Hollywood ladies, including repeated sightings with Rochelle Hudson who, reports stated, was "seen night after night at the Tropics with Allan Lane which spells romance in Hollywood." Seems it didn't take much

Allan between leading ladies in Charlie Chan at The Olympics, *Pauline Moore and Katherine DeMille (Cecil's adopted daughter and soon-to-be Anthony Quinn's wife).* PHOTO COURTESY THE COSTELLO FAMILY COLLECTION

more than a few trip to the Tropics night club to fall in love, at least in the eyes of the press. Another tidbit said of them, "Hounds for making a full-day-and-night of it are Rochelle Hudson and Twentieth Century-Fox Adonis Allan Lane, when they step out together." The piece finished by tattling about how Rochelle "scatters her favors." She and Allan together were nothing serious and the press knew it. The chance to put the spotlight on two attractive Hollywood types was simply too enticing to ignore.

In the same period, a string of mostly forgettable fluff-films with Allan's name attached was punctuated by a few worthwhile efforts. According to newspaper detail, as early as April he was seen around the country in theaters as a mid-list supporting actor in *Fifty Roads to Town* (1937).

"A laugh-spiced romance pungent with danger," this movie starred Don Ameche and Ann Sothern and was set in a blizzard in a mountain lodge. Allan and others were said to "add humor and excitement" to the season's "most zestful escapade."

Charlie Chan At The Olympics (1937) is one of Allan's early movies which made a splash in the theaters. A historically based — though

Allan in Big Business *along with other cast members.* PHOTO COURTESY THE COSTELLO FAMILY COLLECTION

loosely — storyline, the movie utilized actual footage from the Berlin Olympics held the year before. The entire production was unique. Warner Oland, the key character who turned Charlie Chan, the title role, into a cottage industry, was a born-and-bred Swede. Because he naturally had an exotic, somewhat oriental look, Hollywood typecast him and he successfully ran with the image for many years.

Allan's character was pivotal to the storyline, yet his presence on screen was sporadic. The female nemesis was played by Katherine DeMille, the adopted daughter of director Cecil B. DeMille. Within a few months of the movie's premiere, and likely about the same time as it was being filmed, she became the wife of actor Anthony Quinn. Allan had crossed professional paths with her seven years earlier when they played in MGM's *Madam Satan* (1930), both with uncredited roles. The director had been her father.

The next month, Allan was in *Jones Family In Big Business* (1937) or, as the industry ultimately called it, *Big Business*. This film's most redeeming quality, for Allan, was in how his sports persona was used as the plot's focal point. He portrayed a football star returning to his hometown to promote a get-rich-quick oil stock scheme invested in by the titled Jones family. Nearly ten years after Allan Lane, the actor, would have no longer

Allan belting out a tune with his cast members in Sing and Be Happy. PHOTO COURTESY THE COSTELLO FAMILY COLLECTION

played college football — if he had ever really played college football — he was still fit enough to believably take on such a role. The studios continued to pigeonhole him into these characterizations.

Practically simultaneously, Allan was in *Sing and Be Happy* (1937). As the title nearly screamed, this was a musical comedy. While Allan was again a midlist actor, he had an active role and press said he, along with Helen Westley, "head the supporting cast." As Hamilton Howe, member of an ad group, he stole ideas from the star's agency and sold them as his own. With Allan himself only a few years out of owning his own ad agency, clear-cut comparisons were not lost on those who knew his history; the promotional logic of utilizing an actor's background to facilitate a believable characterization was obvious. This was done many times over with Allan Lane.

A back-story during filming was widely circulated. The director, James Tinling, was known for putting out easygoing, escapist fare. The article said Allan owed him a debt of gratitude for how he handled Allan's part in getting the movie to the screen. The original script called for Allan, in the final scene, "to take a heavy wallop on the jaw" from actor Anthony Martin. Anthony played the lead and Allan, as the details explained, was "the heavy."

Tinling, however, had other ideas. "Boys," he said, "I'm not going to do the usual film fight in this — I'm just going to suggest it in light and shadow." He continued, explaining how he would photograph them behind a screen as they shadow-boxed, "instead of making a rough and tumble of it." The director felt this would be more effective in creating the mood. "That's why Lane is smiling broadly," the news piece said, "instead of nursing his jaw."

The Duke Comes Back (1937), originally titled *The Call of the Ring,* rounded out Allan's year. This movie was notable because it was his first flat-out starring role as well as his first picture for Republic Pictures. *Sing and Be Happy* had proven to be his last production for Twentieth Century-Fox.

CHAPTER EIGHT

Movies, Movies, Movies

In the midst of this ongoing visibility, a birth certificate was officially filed for the actor under Allan Lane's legal name, Harry Leonard Albershart. The information for this document was filed twenty-eight years after his birth on September 13, 1937. Details were supplied not by his mother or his father, both legally competent, but by his aunt, Eva Mae Dayhuff Lewis, and there were intriguing discrepancies.

The reported ages for Allan's parents were wrong. Bill was ten years older than Allan's mother, not one year as the application stated. Information indicated Eva, "attended the birth of this child." She had lived with the family then, after a divorce from her first husband, Peter Marks. The record appeared to state there had not been a doctor present. Yet a doctor officially attested to the information in 1937 when the birth certificate was filed, including the doctor's signature.

This effort may have been required for purposes of creating a birth certificate where there had not been one, to support Allan's ongoing working world. Such an unorthodox way of recording a man's birth left space for the unknown as well as for potential mistakes. At the least, it offered concern over how accurate each of those recorded details truly were.

Registration for his Social Security card had been filed a few months earlier on June 30, 1937, giving his address as 2954 Fifth Avenue in Los Angeles. This was a single family home in Aunt Eva's neighborhood — a cute, tidy bungalow only one street away from the home she shared with Uncle Billy. Only basic details were included on that application — his name, address, employer, and the recently-acquired social security number.

The form was signed not by Allan Lane or Harry Albershart but by L. J. Purcell of "Twentieth Century-Fox Film Corp." An included typed notation read, "Employee left our employ during period ending June 30, 1937, without filing application." This was in answer to the direction, "If you have previously filled out a card like this, please state," giving the impression that if Allan had already personally filled out such an application, it had not been connected to his Twentieth Century-Fox work.

Interestingly, a newspaper piece came out six days later that brought all these dates into question as to what might really be going on behind the scenes. "Allan Lane, now appearing before the cameras at Twentieth Century-Fox, formerly made a living behind them when he headed the company of New York photographic illustrators known as 'Allan Lane, Inc.'" The combination of facts may show he left the studio suddenly and without publicity surrounding his departure.

Both filings occurred in the same time period. Social Security itself was in its infancy, created in 1935, and this looks as if the two documents came together in a hurried fashion to fulfill then-current government requirements for a working individual. This shows how the birth certificate was likely required for him to have a Social Security number, which was needed for him to continue to work under contract at an established movie studio.

With this series of events, most public records for a young man named Harry Albershart virtually disappeared. Even though he never literally changed his name, Allan Lane as a professional man on record was officially born at this time, and, for all practical purposes, he took the place of Harry Leonard Albershart, at least in the public's eye. Just about anything could have been listed on his Johnny-come-lately birth certificate, and into the future the truth might never be fully known. This proved to be the case with a great deal of detail surrounding the life of Allan Lane.

Allan Lane's official Social Security application with no mention of his official name, personal address, or any other detail usually included on a Social Security application.

Since everything he did throughout the next two years was for RKO Radio Pictures, it looks like *The Duke Comes Back* had been a freelance effort. Allan played the titled Duke Foster. A newspaper tagline declared dramatically, "Men must fight and the women who love them must sit and wait in fear. Punch-packed entertainment!" Another announced, "ROMANCE WITH A SOCK! A fighting fool in the ring...until a dame lands with a right to the heart." Allan's character was an honest boxer who had to tell his wife he was quitting the ring while he intentionally did just the opposite, taking on one last match to save her father from bankruptcy in the falling stock market.

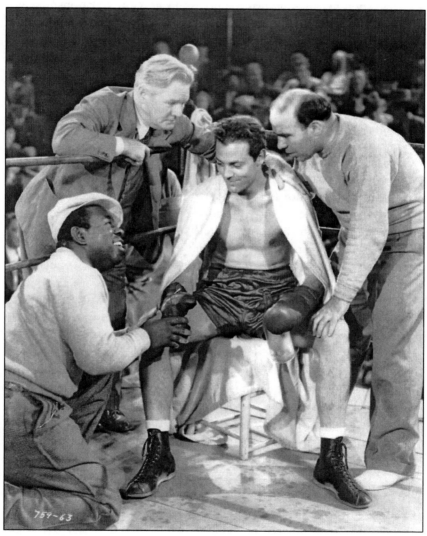

Allan plays a boxer in The Duke Comes Back. PHOTO COURTESY THE COSTELLO FAMILY COLLECTION

The picture was listed as an "adult" film — the subject matter was serious. An official determination that explained how movies were classified, stated "adult" meant "not suitable for juvenile entertainment." None of this really mattered much in the grand scheme. This movie was still the second billing on any theater marquee, something of a forewarning of what was to come for Allan as he moved forward in Hollywood.

Allan soon began what was his first solid romantic relationship since his break-up with Joan Perry. June Travis was five years younger than Allan and, by all accounts, she seemed to be a good fit for him. This was a real romance, not a Hollywood storybook deal. They had Hollywood and the movie world in common, but they also shared one of Allan's greatest passions: baseball. She was the daughter of Harry Grabiner, who was, at the time, vice-president of the Chicago White Sox. She, too, had had a few stops and starts in the film world, and her bona fide first film, *Not On Your Life*, came in 1935.

By 1937, when they began seeing each other, both she and Allan were known quantities for the press and the movie-viewing public. They were seen regularly on dance floors around town and elsewhere. One report from Harrison Carroll effused, "The slickest pair of dancers we've seen around the night clubs recently were June Travis and Allen [sic] Lane. They had everybody in the Century Club watching them the other night." The tidbit finished with an obviously intentional teaser, "Lane's black eye didn't escape observation either...." No explanation was given for Allan Lane being seen in public with a black eye. Since he was working on a boxing picture, however, there is every reason to believe an unexpected upset may have occurred during filming.

June had been a regular on-set at Republic Pictures when Allan was there for *The Duke Comes Back*, and she visited him daily. Republic had officially started moviemaking just a few years earlier, and it offered Allan one of its last half dozen or so productions of that year. The opportunity proved to be good for him, introducing him to a studio operation which would, years into the future, become his home base. For the time being, however, he was simply doing yet another job.

June had recently taken a trip to her hometown of Chicago, and Allan went along. A picture of them was captioned, "Friends of June Travis and Allan Lane, screen players, wonder over a reported romance which is said to have reached the engagement stage. Neither June nor Allan, shown in Chicago, will answer yes or no."

This pair also had something else in common: both were fond of the Great Lakes area. While June grew up in and around Chicago, Allan had spent a good amount of his younger years between Grand Rapids and Traverse City, Michigan. He recently invested some of his newfound money in a small vacation place, becoming something of a "resorter" himself — a little bit like the people after whom his earlier team had been named. He had the cottage furnished with simple pieces, and he hoped June would want to spend time there with him.

Upon returning to Hollywood, June was spotted practically nonstop at Allan's side, and wedding bell rumors really began. "Looks like June Travis and Allan Lane may be making plane reservations for one of the near-by Gretna Greens real soon…" one columnist wrote in early October.

From there, they were known as part of Movieland's B-list "in crowd" whenever there was a major party in town or a special event to celebrate. One summer column, "Snapshots Around Hollywood," said the couple were part of a group of "film folks who helped Vic McLaglen open his new polo field on Riverside Drive," along with "the Andy Devines…Dixie Dunbar and Wayne Morris, and June Lang with mama."

Another romance report in October gave colorful insight into the flavor of Allan's relationship with June, and their particular brand of shared offbeat humor. "It was Allan Lane's birthday and his girl friend [sic], June Travis, sent him a huge box of garden vegetables but without attaching a card. Yesterday Lane reciprocated by sending her a package. The box contained two dozen eggs, all wrapped in cellophane and tied with ribbons and a card which read, 'Here are your eggs. The ham will follow…'"

The Duke Comes Back debuted in November. Newspapers announced, "Meet a handsome new star — six feet tall and oh, so charming!" That he was handsome, tall, and charming may have been worth touting, and the truth, but since he had been in and out of Hollywood for nearly ten years already, he was hardly "new" to the game. This was one of the industry's earliest efforts to promote Allan as a bona fide movie star, and they did so as if he'd just recently walked through their front door.

In December, newspaper columnists hedged their bets as to when wedding bells would ring in earnest for Allan and June. Another one of those "Hollywood Romance Charts," a regular game for gossip columnists of the time, gave the couple 3–1 odds of tying the knot, saying they were, "Running strong; may be in the money."

All this press was not hurting Allan's profile in any way. As of January 19, 1938, it was announced Allan Lane had signed yet another movie contract — this one with "RKO Radio." With the studio beefing up his profile for the press and the public, Allan was still continually called a "former Notre Dame University football star," proving no one cared enough to check the facts. Since this had been added to his biography years ago, and he looked the part, fiction had turned into fact and followed him year after year.

The day after his newest contract was announced, the press continued hot on his romance trail. "Expect an elopement any day now with June Travis and Allan Lane as the principals..." The union did not happen then, either, though their relationship continued on a strong note.

In early April, the press still reported on them as a couple. "They do say that the June Travis-Allan Lane romance which was expected to end at the altar, is cooling somewhat, although both are seen together now and then..."

In a few weeks, June was in Chicago, visiting family. Allan followed her there, and when he came back to Los Angeles, though he was without her, he was smiling broadly. The press reported he had talked her "out of her peeve."

But not for long. Before the end of summer, Allan and June were no longer a twosome. Seemingly for good, even though the bond they had forged continued to hold on by a thread, and if only at a distance. Whatever differences had caused them to teeter on the edge for a number of months had become too much in the final count. Allan was no longer able to breach the divide, and the couple called it quits. He was once again on his own, even though he and June still kept an unconventional open line of communication between them.

As another new year turned the corner, Allan's career in 1938 turned with it...for the better. Despite the seemingly unusual circumstances surrounding his departure from Twentieth Century-Fox, RKO executives obviously saw something they liked and they snagged him next. He was put to work under contract after only one free agent picture in between the two studios. The film promised to him when he first signed, initially known as *Certified*, had not yet begun filming. Instead, they gave him a lighthearted comedy.

Hollywood still seemed determined Allan Lane would become the next great matinee idol. Even when his latest studio wrote his official biography, the press people did everything they could to angle his presence in the movie world by expanding the facts of his life. He was pushing thirty, a bit on the older side for a bona fide leading man in younger roles. When they talked about his origins and birth date, they said nothing more than he was born "on a September 22..." The football hero image was played up in great measure with glorified words that proclaimed, "His saga would be something like — 'From Gridiron to Silverscreen.'" There was no mention that the "football hero" title was more than a bit of a stretch.

There were rumors he was tested for the role of Rhett Butler in *Gone With The Wind* (1939). This is entirely possible. He was the right age, had the right look, was being fast-tracked by the studio's press department, and his every onscreen effort focused on the handsome and debonair image his bosses wanted him to portray. Truth is, there were many actors tested for the role of Rhett Butler, and even more actresses were tested to play Scarlett O'Hara.

Practically all of the Hollywood actors and actresses under contract at the time who had even remotely the right look were in front of a camera to see if they might fit these parts. Contests were held in various parts of the country to discover the next big star. Big names as well as ingénues, debutantes, and country boys came in from every corner of the United States to see if they might have a shot.

In the long run, though, while there were a number of final-count serious women contenders for the part of Scarlett — including Katherine Hepburn and Paulette Goddard, who came close to signing on the dotted line — there were only three men who ever had the slightest chance at bringing Rhett to life, and not one of them was Allan Lane. The likely possibilities were Gary Cooper, Ronald Colman…and the actor who producer David Selznick wanted in the role from the beginning: Clark Gable.

Allan's stock was rising on the marquee, even without *Gone With The Wind*. It had only taken nearly ten years but, finally, Allan Lane was headlining. He started the next year as the costar with Harry Parke in *Night Spot* (1938), a movie that required a heavy amount of physical work. He proved himself in a story combining "drama as well as many hilarious situations." He was well-equipped to employ just the right facial expressions, sight gags, and inflections to make the script believable. One article commended him and his leading lady, Joan Woodbury, for their work in one particular scene that asked for more than their fair share of "dirty work."

The headline read, "Young Stars Are Sunk in Mud for Half an Hour." The lead-in stated, "It's not always glamour, wealth, and ease in Hollywood with the motion picture stars!" The script required Allan and Joan to be quite the method actors. Property men built a tank on the stage and filled it with two feet of what was called "goo" to represent the mud.

Allan's character, Pete Cooper, was a cop posing undercover as a musician. He wanted to be the hero, making a gallant effort to rescue Joan's character, Marge, from kidnapers, who proved to not really be kidnappers. He was assigned to make nice-nice with Marge, a beauty with associations

assumed to be gangster-related. Pete Cooper did eventually save the dam-
sel-not-in-distress, but in the process, he ended up unintentionally giving
Marge one heck of a mud bath.

This one scene alone required over a half an hour of work, during
which time Allan and Joan became soaked through to the skin with the
wet, sticky "mud" substance. They were then finally permitted to get a

*Allan in a tank full of "goo," representing mud, with his leading lady, Joan
Woodbury, in* Night Spot. PHOTO COURTESY THE COSTELLO FAMILY
COLLECTION

bath and put on dry clothing, only to find the scene they had just shot
"proved unsuitable and retakes had to be made." Both were commended for
their professionalism and good humor. "Miss Woodbury and Lane went
through with their unpleasant task a second time with never a complaint."

Allan ended the movie with great professional reviews all around. He
was called "an unusual hero" in one piece, while another stated, "How
Lane rounds up the entire gang and clears the name of the singer after
a series of lovers' quarrels, misunderstandings with the police force and
dangerous brushes with the hoodlums, brings about the exciting climax
and romantic conclusion."

One bit called Allan and Joan "a new romantic team." Since they never
played in another movie together, it is unknown whether they were simply

paired in that one vehicle or if they were intended for a series of movies that never came to pass. Allan would soon prove to be a difficult leading man in other romance pairings.

The evidence of his rising star came in small ways, but those small ways began to show clearly more and more. In some theaters, the proof was in the double-billing afforded *Night Spot* (1938)…when the second-billed

Allan and Joan Fontaine milking every ounce of humor out of Maid's Night Out. PHOTO COURTESY THE COSTELLO FAMILY COLLECTION

movie was also an Allan Lane vehicle, his earlier title, *The Duke Comes Back*. This was done regularly that season.

Allan went right into another assignment, the one he had been initially promised when he signed his new contract with RKO. *Certified* had by this time been re-titled *Maid's Night Out* (1938). Allan played the son of a millionaire who owned a milk company. As Bill Norman, he starred opposite Joan Fontaine who played Sheila Harrison. One tagline easily summed up the plot: "Heiress and millionaire meet and fall in love. She thinks he's a milkman. He thinks she's a maid." Another blared, "Heiress elopes in milk truck! And what a night for love!"

Allan was then a veteran compared to Joan Fontaine, who was eight years younger. The age difference didn't show on the screen, however, and they played well off of each other in this happy, fluffy comedy. The story was a fairly routine "rich-pretending-to-be-poor" concept. Allan was at the top of his game in this silly story, working his part with great comedic timing and infusing punch lines with the right facial expressions and understated physical humor.

CHAPTER NINE

Fate Sealed as a S.O.B.

The practice of running Allan Lane movies on a double billing continued now that he had enough solid features with his name attached. *This Marriage Business* (1938), next in his celluloid repertoire, was played along with *Night Spot* at theaters around the country.

This is where the first public confirmation of Allan having difficulty interacting with a costar showed up — a problem which would become a recurring theme. RKO teamed him with actress Vicki Lester, expecting big things and hot sparks between them on the screen. Without question there were sparks, but not of the sort RKO had desired.

Vicki Lester, the actress, was born Dorothy Day in 1915. She used her birth name in *Vogues of 1938* where she had a bit part. Right after *A Star Is Born* (1937) debuted, her credits resumed, and she was then listed as Vicki, and sometimes Vickie, Lester. She had professionally taken on the name of a character made infamous in *A Star Is Born*, a film that came out the previous year. Janet Gaynor had played that part.

The lady was a beautiful blonde, and the now-Vicki fit right in with Hollywood's image of how a starlet should look. A plan had been hatched to feature her with Allan in a series of ongoing light romantic comedies as soon as her brief part in *Maid's Night Out* (1938) saw the light of day. That was reportedly enough "for the studio officials to estimate that they had a 'find' in the blonde." She and Allan made a pair, physically complimenting each other, but their professional togetherness ended abruptly, almost as soon as it began.

While *Maid's Night Out* was on the screen, Allan and Lester were in the studio trying to be a loving couple in *This Marriage Business*, filmed in late February. Touted as, "A romance, a political fight, an underworld killing, a publicity campaign and an ingenious comedy theme," it was the "debut of a brilliant new leading lady in blonde Vicki Lester."

But there was serious trouble in celluloid paradise. A report claimed, "Several days ago they began working in *This Marriage Business*...since then, the tension has been worse." Allan had no patience for his leading lady. One newspaper article explained, "For Vicki Lester, blonde and beautiful, and Allan Lane may bill and coo before the camera, but off the screen they're not on speaking terms."

Allan with Vicki Lester in This Marriage Business...*not all was happy behind the scenes.*

He criticized her acting abilities, in very specific ways, and other cast members finally had to calm her down after she dissolved into a fit of tears. She told a friend, "When I think I've got to be in his arms now, even before the camera, I could die."

As a result of this disastrous beginning between Allan and Vicki, RKO had to rethink them as a continuing onscreen couple. Clearly there was no love lost — real or playacting. They seemed to not even have the slightest bit of professional, nonetheless personal, chemistry. Reports blared, "RKO finds itself sitting on a bomb." The studio had to bow out of this one gracefully, and sent out press releases to indicate "one of the most publicized romances between two picture people is near dissolution, but they're reluctant to disappoint their fans so will break gradually."

What wasn't publicized was the back-story between Allan Lane and Vicki Lester. They knew each other before the studio put them together onscreen, even before both came to Hollywood and worked for the same studio. As one article put it, "Oddly enough, she had once posed for Allan Lane...when he conducted a photographic studio in New York."

Lester was from New York, and one of her bios related, "Because of

Vicki Lester, aka Dorothy Day; she and Allan just could not get together.

her beauty with the increasing years, she found herself in demand as a model for commercial photographers and artists." That year, she was part of an exclusive group known as "the Twelve Most Photographed Girls In America," posing for various clothing items, magazine covers, and even working as a hand model.

This is where she and Allan were first acquainted. This would have been somewhere in late 1936 before Allan closed shop on his photographic advertising agency. Whether or not they had a romantic relationship that went sour early on, or after they came to Hollywood, each on their own, it was clear they had a personal history between them. In turn, RKO press folks decided that history would create a great backdrop against which they could play up their familiarity. This proved to be a disastrous idea.

Theaters worked overtime to get tickets sold for *This Marriage Business*. In Nevada, "free tickets" were advertised for couples who obtained marriage licenses on the day of the movie showing, where it was called "an ingenious comedy." They announced the number of marriages in the county in the last six months, and declared, "This Marriage Business Is Good!" The title was deemed to be an "adult" movie.

The pair's next film together, in which Allan and Vicki were to have continued their onscreen affair, was slated to be called *It Couldn't Happen Again*. Surely a prophetic title because it was already far too obvious that, indeed, it could not happen again. It barely even happened the first few times. This one was shelved.

Lester and Allan had played in three films together, in total, within about a six month period. By the time the last one was in the making, it was painfully noticeable that while the studio would honor the contracts between the two, they would be required to do so without having the actors closely interact.

While Allan's reaction to Vicki Lester may have been over-the-top and unprofessional, there appears to have been truth to his assessment of her talent, or lack thereof. Later in the year, RKO released her from her contract. Many reports indicated she had been fired, and she did little film work of merit from then on. She returned to her original name of Dorothy Day, did a few more bit parts, and then seemed to fall into complete movie obscurity. She may have married, or come close to marrying, actor Dick Purcell as well as international film liaison and playboy Richard Guinle.

On the other hand, RKO held onto Allan Lane. He was difficult, often downright rude, and usually particular to an aggravating fault, but he had proven time and time again to be a working professional good at what he did. He was able to turn out a solid performance with every picture he was in, whether he played the lead or was in a supporting role.

In many ways, Allan was a Jekyll-and-Hyde sort. He was innately charming, an excellent and well-versed conversationalist, and an all-round self-made man. He could hold his own in the drawing room in the morning, and then in the afternoon speak eloquently with a director, making it clear he fully understood the process of movie-making. By the evening, he was wearing jeans and a work shirt, enjoying solitude and physical labor at his home.

Yet, on a dime he would turn, becoming caustic, rude, and overtly intolerant of everyone around him. Depending on who was in the room with him at any given time, the opinions about him seemed to change on a swiftly rotating basis. Despite his difficulties with co-workers and some executives, still Allan was announced as one of a number of "young players who should gain distinction in 1938," this pronouncement coming from a poll of leading Hollywood directors, including Cecil B. DeMille, for whom Allan had worked in earlier years.

What had been given as the reason behind his steady rise to the top? One major quality…his "engaging personality." Evidence of Jekyll and Hyde once again.

Having Wonderful Time (1938) was an A-list picture filmed as early as January. The production came together when Allan first came onboard with RKO, and hit the screens a few months later. Press notes stated he had "recently turned in a bit of fine acting in this Ginger Rogers — Doug Fairbanks starrer..." The line-up of initial RKO offerings in which Allan was cast show he had barely signed his contract before they put him to work; one film was made right after the other and released almost as fast.

Most of *Having Wonderful Time* was filmed at Bartlett Lake in the San Bernardino Mountains, "where an entire summer camp was constructed with a huge recreational hall and scores of cottages dotted around the borders of the lake to provide an authentic offering." The story was "designed as a study of that unhappy class of New Yorkers, boys and girls, who struggle for 50 weeks of each year, fluttering their wings against the cages erected around them by changing times..." This was possibly a good description of how Allan felt about his life.

Though he was doing well professionally, better than he ever had in Hollywood as an actor, he felt in many ways even more creatively stifled than during his last go-round. He was now in a studio contract that finally offered decent billing. Yet his just rewards, so long in coming, didn't feel as good to him as he thought they would after riding the roller coaster he had to take to get there. Allan was not the "status quo" sort. He had been so busy trying to "make it," and now that he was on the edge of his goal, he wasn't sure that was what he wanted anymore. There was something of a "Watch what you ask for, you may get it" quality to his life.

He was working though, which was preferable to not having money in his pocket. Having work had always been Allan's ultimate goal, so even though it went against his nature, he tried not to rock the boat too much. At any point when he would start to realize he was verging on trouble, he'd do everything he could to consciously rein himself in.

There was something of an outward, professionally environmental explanation for the long, rising push-and-pull of Allan's career as well as careers of other newly-visible performers. Printed in an article in the *Oakland Tribune* in July of 1938 and written by reporter Wood Soanes, the piece was titled, "Newcomers Get Breaks As Stars Break With Studios Over Salaries." Soanes made note, "Whether the blasting of the Independent Theater Owners had anything to do with it or not, there has been a considerable turnover in the lists of important players in Hollywood during the last six months."

Soanes went on to give examples of previously unknown names who suddenly found themselves with elevated billing. "In three cases — all male — the refusal of established stars to accept assignments paved the way for newcomers." There were so many examples that Soanes didn't list all the stories behind each one, but he did state, "Without attempting to go into the histories…the fact that their names are becoming familiar is rather significant…" He finished his bit by giving name to a number of the newly rising actor class, without their attached stories, "Ronald Reagan, Allan Lane, Rosemary Lane, Sigrid Gurie and, if you will, Hedy Lamarr."

Allan was in good company with this group while racking up a notable resumé. His films were played back-to-back in some theaters and, as had

Allan in a predicament as a crafty reporter in Crime Ring. PHOTO COURTESY THE COSTELLO FAMILY COLLECTION

already proven to work well, even on double bills. When his name showed up in a movie roster, it was rarely any longer met with the comment, "Who's that?" Instead, people would often say, "Oh, him!"

When he was next cast as the male lead in *Crime Ring* (1938) opposite Frances Mercer, daughter of New York sports writer Sid Mercer, Allan was lauded as "comparatively new to the screen." This film, initially titled *Cheating The Stars*, was said to be his fourth leading role and her first. The storyline surrounded an actress who posed as a fortune-teller to trap racketeers. Allan was the reporter who hired her to unmask thieves running a fake racket of women who took the money of unsuspecting customers.

The film, "an attractively crisp and novel motion picture treatment," was set to break new ground, exposing "ingenious methods by which fake fortune tellers manage to surprise their credulous clients…" A lot of research was put into the script to make it accurate and believable, "strikingly" revealing any number of ways fakers managed to lull gullible targets into their trust, and then bilk them for their money in the name of being able to "see the future."

Allan was noted to have "scored in several recent RKO offerings" and reports said he was "ideally cast as the resourceful newspaperman." Frances Mercer went to great ends to be believable, saying she visited "three soothsayers" to research her role. These seers told her she would "climb to the top of films in the next three years" if she worked hard. While she did end up having a decent career — much of it in TV — Frances never did "climb to the top" of films.

Allan felt he was doing well enough to finally enjoy the fruits of his labor. Though he remained careful with his money, he became a member of Lakeside Country Club and began playing in benefit tournaments. He had already done a few other benefits, namely the 1937 Trans-Mississippi Golf Championship in Denver at the Cherry Hill Country Club, as a representative of the West Coast and Lakeside Country Club.

In July of 1938, soon after *Crime Ring* hit the screen, Allan led the pack at the Lake Arrowhead Golf Tournament, again representing Lakeside. He was called a "Class A performer." His abilities on the golf course, while maybe not quite on par with his abilities on the football field or baseball diamond, were still far more than adequate. Benefit organizers who saw good reason to include up-and-coming Hollywood types in their efforts were happy to have him along. Allan had a five handicap, and reportedly shot a sixty-eight when he had been in New York not long before.

He was a fan of just about every sport known to man, and if he could have a hand in something going on in the sports arena, away from the screen, Allan took the chance. That included wrestling. A professional by the name of Danny McShain was in the spotlight that summer. Known then as "The Wild Irish Rose," cocky and over-the-top and one who didn't often play by the rules, Danny had won the NWA World Light Heavyweight Championship the year before. He was only just beginning in a career which would support him throughout his life.

Allan was highlighted as part of Danny's world in August. Danny was "hanging out in Hollywood" and Allan, called "a movie actor" who was trying to play director, attempted to draw Danny into the movies. He did appear in a few films, though little of note. Nothing came of his association with Allan and no specific projects were named.

Fugitives For a Night (1938) was next on Allan's quick turnaround picture list, in which he supported Frank Albertson and Eleanor Lynn. Originally titled *Birthday of a Stoodge* [Stooge], the story told of a murder mystery and the goings-on inside a movie studio.

Allan's role was unfortunately right on target insofar as what he was becoming known for in the movie world's insider circles. He played John Nelson, a "conceited star" who is frustrated with his place in Hollywood. He believed his studio wasn't doing enough to advance his career. Original casting occurred in June. One piece indicated actress Adrianne Ames, "who hasn't been working on a lot in over a year, checks in at R-K-O for the femme lead...opposite Frankie Albertson and Allan Lane." Since Eleanor Lynn appears to have carried the female top billing, either Ames was flatly demoted or the script called for two ladies of differing characters to carry the picture — one in a supporting role.

Danny McShain, pro wrestler and Allan's friend.

The script was written by Dalton Trumbo who in a few years would be caught up in his own real-life drama as one of the "Hollywood Ten." In this film, Trumbo showed his contempt for the world in which he made his living, representing the movie environment in an all-around negative light. He wrote almost all his characters to be, at the very least, blatantly unpleasant. Little was said in the press about Allan's performance, one many felt he could practically "call in" with little effort required.

This was second billed on the country's movie screens, often following the lead of A-list stars and their top-promoted work. The process helped the likes of Allan since he would be seen, one way or the other, by moviegoers who otherwise came to see the big names. It also served to make clear the reality that Allan Lane, and those in line with him, was a B-list actor. He would have little chance of headlining in the sort of features in which he played while a star such as Robert Taylor in *Broadway Melody of 1938* was his lead-in.

Allan's work in 1938 rounded out with a movie called *The Law West of Tombstone*. This marked his first Western — a genre in which he would ultimately achieve the sort of stardom he only looked to achieve in those days. He didn't star in this one, and, in fact, as outlaw Danny Sanders, Allan ended up dead on the short end of a gun being fired by a young cowboy, played by Tim Holt. Holt was skimming twenty years of age,

Pacific Liner *theater poster.*

and though he would ultimately become a cowboy star in his own right, in this rather unconventional picture he was Harry Carey's sidekick. The movie received little note in its day, bringing up the bottom of a two-and-sometimes-three-picture theater bill.

Allan's initial movie of 1939 was *Pacific Liner*, the story of the "professional and romantic conflict of the men who work in the engineer room of a big liner." Made in late 1938, this debuted in January. The storyline surrounded a cholera breakout, and during filming — whether for promotional purposes or simply because someone decided it was a good idea — RKO made sure there was a physician on set to "dose the cast with cold preventives." The brass went so far as to make sure "every set worker had to have a shot in the arm."

This was yet simply another low-man-on-the-totem-pole role for Allan. The part of Bilson didn't do much for his stature in what had been a resumé with growing promise. He seemed to be treading water until RKO could find a solid starring vehicle that fit him well. Until such happened, he churned out one average performance after another, easily showing up for work each day and collecting his paycheck before he went home and waited to do it all over again the next day.

Allan felt as if he were once again in danger of being lost in a studio system backlog of combined new and established actors. He found himself somewhere in the middle of the heap, an uncomfortably familiar feeling. He'd been in this position before. Each time, he had managed to bring up his profile at least a notch yet had never managed to reach the apex.

CHAPTER TEN

Moving Up in the Movie World

About this time, June Travis still seemed to be trying to figure out where her relationship with Allan had gone wrong. For so long they edged on the "on-again, off-again" seesaw. She had finished her latest picture titled *Federal Man-Hunt* (1938), which came out at the end of December. A month later, she left Hollywood to return to Chicago. News reports indicated she "deserted Hollywood temporarily at least to come home and 'think things out.'"

Her interviews showed her to be in emotional conflict, pondering any number of personal issues while looking for "something to do." She didn't know whether that meant college, writing, going into a business career… or returning to Hollywood and the movies.

She was also confused as to what to do in her romantic life. The things she was "thinking out didn't exclude romance — and Allan Lane" whom she considered to be very attractive, and she counted him as a good friend. Yet despite their friendship, she was concerned about the difficulties of sustaining a meaningful relationship in Hollywood. She stated, "So many marriages out there land in the divorce court."

June had a lot on her mind — and Allan was not the least of these thoughts. She finished her public soul-searching with, "I just can't say what I'm going to do — I don't know. And I left Hollywood to come to think it out." This particular interview was the most insightful glimmer into what sort of relationship Allan and June had shared.

Allan went on with his work. His next role, in *Twelve Crowded Hours* (1939), gave him a meatier opportunity than many of his most recent efforts. He found the experience to be, if not overwhelmingly satisfying, at least engaging. He supported Richard Dix and Lucille Ball, with whom he had already worked, though briefly, in *Having Wonderful Time*. Ball had bounced around the movies for over five years but only recently had any roles of note. She had been cast mostly in parts that showed her as little more than pretty woodwork, not receiving a cast credit.

This movie gave her more visibility, though she was still far from the superstar she would ultimately become. There is evidence RKO tried her

Lucille Ball, Richard Dix, and Allan in Twelve Crowded Hours.

out with Allan to see if they might make a good team, having them come up the ranks together and then play opposite each other in lesser roles. In this one, they played brother and sister. The romance aspect wasn't in play but their chemistry together was workable.

Next was *They Made Her A Spy* (1939), peddled as, "Uncle Sam's answer to espionage," and "Uncle Sam cracks down on spies!" This was an April release intended as a vehicle for yet another new romantic screen pairing for Allan. This and his previous film were out in the spring, though both had been made at the end of the previous year. A few months earlier, it was announced he had been offered, and had accepted, "a new term contract" with RKO.

He had played nice-nice well enough, and long enough, to be kept on by the studio. RKO's repeated efforts to find him a solid onscreen love interest seemed to indicate the direction in which they wanted his career to go. This time he was thrown into the mix with Sally Eilers. Each actor already had a string of relatively successful films, so RKO saw them as a potentially good romantic team. Eilers had been a Mack Sennett discovery and was a good friend of Carole Lombard. Married to producer Harry Joe Brown, they had a son, Harry Joe Brown, Jr., who at only four years old was given a bit part in the production.

Movie poster for They Made Her A Spy…*Allan made the cover.*

There isn't any heavy evidence RKO worked hard to make Allan and Sally a recurring twosome after this film was out of the gate and in theaters. Either the pair didn't have much in the way of chemistry or timing didn't work. There didn't seem to be anything blatantly negative between them; their pairing was simply an idea that didn't pan out. One review said the movie showed a "warm romance between the two," proving they had done their jobs well in front of the camera. Allan went on almost immediately into another project, while Sally didn't appear onscreen again until the fall. She didn't collect but a handful of credits to her name after *They Made Her A Spy* and was said to never have reached the potential the studio originally expected of her.

There was still activity behind the scenes between June Travis and Allan. They were seen and photographed together, obviously more than casual friends. They cared for each other but things seemed to be stalled. The concerns seemed to be more on June's side than on Allan's. She never said anything against him. She had, in fact, only the best words for him and their time together. Yet she dragged her feet, and even their friends didn't know which direction the couple would go. Allan was quoted during this period saying firmly, "It takes two to make a bargain."

The next movie in line had Allan once more playing alongside Lucille Ball, this time in another "adult film" titled *Panama Lady* (1939). He was touted as a "rising young leading man." He had been called variations on this many times before. One newspaper piece made note of the nearly back-to-back films for him and Lucille Ball as a pair, though the change in this storyline had them interacting much differently. "Having recently appeared as brother and sister in *Twelve Crowded Hours*, Lucille Ball and Allan Lane now come to the screen as lovers in *Panama Lady*."

An entertaining story came about during the making of this movie. One of the other "stars" was a "brilliantly plumed talking macaw" named Lucy. Having a bird with this name proved to be quite a problem since Lucille Ball's character was also Lucy... not to mention her real name, as well. Every time the name came up in script dialogue, the bird would answer in a "penetratingly-raucous voice." This played havoc with the sound department, which could not keep up with the rest of the dialogue in the wake of the bird's wild squawking.

Allan with Lucille Ball in a romantic clinch for Panama Lady.

Lucy the bird — not the actress or the character — was fired then-and-there. In her place, another macaw was hired. This one was named Pete. Clearly Pete would not be any sort of competition for the movie's female lead, aggravating or entertaining or both.

Being seen at movie premieres was one of the ways the studios got publicity for their most promising actors and actresses. Allan was a part of this game, and in May, he was amidst a large contingency of well-knowns and hopefuls who walked the red carpet at Grauman's Chinese Theater.

The movie was *Rose of Washington Square*, starring Tyrone Power, Alice Faye, and Al Jolson. The bona fide stars in attendance were blinding — Power and his wife, Annabella, Claudette Colbert, Elsa Maxwell, Marlene Dietrich with Eric Maria Remarque, Irving Berlin, Ruby Keeler, and a host of others not as well known, like Allan. Allan attended with starlet Judith Dickens, who had a bit part in *Young Mr. Lincoln* (1939), set to come out soon thereafter. Judith was never heard from again as a Hollywood player. An uncredited actor in *Young Mr. Lincoln* was a boy named Jack Kelly. He would grow up to become one of TV's best-known Western stars on the show *Maverick*.

As Allan delivered to the screen one solid film appearance after another, official word came out that he finally intended to complete his college degree. Reports said he had registered for the summer term at UCLA, "a first step toward a college degree he missed by two years."

Allan's college efforts, or lack of college efforts, have forever been a mystery. Besides the widely circulated false information about him and Notre Dame, he was also said to have attended Texas Christian University as well as a few other institutions of higher learning. His new educational foray as reported would have made sense only if he had already put in two years of college somewhere. Since public records of him attending any college have been proven false, one after the other, the idea that he would complete a degree he may not have started seemed to be yet more studio fodder to beef up his public persona. UCLA verified there were no known records for anyone named Allan Lane or Harry Albershart.

This particular article went in-depth, including alleged rumination from Allan himself on how he felt about continuing his education. "It's never too late to go back to school," he was quoted as saying. He wanted to get his science and liberal arts degree, using "leisure time" to attend classes at night and between pictures. He explained what spurred him on to make the effort, despite his intense work schedule. "A trip back east, where I associated with scores of persons from every walk of life, opened my eyes to how narrow one can become if they get the idea that the entire world and everything of interest is bounded by Hollywood and the motion picture business."

This comment would have related to his stint in New York City a few years earlier — evidence of a period where he definitely did spend at a distance from the Hollywood community. The piece continued, reportedly in Allan's voice, "I made up my mind then and there, that I would not permit myself to become just an actor, with no knowledge and no interests outside that profession."

Such a comment would have been logical for him, backing up his well-known desire to be more than simply a pretty boy in front of the camera. He really wanted a chance to bring out the more cerebral and creative side of his personality. The sentiments sounded suspiciously like something he might have said, blatantly and without apology scorning the "narrow-mindedness" of Tinseltown as well as the expected avenues open to him via the movie world's mindset. He was known to see that as little more than a myopic way of life focusing only on the external.

Allan Lane seemed to be in turmoil again.

Unfortunately, the rest of the article heartily restated his "history" with Notre Dame where, it said, he "lettered in football, basketball, and baseball," and then afterward signed with the Cincinnati Reds. Again, loose speculation is required to find a way around what his truth really was versus how much was made up for the sake of an official biography. It's entirely possible Allan's direct quotes were interspersed with a tailor-made background. Also possible he might have always intended to go to college, even if he never got there. Or maybe he got there, wherever "there" may have been in terms of a physical institution, but did not finish his degree.

Allan made no less than six films for RKO in 1939 with recognizable parts. In most, he was a solid mid-list supporting actor, and in a precious few, he was the leading man. His studio seemed to have faith in his ability to do the job yet wasn't quite certain he was the man to ratchet up a few notches and hang their hat on for any number of stand-out lead roles. Since he had signed with the studio, he had starred or co-starred in a handful of pictures. This felt like an ambiguity and continued to discourage Allan. He was all the more determined to stay the course.

There was something a bit odd about the last two films for Allan in 1939. In each movie he played a character named Steve Kendall, though one story was not a follow-up to the other. Allan either looked like someone of that name to the story writers, or scriptwriters simply weren't creative, or coincidence was high that summer and they really liked the name. However it came about, the name, Steve Kendall, showed up twice on Allan's resumé, one right after the other.

In the first go-round, Allan's Steve Kendall in *The Spellbinder* (1939) is a supporting role, at best. The film's star was Lee Tracy, who was eleven years older than Allan and already had an extensive career under his belt. He had started in movies in 1929, and ten years later he found his way to the head of the class, while Allan was still diligently working to try and keep the teacher's attention. This film didn't even do anything for its star, though, and reviews were lukewarm.

In *Conspiracy* (1939), Allan, aka Steve Kendall, was the star, and he did a credible job in making this one entertaining. The movie was "a strange romance" where he played "a young American sailor." Along with "a European girl who tries to save his life," they were "pursued by secret police" in a European dictatorship seaport. *Motion Picture Herald* called

Allan "handsomely proficient." Linda Hayes, "a charming newcomer," was his romantic co-star. Yet again, this was second-billed, called a "companion feature," along with A-list actors, Carole Lombard and Cary Grant starring in *In Name Only* (1939).

The same month *Conspiracy* hit theaters, and as the press called him "one of RKO's best bets" despite his see-saw career, Allan played in a trio

Conspiracy, starring Allan, Linda Hayes, and Robert Barrat as the "second feature."

bowling tournament in Hollywood. This lent credibility to earlier news bits, when he was much younger, about his ability to work the lanes. He played the game with Ned Day from Milwaukee, the American National Match Play tournament champion, who had recently made a big splash. Day was known as the "first genuinely famous bowler." In the game Allan shared with him, on August 17, Day set a new world record, scoring 834 for three consecutive games. Rounding out the trio was actor Harold Lloyd. This stellar game was touted in Day's publicity for years and years to come. For Allan, it was simply a bit of fun, exercise, and another snippet to keep him in front of the press.

Age continued to creep up on Allan in an industry where age wasn't usually an attribute. He was already in his early thirties — not remotely

an ingénue anymore. He had run circles around the studio block more
than once, and he knew the course in great detail. Having come and gone
from Hollywood twice, with new image makeovers each time, he was on
his third round at trying to make a break-out name in the movies. He was
known in the picture world — a point not in question. What he hadn't
been able to achieve yet was honest-to-gosh stardom. He was hardly
a newbie but he had not become
anyone's idea of a household name,
either.

The country was just barely
finding her way out of the
Depression. The United States
was on the edge of jumping into
what would become the Second
World War. And actor Allan Lane
did his level best to keep a steady
foot in an industry that changed
its highest profile personnel with
each new moving picture. To say
he was dispirited was more than a
monumental understatement. This
was not what Allan had hoped for
when he first tried his hand at the
movies over ten years ago.

*Champion bowler Ned Day the year
before Allan played with him and
Harold Lloyd in a tournament in
Hollywood.*

As the new decade came into
being, Allan found himself changing his home studio once again.
Just months earlier, the press applauded him as a star for RKO, boldly
stating RKO regarded him as a valuable "find." Not only was he handsome with an "abundance of charm," he had a "natural understanding of
histrionics." This was what RKO reportedly saw in him, believing him well
equipped for the "competition with modern screen hero types."

It had only been two years since he had been signed at what was termed
a "steep salary," in January of 1938, and under a "long-term contract." He
had been seen in one after another comedy or drawing-room romance,
usually with him in a lead or costarring role. Having played something to
the tune of "twelve leads in fourteen pictures," many with a lighter theme,
he had proven to be more than adept at comedy. He was good at delivering
punch lines at just the right moment. He knew how to utilize his facial

expressions to draw the most laughs out of any script. And he was never afraid to take a fall for the sake of the story's humor. Physical acting was right up his alley.

With the entire world in turmoil, the entertainment industry, often a fantasy mirror of what was happening in reality, seemed to be facing another evolution. Tensions were high in the real world and the general

An uncharacteristically friendly family photo with Allan's mother, Anne, Allan, his father, Bill Albershart, and his sister, Helen, probably taken in Los Angeles between 1940–1945. PHOTO COURTESY THE COSTELLO FAMILY COLLECTION

population looked to the movies to alleviate their fears, if only for a few brief hours. People demanded amusement to take their minds off the potentially impending doom that seemed to surround them everywhere.

Light comedies were the sort of feature in which Allan played most often these days. He fit the bill as required of him, though he was unhappy with the direction his career, and his life, had taken. He had worked with the studio to broaden his appeal and expand on the idea he would "gain distinction" that year. He had hoped RKO would help him work his way into getting behind the camera as a director but the studio didn't see eye-to-eye with him on that goal.

One article said of him, "Older in experience than most of his contemporaries, he chafed at what he thought was slow progress, but now admits that the movies, like the fight game, are smart to train the star-contenders slowly." This was "press speak" for what was his blunt reality. Allan Lane was not moving up the ladder fast or in the way he would have wanted had he been able to specifically direct his career, rather than have a studio direct it for him.

In the midst of his professional concerns, personal and romantic issues continued to tail him. His father had moved to Los Angeles from Indiana after his second marriage failed. He was renting a room, and as of 1940,

Sexy Judy Malcolm, another of Allan's many "dates" around the same time as he was being called "one of the finest physical specimens in Hollywood."

he told people he was a widow even though Anne vas not only still very much alive but living in the same city. This created family tension Allan had to work around. Now that his dad was geographically near him, their relationship splintered even more than when they had been separated by distance. He protected his mother whenever and however he could, and he and his dad drifted further and further apart.

On the romance front, Allan seemed to have moved on, even though there were rumors June Travis had had second thoughts about breaking up with him. She'd left Hollywood behind her and now called Chicago home. One article revealed her introspection about the recent events in her life. "The things the red-headed movie starlet…was thinking about didn't exclude romance — and Allen [sic] Lane…" One thing this snippet indicated…their break-up had been amicable, seemingly even a little bittersweet.

June proved she was the marrying sort of girl, though marrying in the movie industry had given her great pause. She ended her film career that year, and in 1940, wed Chicago businessman Fred Friedlob. June Travis Friedlob never looked back. Though she did appear onscreen a few more times in her life, she ensconced herself in the local theater circuit and became a well-loved socialite and patron of the arts. Her wedding ended any chance for reconciliation with Allan.

Allan missed hardly a step, at least publicly. He was called "one of the finest physical specimens in Hollywood," and was seen with Judy Malcolm at Bert Gordon's Mad Russian Café soon after its premiere opening. Malcolm, an actress and stuntwoman, had been Milton Berle's main squeeze and she and Berle had recently been slated to be married. Allan also stepped onto the dance floor with Ann Sheridan at the Bamba Club. He wasn't a man to take a relationship lightly, and most of the sightings of him with a beautiful lady continued to be nothing more than flashes of a camera's light bulb and a few words in a gossip column the next day.

Attracting beautiful women was easy for Allan. He could do that without effort. What he wanted to focus on was his career. He felt it might be time to alter his tactics, and work on a new effort to secure his place in the movies. Allan Lane planned to become a star, one way or the other.

CHAPTER ELEVEN

Horsing Around

Whether truth or fiction, or a combination of both, publicity efforts had become more important to Allan's resumé now that his focus had become more defined by the studios for which he worked. He was in his second decade, and then some, in an effort to make a name for himself as a movie star, and press attention was crucial to him since he had finally gained notable visibility.

Yet now that he had that ongoing experience, Allan knew how the promotional machine worked. The gossip tidbits could go in his favor, or go against him. Managing his image was as much a part of his job as was doing well with the roles he was given. He was determined to veer public mention of his name toward more in-the-moment sports-oriented events and celebrity benefits, rather than salacious tidbits about studio-arranged dates with every new starlet in town, or serious relationships. All this took up far too much of his publicity real estate. Who he dated and what went on his personal life was nobody's business but his own.

He became an even more actively visible golfer, known to have rock-solid ability in the amateur set, garnering enough clout to be considered part of the Hollywood sportsmen's community. Allan's membership at Lakeside Country Club in Los Angeles allowed him to play not too far from the address he called home on San Marino Street. He had apartment-hopped quite a bit since his latest return to town, not having found anything more permanent he liked enough to put down solid roots. At least for now, he was only about four miles from Aunt Eva's home, where his family still congregated during downtime and holidays.

New Year's Day 1940, found Allan playing for the cameras and an eager audience at Lake Merced Golf Club in San Francisco. He wasn't officially working for the lens in that capacity, yet he had a new persona to cultivate and he spent a good deal of his time doing exactly that. While his track record proved he hadn't been easy to pin down to one place for any length of time, the product he put out over and over again had garnered him a growing and appreciative audience. The studios with which he had worked, and the ones he hadn't yet contracted with but might someday, all kept an eye on him.

That January, he was part of a $5,000 match play tournament, teaming for a few rounds with Sir Walter Hagen, a famous golfer who had won the PGA Championship five times, the Western Open five times, and a number of wins at both the U.S. and British Open. Allan and Hagen played with actor Richard Arlen. Days later, Allan was again with the same men at Orinda Country Club, also in San Francisco. This was a multiple day tournament to benefit the Finnish Relief Fund Drive which had been created a few years earlier to offer "moral and financial assistance" for the people of Finland against what was seen as an assault on that country by Russia.

Allan continued to play heavily in benefit tournaments throughout the year. During this time, the tides of personal fortune turned for him. His maternal grandmother, who had lived with Aunt Eva and Uncle Billy, passed away, leaving a void in the family. Aunt Eva had moved up in economical stature, becoming one of a rare breed: a professional woman. She studied hard after moving to Los Angeles and acquired her degree as a "chiropractic doctor." This was a relatively new field in 1940, having been officially recognized in 1895. The image of a chiropractor had since received a good deal of legitimatization to separate the "quacks" from those like her who had taken on formalized schooling.

Now going by the name of Dr. Eva Lewis, she had built up a well-respected business. To accommodate her growing practice, a small wing was built on the back of the house and her degree was hung on the wall before she opened her doors to paying customers. Clients would visit her in her home office for treatment for all sorts of ailments.

This, along with Billy's income from working for the studios, gave the couple a respected place in the community as well as a stable address for family members to call home whenever needed. And the majority of the family — including Allan, his sister, his mother, his grandmother, and even siblings and cousins — regularly spent extended periods of time at 2914 Fourth Avenue in the Jefferson neighborhood of Los Angeles. Grandmother would be sorely missed.

This location was the clan's emotional anchor. That spring alone, there were six people living in the house — Eva and Billy, Eva's brother Charles,

Allan's mom and sister, and divorced cousin Esther Wolter Dodd. In between apartments, sometimes-vagabond Allan also hung his hat there from time to time.

A month or so later, Allan found himself in the hospital. Cedars of Lebanon housed him for a short time as he recovered from an emergency appendectomy. The need for surgery had come upon him suddenly. Unfortunately, he had earlier volunteered — in fact he had been the first to volunteer — to play the day after his admission to the hospital in yet another Finnish Relief Fund benefit tournament. That, thanks to his health and personal situation, never happened.

Grand Ole Opry *1953 re-release theater sheet...not Allan's usual fare.*

He recovered quickly enough. By the summer, Allan was back in the movie game, having secured a standard "picture commitment" with Republic Studios. He had previously worked with Republic as a freelancer, so their way of doing business wasn't foreign to him. This contract simply meant he would work for them now on a non-exclusive, picture-by-picture basis. In between, if an opportunity came his way, he was also allowed to do pictures elsewhere.

His first newly contracted Republic picture was hardly his usual fare. *Grand Ole Opry* mixed "politics, girls' baseball and hillbilly music." The only part with which Allan was intimately acquainted was baseball...and even then, it was far from a girls sport for him. Despite the "slapstick to the accompaniment of hillbilly music" storyline, Allan managed to play his usual type, that of an urbane, handsome gentleman.

In many ways, Allan's luck had drastically changed with the move to Republic though he may not have realized this then. His next vehicle proved to be the sort in which he would make his ongoing mark on entertainment history. He had no clue, however, when he took the role. He was simply making sure he had ongoing work.

This was the year Allan Lane was introduced to the idea of the movie serial. The concept had been making rounds in Hollywood for decades. Serials and recurring themed movies were easy ways for the studios to pump out short, moneymaking, cliff-hanging storylines that proved to bring audiences back for more, time and time again.

Until this juncture, Allan had been showcased primarily as an upper-

Allan as Sergeant King in King of the Royal Mounted...*always in danger in an action-packed serial.*

class gentleman in single-run movies. He had been able to hang on in an atmosphere that easily spewed out leading actors on a weekly basis, if not faster, and tossed them away just as quickly if they didn't fit the bill. Still, Allan had never lit the world on fire in that sort of movie. He was unhappy and unfulfilled. This wasn't what he was looking for the last time he had returned to Hollywood five years before.

About to pack it all up yet one more time, give up entirely, and head out to find another line of work — after all, he had remade himself once already and he was confident he could do it again elsewhere — fate intervened, again in the guise of Republic Pictures, this time with serials. Sensing they might have a star in this actor if they handled him right, Republic executives changed gears with Allan. He had been previously under-utilized or, at least, improperly utilized for his personality type.

King of the Royal Mounted (1940) was another single contract deal with Republic for Allan. As a serial, often called a "chapter play," the story was made up of twelve installments and filmed between June 18 and July 12. Each episode was packed with thrills, action, and a lot of fisticuffs. Serials — Westerns or those set in an exotic location — were primarily created for youngsters. The kiddies would be dropped off at the theater for a roundabout noon, sit-in-the-seat time. They would see a feature film, cartoons, previews of coming attractions...and the serial, which, at its end, would promise an exciting new installment for the following Saturday afternoon matinee. Then the kids would wait all week in great anticipation to do this all over again.

Hiram S. Brown, Jr. was Allan's age and nicknamed "Bunny." As a producer in charge of RKO serials, he needed just the right actor to take on the characterization of Sergeant King, based on the *Zane Grey* comic strip. Allan, whom Bunny remembered as being tall, good looking, and well built, and who had most recently worked primarily for Republic, seemed an excellent fit. Bunny signed him as the lead.

William Witney, the serial's director, was not impressed with Allan as a man. He was reported as saying a production with Allan in it, from beginning to end, was not a happy experience. While Allan's initial interview went well, once he was signed to a contract, the pleasantries were done. Witney never did like Allan personally and he rarely missed a chance in an interview, in the moment or as time went on, to make his displeasure well known.

There were six years between the men, with Allan being the oldest. Since Allan didn't take well to strong personalities telling him what to do, the idea that a younger man having final say over the way in which he did his job didn't sit well with him. The pairing equated to two roosters in the henhouse. Other stories reported that Witney didn't care for Don "Red" Barry either, the first actor to bring *Red Ryder* to the movie screen. Barry was not known to be an easy man to deal with, maybe more than Allan, so whether all of this in general was a commentary about Allan Lane, Don Barry, William Witney — or all of them — is unknown.

Soon after the initial signing and even before shooting began, an article headline blared, "Star found," and went on to explain, "Mounties are healthy men. When Republic was casting about for an actor...the studio was obliged to make a long and diligent search. The actor who won the prize role from more than a hundred candidates tested, was Allan Lane, who stands six feet three in his stocking feet." Other actors had already been placed in the supporting roles, so finding the lead had been the clincher. Allan Lane was set.

Promoted as "the greatest thriller ever filmed," there was little concern over Allan's personal interactions with production executives once the first episode hit the screen. Despite the clash of personalities while on the set, the product hit the screen with lots of attention in its wake. Ads gushed how the new twelve-chapter serial was "greeted with whoops and enthusiasm by the young serial patrons" and the first installment, "'Man

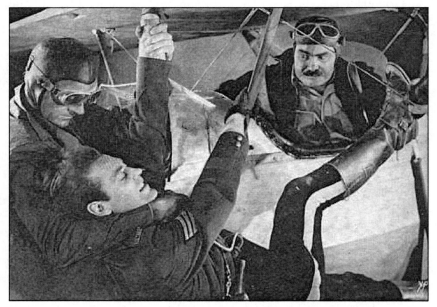

Allan as Sergeant King braving death in King of the Royal Mounted... *hanging out of an airplane!*

Hunt' came off with a flying start." Singled out, "Allan Lane as the leader of the Mounties gives a magnificent performance as the virile, handsome hero who braves death many times to accomplish the final destruction of the enemy group."

This Saturday afternoon movie serial would prove to be Allan Lane's saving grace as a professional actor, while becoming only his first in a succession of ball-and-chain onscreen vehicles.

Serial installments were usually filmed within a short period of time. According to Chuck Anderson, owner of "The Old Corral" website, serials were put together based on the different location work needed. Town shots would be filmed, exteriors, stagecoach chases, and on and on. Once the production work was completed, the director and editor would put it all in order.

These relatively quick jobs offered a studio a long-running opportunity to garner new and returning viewers eager to see the next piece of a story that had already hooked them. For an actor, they were a chance for consistent visibility and a short-lived but steady paycheck. This meant that while he was being seen on the screen, Allan's comings-and-goings in his personal life continued to be of interest to the hungry gossip-seeking public. His dating history, while not necessarily a topic of conversation on the tip of every columnist's tongue, still usually received honorable mentions in many "this-and-that" lists of who-was-seeing-who. Whenever he played in a sports-related benefit, those details also hit the papers.

William Witney, who became known as one of the leading developers of low-budget serials, related in an interview with the *New York Times* how serial productions worked. "We'd start shooting as soon as the sun came up and shoot till after the sun went down, and we did it for six days a week." He said in the same article that such serials in the 1930s, a few years earlier than *King of the Royal Mounted*, "…were shot for $175,000 to $225,000 or more, and many were produced in a month or less." Witney said the process traditionally took fifteen to eighteen days to shoot an entire serial of twelve to fifteen episodes.

This explained how Allan Lane was publicly seen as a "star" when his first experience with serials hit the screens, about August of 1940. But by December of that same year, a news tidbit blasted, "Alan [sic] Lane used to be a contract player with RKO. Now he's selling automobiles. He's making twice as much."

What detail failed to explain was how Allan had worked nearly non-stop for a number of studios, including RKO, prior to this period. He had done serial work in the summer that premiered in early fall. By the time 1940 closed, as an actor he was already technically out of work in Hollywood, even though his action-packed appearances on screen continued to be shown to the masses nearly every Saturday. When read between the lines, the gossip also made clear that Allan Lane was not a man to while away his time. He was always working, no matter what he had to do to get his all-important paycheck.

Early 1941 newspaper ads for *King of the Royal Mounted*, described as a "continued serial," reported that the series debuted in the fall of the year before and was still playing strong, and playing often. In fact, the entire program had just opened in early January at many theaters across the country. Though Allan's movie work may have been sporadic, his visibility was, for the most part, ongoing.

Since he had gone from picture to picture, sometimes with no work in between jobs, kiddies may have been chomping on popcorn and delight-edly watching him take care of the bad guys, while adults were literally buying cars from him in Los Angeles. Whether or not he was making pictures, Allan continued to have financial obligations. That never stopped. The visibility on the automobile showroom floor would not have hurt him in any way, especially since his stint as a car salesman did not last long. He would have been an asset to the dealership as well.

Allan needed to be useful; that was his nature. He needed to be doing something he felt gave his life purpose. He had known hard work since childhood, and not only was he responsible for himself but he was also always taking care of someone in his family.

His nephew, Tom, said whenever "Uncle Harry" had money in his pocket, his mother never wanted for anything. She was married but there were troubling family concerns at play in that relationship which created not only emotional tension but, at times, financial difficulties as well. To the best of his ability, Allan always ensured she had nice things. "Whenever Uncle Harry was working," Tom Costello said, "Gramanne would get a new couch, or a color TV set, or whatever. He took care of her."

Late that year, Allan once again proved that who he dated, or worked alongside, often correlated with who he might know from the sports scene. June Travis, Allan's almost-love, was the daughter of Harry Grabiner with the Chicago White Sox. Frances Mercer, daughter of sports writer Sid Mercer, had been one of Allan's co-stars. And now he was dating actress Florence Rice, daughter of sports writer and sports commenta-tor Grantland Rice. She was then fresh out of a divorce from "B" actor Robert Wilcox, who would ultimately gain infamy as the husband of Diana Barrymore.

Allan and Rice were spotted on a number of occasions on the dance floors in and around Hollywood, once in particular at the then-popu-lar Hollywood Bar of Music on what was at the time named Beverly Boulevard — dinner, dancing, and a show. The place was known for the "dueling piano players" seated opposite each other at twin baby grands. Louella Parsons, famed gossip columnist, made note of their pairing on a particular evening in November.

Allan's dancing ability had never been in question and that was often how he shook off whatever ailed him. Dancing was in ways yet another sport for him. Though his contract had been nixed and he had no active studio work at the moment, that made little difference to an entertainment-hungry audience looking for every little detail about the stars of the silver screen.

In fact, fans may not, for the most part, have even realized there was anything different in the professional life of Allan Lane, since his hit serial still played in movie houses across the country and he still received

Another of Allan's many pretty female companions, Florence Rice.

between 8,000 and 10,000 fan letters a month. Allan took advantage, and except for anyone who may have bought a car directly from him in Los Angeles in recent months, he remained known as a Hollywood actor. He stayed publicly visible on the promotional scene and, as a result, most moviegoers had little idea Allan Lane had been forced to peddle vehicles to make a dollar, and had stopped, at least for the time being, chasing imaginary movie bad guys.

If crowds paid attention, though, they probably recognized his absence soon after. *King of the Royal Mounted* continued on screens around the country but they were now repeats of the entire serial. Allan didn't get a lot of solid new work throughout 1940. Since he was not obligated to any one studio, he took roles from wherever they were offered to him. As a result, he had only three official credits to his name that year. One interesting project was a short released the first week in June. The entire work was cast and shot in days. *Coffins on Wheels* (1941) was a free-standing part of a series under the title *Crime Does Not Pay*.

There were multiple purposes for this series, which had begun in 1935. Each segment took about twenty minutes or less to tell the story. Besides serving as a public service announcement to prove to the viewing public that honesty was the best way to go about their daily life, there was a practical end as well. These shorts were used as a training ground for promising new talent to show what they could do. In *Coffins on Wheels*, Allan represented the law in a story which revolved around an excited teenager ready to buy his first car. His innocence was put up against a seasoned crooked car dealer to prove, though with disastrous consequences, that *Crime Does Not Pay*.

Allan used his professional off-time to get into the celebrity bowling scene. The American Bowling Congress Tournament, known as the A.B.C. Championship, "went West for the first time" and was held in Los Angeles in June. Allan was part of a large group of celebrities who attended as spectators. Others who enjoyed the event were Carole Landis, Nancy Kelly, Jane Withers, Eddie Foy Jr., and Red Skelton. Many Hollywood types were avid bowlers, a quite popular sport at the time. Allan had played since he was a kid, competing on many levels in earlier years. There were 5,797 five-man teams collected together from 865 cities across the country entered in the A.B.C. Championship tournament.

The next year was another lean one for Allan. He contributed, if only as a warm body, to *All-American Co-Ed* (1941), a Hal Roach production. Press was promising and it was billed as "The Season's Greatest Musical." Advertisements blared, "Hit tunes! Gals! Gags! Wow! What a Show!" Allan was simply credited as the "Second Senior" in yet another dancing-and-singing vehicle. He had just celebrated his thirty-second birthday when the movie came out. Hollywood was apparently not too worried about the fine details. Even though he wasn't anywhere near a traditional college senior at any school, the age disparity didn't hold him back from getting the small part. The film for him was nothing more than a few extra bucks in his pocket when he needed them. Once again, his character didn't even get a name.

Before the year ended, Allan phoned in one more bit part as a bayonet drill instructor in *Military Training* (1941). Another Hal Roach effort, this was put together in conjunction with the U. S. Army Signal Corp in cooperation with the United States government. The country was getting in deep with the Allies. With war raging, just about everyone, even in Hollywood and on celluloid, did what they could to aid the effort. This wasn't a theatrical film and none of the actors — including the likes of Alan Hale, Jr., Alan Ladd or Allan Lane as well as all the others — did it for the credit. The characters didn't have names, only titles and functions. Also known as *Training Film No. A 3*, it was exactly that — a training film.

CHAPTER TWELVE

Serials Are Serious Business

Allan certainly wasn't prolific in his screen work in the early 1940s, so when he learned Republic wanted to remix *King of the Royal Mounted*, he was all for it. This began the period when Allan's future in serials expanded, not because he made much of anything new but because what he made in 1940 was being used to the best advantage. In fact, Allan himself did little during the early part of 1942, yet by the end of April, *The Yukon Patrol* (1942) had been released by Republic Studios and things finally began to turn around for him as an actor, slowly but methodically. Finally.

The Yukon Patrol was an hour-long, and then some, feature version of *King of the Royal Mounted*. One tagline screamed, "ROMANTIC ADVEN-TURE…in a land where men fight to live…and love!" Whether or not he knew it then, Allan was in the middle of a heavy-duty career makeover.

This series was milked for all it was worth. Actor Bob Kellard, billed at different times as Robert Kellard or Robert Stephens or Stevens, was well known to Allan. They got along famously, anticipating each other's lines and even their ad libs. He was called Allan's "sidekick" in the initial *King of the Royal Mounted*, and though he received no credit, he was also seen in *The Yukon Patrol*. Press said the two were "pals in the Republic picture" as well as "pals in real life." They enjoyed working together and reports said, "…during the filming of *King of the Royal Mounted*, the ribs sallied back and forth between them at high tension speed."

Allan's next contribution to the screen from this general storyline came out hot on the heels of *The Yukon Patrol*, which the studio had used as something of a promotional tool. *King of the Mounties* (1942) was Allan's second King cliffhanger. In July, Allan sent a letter to Republic and in it, he authorized the studio to "use any and all stock material taken from your former photoplay entitled *King of the Royal Mounted*, Production #998, for which my voice was recorded and my person photographed in and for your present photoplay *King of the Mounties*, Production #1195."

This official typed letter was signed by Allan and dated July 28, 1942. For a grand total "in hand paid" of $162.50 — the amount written out in longhand and in numbers — he allowed "said sound recordings of my voice and photographs of my person used in your former photoplay..."

authorized by him to Republic, their licensees, exhibitors, successors and assigns, "for motion picture purposes and only in connection with the exhibition of said photoplay..."

Essentially an assemblage of older material with a hearty amount of footage taken from the original product, theaters screened this in October as a new offering. *King of the Mounties* again brought Sgt. Dave King into the limelight, with Allan in the title role. Billed as a follow-up, it became, in its new form, a debut offering as far as audiences were concerned, and they ate it up. The amount he was paid for this endeavor would equal somewhere

Allan's friend, actor Bob Kellard.

in the neighborhood of $2,500 today. The benefit to his career ultimately proved to be priceless.

Considering the date of the letter Allan penned to authorize material from *King of the Royal Mounted* to be used in a new effort, he appeared to have lived off old paychecks for all of 1942 and into early 1943. With his pocketbook getting lean, he was willing to take what was offered to him, when it was offered. Throughout the year, he moved between Warner Bros., Republic, and Twentieth Century-Fox to find work.

In early 1943, he had another barely-there credit added to his resumé via Warner Bros. Playing nothing more than an unnamed Marine in this one, titled *Air Force* (1943), the movie starred Gig Young, one of only a few known names to get solid billing. The others, such as Harry Carey, Arthur Kennedy, and John Garfield, were part of a list of characters seemingly drawn together to take on another war-time production, not to give themselves major billing. The tagline read, "Air Force bomber, 'Mary Ann,' takes off for the Pacific with the crew battling against heavy odds."

Air Force came out in March of 1943. Almost immediately after, Allan was featured in his second Western role and his first Western serial. *Daredevils of the West* (1943) was a Godsend, giving him new money to live on. Newspaper ads announced the first chapter coming out in a number of

Daredevils of the West *theater card featuring Allan.*

east coast theaters in early April, saying the "new thrilling serial" had been filmed the month before. This one was applauded as a "serial story studded with stirring action and dangerous adventure" from Republic Studios.

Serials were made for the most part to babysit and entertain kids who loved a make-believe world of action and adventure. There was lots of action and lots of adventure; rough-and-rowdy fight scenes; and bad guys and good guys with the good guys always ultimately winning the day — though never before about an hour's worth of fisticuffs and cliffhangers to make the winning all the more worthwhile.

Though the entire effort had taken time to work out the nuances, public reaction to Allan's performances in *King of the Royal Mounted* and subsequent iterations proved to studio bosses they had someone who could hold his own in this sort of action adventure genre. Republic hired him again, and this time they seemed to understand what kind of an actor they had in Allan Lane. Here could be Hollywood's newest action hero.

Daredevils of the West was an all-Western "chapter play." With twelve installments, again shot in quick succession and released almost as fast, the work gave Allan a short-but-sweet ongoing paycheck as well as renewed visibility. Republic had a reputation for offering moviegoers remarkable and exciting stunt work, non-stop action, special effects, and nail-biting fight scenes.

Allan proved he was capable of all that and more — he was thoroughly able to rise to the occasion. William Witney, who might have resisted having to work with Allan again if he had been the one in the director's seat, was serving in the Navy. His co-director on most other Republic serial efforts, John English, went solo on this one, a fortunate turn of events for Allan. These two men had worked together before and there was no evident conflict between them.

There was an intriguing and unique side story to *Daredevils of the West*. Gossip columnist Jimmy Fidler reported it had been Allan — an "erstwhile New York photographer" — who gave female costar Kay Aldridge her first job as a model back in the 1930s. A predominance of Allan's photographic work back then, in addition to high-visibility advertising clients, had been female models looking for the best possible portfolios to present to Hollywood. Kay proved to be yet another of the many beautiful young ladies with whom Allan had a history.

He had done his job as a photographer well, and she obviously made it to the screen. Years later during a panel discussion at a fan convention, Kay admitted to knowing Allan in the early days. She said, "I first met Allan Lane in New York when I was a model and he was a boy model…" That he had modeled is fact. That she had modeled for him when he was behind the camera was also fact, though she did not mention this detail those many years later.

Kay had a bit part as a model in *Vogues of 1938*, the same film in which Vicki Lester appeared, also as an uncredited model. This puts two of Allan's previous modeling subjects in the same vehicle, the same sort of role they played in real life, and in a logical timeframe. Only a year-and-a-half or so later, the timing showed how these people crossed each other's paths at nearly the same time and for the same reasons.

So when he again came in contact with Kay, they found themselves as costars, and the press called them "the serial king and queen." Ads screamed, "12 episodes of punch-packed, hair-raising, thrill-crammed action!" The top brass planned to put the pair together in more starring vehicles but, again, fate had other plans. They were a well-matched pair and got along without major issue, but Kay left the studio, leaving Allan Lane without a female costar. While his work for the most part didn't require the romantic interaction his earlier drawing-room romantic fluff movies had, these serial plots still needed a female to play opposite the hero and offer the feminine touch.

A young Kay Aldridge, about the time she would've first met Allan.

One of the uncredited actors in the cast was a man originally known as Harold J. Smith, a Native American from Canada and the son of a Mohawk chief. After he began acting under the name of Jay Silverheels, he did extensive background work before ultimately becoming forever a part of the collective TV-watching mind as Tonto, sidekick to TV's now famous *Lone Ranger*. At this point in 1943, however, Silverheels wasn't even ten years into his career.

That fall, *Daredevils of the West* played in many theaters on a double bill with *King of the Mounties*. Special notice was made that both starred "he-man Allan Lane." Chuck Anderson, who runs the well-researched "B" western website "The Old Corral," thought this unusual but speculated how Republic may have wanted to "sweeten the deal" for theater owners. Allan's hard work had only taken nearly fifteen years to show real success, but he was finally an unquestionable lead actor, which certainly catered to his physical type and screen abilities.

Allan's third onscreen offering that year returned him to another gentlemanly role. Put out by Twentieth Century-Fox, the studio was one he had done a lot of the same sort of work for in the past. His part in this film was unfortunately, again, largely forgettable. A down-the-cast-list appearance with Laurel and Hardy in *The Dancing Masters* (1943) did little to further his adventure-seeking, "he-man" career. From Allan's professional perspective, the problem was that this was a starring vehicle for the established team of Laurel and Hardy. Their films rarely needed explanation, and audiences didn't go to see anyone but them. Ticket buyers were shoo-ins for the fans of the duo and those fans usually cared little about other actors in the cast. *The Dancing Master* was released in November.

Offscreen, Allan kept busy with his other love: sports. Chuck Anderson from "The Old Corral" mentioned three *Los Angeles Times* articles, from November 9 through 11, which told of Allan involved in Negro League All-Stars baseball at Gilmore field in Los Angeles. Called a "movieman," his name was spelled Alan Lane and he headed up "Alan Lane's Major League All-Stars."

Allan's team was part of the California Winter League, which, according to Mr. Anderson, "existed from prior to World War I through the mid-1940s." The Winter League was "America's First Integrated Professional Baseball League," according to author William McNeill, and operated in Southern California from 1910 until 1945. Alan Lane's Major League All-Stars included Johnny Lindell of the New York Yankees, Al Zarilla of the St. Louis Browns, and Vern Stephens, also from the Browns.

The next year, he had the male lead in *Call of the South Seas* (1944), a second-billed feature for Republic in which he sported a moustache, likely the only time Allan was seen onscreen with facial hair. His lovely dark-haired costar was Janet Martin, daughter of a well-seasoned stage concert singer. At five-feet-five-inches and only 110 pounds, she was a striking complement to Allan's height and coloring. The movie didn't get a lot of attention, but Allan and Janet had no problems working together, and they made an attractive pair.

Feast or famine, whether during a busy year as an actor or selling cars, either way, Allan remained concerned about how well his family got along. While he knew Aunt Eva and Uncle Billy would never let his mother or sister do without a home or food, he still considered himself responsible for their overall well-being. When he couldn't keep up his end as their caretakers — in total or even with partial input — he felt as if he was failing them.

The last few years held great significance for Allan's sister Helen. Reading between the lines shows those years had not been easy on her. She and Clarence Wolven had divorced. In May of 1937, she remarried, this time to a man named LeRoi Gant Brennan. That union lasted less than a year. By 1940, she lived with Aunt Eva and Uncle Billy in a full house that included her mother, a cousin, and an uncle on her mother's side. Her mother and Will Costello were together until his death, though they had divorced by 1940 and were then living apart. Later, they were together in Eva and Billy's home, but in different parts of the house. Obviously Helen wasn't the only one in the family having relationship issues.

She resided with Aunt Eva and family for the next two years and didn't care to publicly recognize her marriage to Brennan, evidenced by how she still lived under the name of Helen Wolven. She did the best she could to support herself while contributing to the family household by working as a sales lady at a local department store.

Helen's life changed yet again on Valentine's Day in 1942, for the better

Call of the South Seas...*Allan with a moustache.*

in many ways. She became the wife of Roland Hower, her second cousin. From the start of their marriage they chose not to have children because of their close bloodline. Roland was a sweet man but he had trouble communicating. One of his issues arose from a physical condition he couldn't control. Roland had Tourette syndrome, and his niece Pat recalled his horrible tics which he, and all around him, simply had to live through.

This made it difficult, sometimes impossible, for him to properly take care of his wife. Though they had a good personal relationship, they often had trouble making ends meet and keeping a household together. The couple didn't always live in the same place, and it wasn't until about four years after they wed when they began to claim the same home address. For the first few years of their marriage, she lived with her family, and he lived with his mother.

This is where Allan came in yet again. Even when his work was sporadic, he did everything he could to help his sister, as well as his mother, ensuring neither of them ever needed any of the basics. As long as he was breathing, they would have a home to live in and food to eat. Years earlier, Roland had worked as an auto mechanic as well as a poster maker for a theatrical advertising company. Then, he did odd jobs, sometimes for one of the movie studios — as he also did during his marriage to Helen. As Allan became more secure in his position in Hollywood, his family's comfort level also rose.

A little less than three weeks after his sister's marriage to Roland, Allan signed a Term Player contract with Republic. This promised him a regular paycheck and the security of knowing he was bound to have a job on an ongoing basis, year-to-year, for as long as the contract held up. He was forbidden to appear in any other studio's films without express permission. On the other side of that coin, he was saddled to Republic and only Republic. The studio could use his services whenever they cared to do so, and, for the most part, however they cared to use or not use his services. Either way, for that first year his salary was a weekly $250.

When he was away from the cameras, Allan had his pick of beautiful young thespian hopefuls from whom to choose. One of these ladies was a Universal contract actress named Ramsey Ames. She had gotten her start in movies in the early 1940s, just a few years earlier, thanks to a chance meeting with Allan's nemesis, Harry Cohn. Allan was seen now and then with Ramsey at the Mocambo. While their get-togethers may have been no more than photo opportunities, one now-gone picture told a back-story. Allan looked utterly smitten. Since she wasn't a Republic actress, their romantic alliance may have been real, even if short-lived.

His work in serials had caught fire and given him that one specific quality he had lacked up to this point: an identifiable persona all his own. Seems he had finally found his niche. *The Tiger Woman* (1944), which came out as early as May 18, 1944, was pure "B" movie kitsch from the get-go. Many newspaper ads gave Allan top billing, above Linda Stirling, even though the serial had initially been created as a vehicle for her. She was the heroine in the title role.

The storyline required viewers to suspend any belief in day-to-day reality. The story told of a young woman lost in the South American rainforest. She found her way to a tribe of natives and became their leader. What had a white woman been doing in those parts in the first place? That was the initial point of the plot. Possibly a lost heiress named Rita Arnold but viewers had to go see all twelve installments to get the full story, and frankly, not many really cared about her history. They went to see the nail-biting, cliff-hanging action, and Linda Stirling in her skimpy costumes.

A "B" Western tale without the Wild West, this one centered on bad guys trying to steal land that belonged to the good guys. Of course. Allan, as Allen Saunders, an engineer for the Inter-Ocean Oil Company, ended

Allan with The Tiger Woman...*props and costumes show how unrealistic the plotline was, though no one really cared.*

up fighting the bad guys alongside *The Tiger Woman* to victoriously save the day. Duncan Renaldo played Saunders's partner, Jose Delgado, a number of years before he became forever-after known as The Cisco Kid.

The suspension of reality was exactly what audiences were looking for when they gave their money to the ticket-taker for one of these weekend afternoon matinees. This was Republic's most expensive serial that year, based on the number of installments, and it was filmed between mid-January and late February.

The reaction from theater-goers, as well theater managers, was reportedly so enthusiastic after Allan completed this effort — his third serial for Republic — that Herbert Yates, the studio head, "recognized the fact that a top action star had been born."

Seems the evidence was cumulative. As proven by his career path to date, in no way was Allan an overnight sensation. Republic had had their first shot with him years before. Though they had liked his work then, they hadn't seen the merit of repeatedly utilizing his talents until they finally put him in something to emphasize his ability to act and react in physical settings, rather than play nice-nice with beautiful ladies in high-brow settings.

It was now clear to Republic they had a solid property on their hands. Allan shined in these action-filled stories. He had made more of a mark for himself in the last four years than he had in the eleven or so years he'd so far spent up to this time, working in and around the industry in one way or another.

During the end of filming of *Call of the South Seas*, he received word that Republic was eyeing him for a set of western scripts that would soon need a new starring actor. This was clearly good news, proving he was on his way up in the entertainment world. The news also showed that if Allan Lane planned to make his living as an actor, and he wanted to climb the ladder in Hollywood, his fate was now sealed. In the eyes of his audience, he was to become a fast-moving, always on the go, Western-type good guy of extreme action and few words.

CHAPTER THIRTEEN

On The Upswing...
Career-wise, At Least

Allan jumped into the opportunity to finally be a star with both feet... and his fists. Though Republic had apparently slated eight scripts for Allan, *Silver City Kid* (1944), initially known as *Red Gulch Renegade*, proved to be the first of six pictures he made for Republic over the next year. Whether it was six or eight, the effort proved to be a second image makeover for him with the studio. He had shown them he could handle serials. Now he would star in serials as he rode the range on a horse named Feather.

He took over scripts originally meant for Don Barry. These already-written programmers were for Republic's "Action Western" series. Barry was being groomed for meatier roles, leaving these vehicles open and ready for a new actor to tackle. Allan's salary didn't change but his visibility did. His first female costar was Peggy Stewart, a popular actress nearly twelve years his junior, with about a dozen or so appearances already under her belt.

Years later, Peggy's comments about Allan became some of the best-remembered recollections of his real-life character and personality. In *Allan "Rocky" Lane, Republic's Action Ace*, written by Chuck Thornton and David Rothel, her reminiscences spoke of how "dull" he was. She called him "the *dullest* man I ever met." She said he didn't have a good sense of humor "on the set" but he was "a very giving person; he was a very charitable person and all those wonderful things."

Peggy gave an example to illustrate his lack of humor while on the set. She had given him a nickname. "I called him Bubblebutt and he didn't think that was a bit funny." She said she said it "in jest" but her joke didn't "get through to him at all." Peggy didn't have any issues "with him being hard to get along with. Allan was pleasant enough to get along with." Her commentary, taken in context of his life at that time and his background, was on the mark. "So you just took Allan for what he was. As an actor doing his business or trade, he was one hundred per cent professional."

Allan was a professional. He took his work seriously. He did not handle criticism well and wasn't confident about his appearance, in spite his placement in earlier roles as a matinee-idol type. In 1944, Republic was rolling out Westerns one right after the other, and Allan was a hot property for

let . . . and the boots
addles left by the pio-
of the Westerns of
day. .

BRONCO BILLY
DUSTIN FARNUM
WILLIAM S. HART
TOM MIX
BUCK JONES
i a heritage of artistry and
. . . in entertainment and bril-
duction . . . that Republic is
 carry on to greater heights.

. . . ROGERS, AUTRY, ELLIOTT AND BURNETTE WELCOME A FIFTH MUSKETEER TO RIDE ALONG REPUBLIC'S HIGHWAY TO FAME!

THE SILVER CITY KI
STAGECOACH TO DENVI
JESSE JAMES' LAST RI
TRAIL OF KIT CARSON
SHERIFF OF SUNDOWN
THE TOPEKA TERROR
CODE OF BILLY THE KI
CORPUS CHRISTI

Early introduction of Allan Lane as Republic's "New Cowboy Star" with the ad announcing "a series of eight" presentations. PHOTO COURTESY THE COSTELLO FAMILY COLLECTION

them. Next in line for him, as well as for Peggy Stewart, was *Stagecoach to Monterey* (1944), in the can and on the screen no more than a few months later. Allan played an undercover United States Treasury agent in the days of the Wild West. The press called it, "A two-fisted western packed with excitement." This storyline gave Allan every opportunity to cement what would become his signature moves as a rough-riding, hard-shooting, and knock-'em-down fighter for justice.

He was also being called one of Republic's most handsome Western stars despite his lack of self-assurance. His looks were one reason he had been targeted for these roles, in addition to the fact he was always willing to take a punch, and he could easily move right out of one scene and into the next. Serials were fast-paced and usually somewhat short on plot, but action in the form of a tall, well-formed cowboy was always at the forefront.

This sort of work suited Allan's personality well. In earlier iterations as a movie actor he had proven he could act and carry a scene — be it comedy or drama or a musical — but he had never done well with in-depth interactions with the other characters. Serial Westerns gave him an opportunity to shine on his terms. Most of his life he had relied on himself to survive, and now, in his new place in Hollywood, he had been given a platform on which he could be his own man and earn his living doing so.

Movie poster for Stagecoach to Monterey.

One observer had said he was "sort of a loner." This was a polite understatement. Yet the rest of that commentary spoke of how good he was as an action hero. Allan was often noted for his work ethic on the one hand, and given darker marks about his personal side in the next breath.

Sheriff of Sundown (1944) rounded out the Allan Lane offerings for 1944, coming out just before Thanksgiving. He was again paired with Linda Stirling and Duncan Renaldo, apparently a studio tactic intended to draw fans of *The Tiger Woman* back to the screen for this "reunion" of sorts. The ploy, if that's what it was, worked, and Linda appeared one more time alongside Allan in his next screen vehicle.

Allan was now working regularly. He knew from one day to the next that his bank account would not go hungry. He was confident he could reliably help to support his family. These facts gave him comfort. An article stated he was:

...a lucky man — having carried out three of his ambitions. His first ambition was in the field of sports. He succeeded in playing with the Cincinnati Reds and the Brooklyn Dodgers. Then he decided he'd like to

develop his hobby, photography, into a profession. He opened an illustration studio in New York and was very successful until he decided to close shop and go to Hollywood, thereby pursuing a third ambition. Needless to say, this time he succeeded, too.

As usual, the sports information was included in Allan's line-up of accomplishments, no matter how often or how much detail was stretched

Movie poster for Sheriff of Sundown.

to fit needs of the copy at any given time. The other two "lucky" factors attributed to him — his professional work in photography and his efforts in Hollywood — these had fleshed out to be true. Yet, he had definitely taken a while to get to the point where he was in early 1945 — on the verge of solid Saturday matinee Western movie star status.

The Topeka Terror, a 1945 release and one of the last scripts he had taken over from Don Barry, came out in January with Linda Stirling as his co-star. Shooting began on September 28, 1944 and the production wrapped on October 5. Allan had an ongoing filming schedule, with projects backing up and awaiting release. Republic was keeping him busy.

Another player was a young girl named Twinkle Watts. She was born in 1933, so the entire time she professionally associated with Allan, in about a half a dozen features from 1944 to 1946, she was a young girl.

According to *Allan "Rocky" Lane Republic's Action Ace*, at a film festival in 1988, Twinkle was asked what she thought of Allan. Her recollections were those of an adult looking back on her childhood. She said he had been "a serious man, maybe too serious...After all, they were paid to take it seriously." He always treated her like a little girl, she recalled, which is exactly what she was at that time.

Allan and his lovely female co-star featured on a movie poster for The Topeka Terror.

By late 1944, Allan was already on the far side of his mid-thirties and had no one with whom he could share his rising good fortune. While he had never had a problem finding romance, a solid lasting relationship had always eluded him. He knew he wasn't easy to get along with — that was no one's secret, least of all his own.

He dated regularly. Lately it was a here-and-there with June Storey as well as other sweet young actresses, many of them new-hires for Republic. These types of get-togethers dotted his publicly-announced romantic efforts. Never anything serious. In fact, nothing much was really real. That is, nothing until Sheila Ryan entered the picture.

When all five-feet-five-inches of this beautiful lady came into his life, long and slender and sexy, Allan was cautiously optimistic. Sheila was born in Kansas, and logically they should have shared a Midwestern sensibility, except by this time, they both had a healthy awareness of Hollywood's official indoctrination process. The Midwest in them had long since fallen by the wayside.

Allan was thirty-six years old. Sheila was twenty-five. She was nearly twelve years his junior. She already had an extensive dating record prior to meeting Allan but had not yet been married. She and Mickey Rooney had garnered a lot of attention together. She also spent time with then-actor Steve Crane who had recently had a go of it with Lana Turner. A few years earlier, she flew with Howard Hughes to Nevada's Cal Neva Lodge — chaperoned by her mother, of course. She also walked around the block with producer William Girard, who did *The Caribbean Mystery* (1945) in which Sheila co-starred. In her six or so years in Hollywood, Sheila Ryan had not been at a loss for male attention. One article said she was her studio casting director's "favorite 'other woman.'" Yet for Allan, then and there, she was the only woman. He was willing to become a married man for the third time.

Why she decided Allan Lane was the man for her, the man with whom she would leap into marriage, is unknown. And they did leap into marriage; they were not that well-acquainted before they tied the knot. Even Sheila said theirs was "a very brief courtship."

She attended Hollywood High School and started her career with the best of intentions, signing a contract with Paramount while she was still in school. Then she went with Twentieth Century-Fox. Finding a good deal of work coming her way early on, she was onscreen with seasoned names — the likes of Laurel and Hardy, Warner Oland, and Cesar Romero. From there, she went to RKO. By the time she and Allan were on the way to the altar, she had become primarily a "B" Western actress, and articles indicated she was "free-lancing."

Her story was somewhat similar to Allan's in that way. Although Allan's star seemed to hang a slight bit higher than hers at the time, Sheila regularly got the gossip tongues wagging. They worked in the same movie genre and moved in comparable social circles, crossing paths both professionally and privately.

In early October, a newspaper report said, "Film actress Sheila Ryan, often reported engaged, made it definite today." This comment alluded to her lively love life — she repeatedly teased the press with her plans to make her way to the altar with one man or the other. "She is going to marry Allan Lane, star of western pictures."

With Allan as her intended, she finally did add a wedding band to her jewelry collection. Newspapers wrote of a unique ring that had been given to her by her family when she was twenty-two. The piece consisted of gem stones from her great-grandmother's ring, her grandmother's ring, and her mother's ring. The intent was to have her own gems added when she married. Whether or not this was the ring she wore when she and Allan wed is not known.

Reporters kept an eye on the couple as their hastily made plans were put into action. The first official public reports of their impending union came out the day before on October 4, 1945. They drove from Los Angeles to Las Vegas the next day, and in the early evening, married at the Little

Sheila Ryan about the same time as she and Allan first got together.

Church of the West. Republic Studios made the announcement. Reverend Albert C. Melton officiated, a Congregational minister who performed most all of the Christian weddings at that church.

No one from Allan's family was known to have attended. Sheila's mother, Edith Golde, her stepfather, Charles Golde, and her grandmother accompanied the couple on the trip. After vows were spoken, the newly married Mr. and Mrs. Harry Albershart were showered with confetti as they left the tiny chapel. Wide smiles were seen all around.

But that happiness did not last. Little more than a few months later, the press was once again hot on Sheila and Allan's trail, this time for not-so-wonderful reasons. The marriage happened on October 5 and by early January of the following year, all of Hollywood was aware their union was over. Sheila made her feelings quite public, and gossip columnists and news services snatched up every circulated detail.

They weren't a high-visibility A-list couple but were each separately well-known enough to be good copy together. Allan had his own following, and Sheila was in the process of building hers, so any

Allan's wedding to Sheila Ryan at the Little Church of the West in Las Vegas. PHOTO COURTESY THE COSTELLO FAMILY COLLECTION

even remotely salacious detail of what had gone on behind closed doors between them was at least good filler, if not downright great reading material. Sheila told the world she and her new husband "differed on practically everything."

Official Splitsville was announced on January 18, 1946. "The wedded bliss that Sheila Ryan and Allan Lane of the screen sought in a Nevada elopement a little more than three months ago failed to materialize, and so their marriage was at an end today. The actress said a clash of careers was not to blame for the rift. It was much broader than that. She said she intends to file suit for divorce in the immediate future."

And she did exactly that. In less than two weeks, Sheila had hired well-known Hollywood lawyer Oscar Cummins. Two days later, he filed her divorce complaint. Cummins had represented, amongst others, Jean Harlow a dozen or so years earlier when her husband, Paul Bern, died under mysterious circumstances. The death was ultimately ruled a suicide, but in real time, details took a while to gel, and when the tragedy occurred, Harlow needed solid legal representation at her side.

This time, Cummins was only working a divorce, but he still made

Allan and Sheila were showered with rice by Sheila's mother, stepfather, and grandmother as they left the church. PHOTO COURTESY THE COSTELLO FAMILY COLLECTION

sure his effort held a heavy punch. Sheila's mother was an adult education supervisor for the Works Progress Administration (WPA) and her step-father worked in the special effects department for Walt Disney Studios. They had enough money to ensure Mrs. Golde's only child had excellent legal coverage, and Sheila petitioned for dissolution of her marriage to Allan under the grounds of "mental cruelty."

Sheila claimed Allan "had a very rigid plan for me. He wanted to control everything I did. He criticized me sometimes even for things he thought I would say." She also made note how the two of them could not agree on anything and "he thought he was prettier than me." She spoke of how critical Allan had been of her, and how he said he wanted her to "quit pictures." Her mother "corroborated" her daughter's claims.

In another statement, her words were as blunt but much less harsh. "It simply was a difference of opinion on practically everything. We couldn't be happy together, so what's the use of dragging things out?"

They had set up their marital home in what had been Sheila's apartment. Allan quickly moved out into "another dwelling near by [sic]" and less than seven days after Sheila's last public statement, on New Year's Eve, he was in a car crash.

Physically, and maybe emotionally, the accident did quite a number on him. Gossip columnist Harrison Carroll was quick to put into written word what many were wondering. "Allan Lane's bandaged head has nothing to do with the breakup of his marriage to Sheila Ryan. He was in an auto accident." A few weeks later it was announced it would be a month "…before doctors can decide whether or not Allan Lane will require plastic surgery to remove the scar on his forehead…"

In the midst of all the turmoil — and it really was anyone's guess as to how that car accident came about and Allan's state of mind at the time it occurred — he stayed quiet on his end of the marriage battle. He did not contest Sheila's terms or her public remarks, and he didn't make any commentary to the press about her or their time together, good or bad.

Erskine Johnson, Hollywood columnist, a few years later made note of the concept of "mental cruelty" as it related to Tinseltown divorces. His definition helps put the conflict between Allan and Sheila somewhat into context of the business they were in, their age disparity, and their personality and lifestyle differences. "Hollywood divorce petitions," Johnson explained, "usually carry the charge of mental cruelty and let it go at that without specific details…"

And there were no specific details bandied about for Allan and Sheila's split. The same article had gone on to explain how movie couples usually worked all this out — the individual charged was almost always the man, and he didn't take it any further. Instead, he simply let it slide and went with the flow.

Sheila had filed. She dictated the terms. Allan followed suit. Theirs had been a marriage even Sheila publicly noted should have never happened. They were unsuited for each other and did not have anything but Hollywood in common and the fact that they were both beautiful people. When all was finished and the union dissolved, she had a simplistic explanation. "We're simply incompatible."

More than a slight understatement. Everyone, including Allan, knew he was a man with a forceful personality, a defined belief system, and high, even sometimes unrealistic expectations of everyone around him, including himself. He was a decade older than Sheila; that alone would have had great potential to cause problems. Allan came from a place where the wife was the heart of the home, and the husband was expected to be the breadwinner. Even though the equation hadn't always worked out well for his mother, that had always been her intent, and his mother was his role model for the lifestyle he so deeply wished to live. Realistic or otherwise, he wanted a woman who would always complement him and be at his side to support him.

Sheila, on the other hand, was modern. She was trying to find her way up the Hollywood ladder, and becoming a traditional wife seemed to not be in her plans then. Her role model — her mother — was college-educated and a working lady. Sheila seemed to discover, too late to avoid divorce court, that she would do best with a man of a different stripe than Allan, a man who would stand with her, next to her, and not in front of her.

Allan demanded to be the sole breadwinner. Though Sheila had claimed there had been no clash of careers at the time of their union, Allan was finally making good regular money. She had not yet been as professionally successful. It had only been a handful of years earlier when she had been doing bit parts under the stage name of Betty McLaughlin.

Allan was on the cusp of a lucrative, headlining livelihood. Within barely a few months, he would take over the popular role of *Red Ryder* from the latest actor to star in it: Bill Elliott. At the time of their divorce, Allan was in the early days of contracting and planning a new stage of his career. In his mind, it was not unreasonable to expect his wife to take on a supporting role in a success that had been so long in coming for him.

One thing they did agree on was how they should dissolve their living arrangements. Columnist Louella Parsons reported, "When Sheila Ryan and Allan Lane decided to call it quits there was no embarrassment about who kept the apartment. Allan had subleased his own apartment when they married and he was able to get it back, so he just returned to his old quarters."

On February 22, 1946, Sheila Ryan was granted an interlocutory decree of divorce by Superior Judge Thurmond Clarke. This one wouldn't be contested by either side and in less than three months, the press was touting another soon-to-be-expected trip to the altar for the ex-Mrs. Harry Albershart. She planned to marry screenwriter and sometimes-actor Fred Brady. The romance was called off nearly as fast as it was announced, however, and Sheila did then marry actor Eddie Norris a year after her relationship with Allan ended. Her wedded bliss with Norris lasted a bit over a year, and she was again in divorce court. A few years later, she married one more time. This marriage, to actor Pat Buttram, lasted through to her death.

The relationship between Allan and Sheila Ryan had been a hasty affair and seemed doomed from the start. It was quickly dissolved, as if they had never been together. As if they had never known each other. This had unfortunately become Allan's life script.

CHAPTER FOURTEEN

Lights, Camera...Stardom!

With three divorces behind him, Allan decided to give up on romance, at least for awhile. He kept busy with work and sideline activities related to publicity and charity benefits. He became visibly active with the Motion Picture Relief Fund. The Fund, as it was called in the business, was an organization set up in 1921 to raise money to help actors and others who made their living in the industry. When they became too old to work anymore, gravely ill, or found themselves in the midst of hard times, they could go to The Fund for help. Their motto was, "We take care of our own." Insiders took this effort seriously and many offered their time, services, and finances to help their comrades. At any point, by the very nature of their business, any one of them might be in need of what the Fund selflessly offered.

It was not only benefits and appearances that brought in much-needed financial support but there were also products designed for this purpose. One was the Hollywood Starstamp set, along with an album designed exclusively to hold individual stamps — like postage stamps but with a picture of a movie star. The stamps were to be placed along with the star's name and affixed to the assigned spot. Anyone who was anyone in Hollywood was featured in this album. The product was the brainchild of actor Jean Hersholt, and put together by Harlich Manufacturing of Chicago. Hersholt was the organization's president. His tenure began in 1939 and ran until 1956.

Each individual featured in the album, along with their stamp, was required to sign a release to allow their name and image to be used for that purpose. A blanket release was issued and the signatures were collected. The effort took shape in 1946 and was publicly issued in 1947. Releases were valid through the end of that year. The stamp book had been expected to grow in subsequent years.

The album was given a fancy design, with embossed signatures on the cover and signatures imprinted inside the album for each individual star stamp. There were also separate stamps for Academy Award winners, historical characters, Western stars, and other genres. Allan was included amongst a page full of Western picture actors. As a group, each were required to sign a "unique document" in addition to the release, expressing their willingness to have their face and name used. Allan's stamp number was "W205."

The endeavor was meant to be a fun exercise for movie lovers and children of all ages, and came with directions as to how to adhere each stamp,

Hollywood Starstamp Album.

as if it were a "quiz" and the individual was being tested on their movie and movie star knowledge. If the stamper didn't have all the answers, no problem; a cheat sheet was included in the back. Allan happily contributed his name and image to the effort.

That spring brought more evidence of his charitable efforts, though he was secretive about most of the time he spent behind the camera with the less fortunate. He did not do it for publicity. In fact, he became openly angry if a columnist or newspaper article leaked any details of these visits for needy fans. Yet, invariably, here-and-there something would come out. Allan often donated his time to the concerns or entertainment of children, whether it was in parades or visits to sick kids in hospitals, or stopping by local schools.

In March, he did just that, going to see the kids at Encino Elementary School, near where he lived. They had a pet show, and Allan congratulated winners and handed out ribbons for the winning pets. This wasn't a glamorous use of his time, and definitely not a profitable one, but he enjoyed every minute he spent with the kids. He would go home after such experiences and feel as if he had done something worthwhile, something beyond just putting in his time for the sake of making a movie.

Western starstamps including signatures with Allan near the top on the right.

The scar from the car accident a month or so ago had begun to heal nicely without plastic surgery, and Allan got back into living life on his own terms, again without a partner. The apartment he returned to after he and Sheila divorced soon became a thing of the past. He purchased a small, "rambling" ranch in the Encino foothills and furnished it in ways which represented a lifestyle he had never before been able to live. He was said to have decorated "mannishly in leather and wood, and filled [it] with Western gimcracks." Those "gimcracks" were cowboy knickknacks of every sort. For example, he kept ten-gallon hats stacked on shelves in his bedroom.

He also owned "dozens of firearms, many of them relics from pioneer days," which he kept "scattered around his bachelor home." Several of his guns were visible, but most were put away in cabinets and drawers. He was said to "at the drop of a hint," go out into his backyard and share target practice with any guest who showed interest.

This home was where he cemented his love for owning, and training, horses. The horses would soon become his passion…even his obsession.

Allan showing off his closet with hats on the top shelf. PHOTO FROM MOVIE GUIDE AND COURTESY TINSLEY YARBROUGH

Western roles now came Allan's way fast and furious. Finding recognition for a single genre had been a long time in arriving, but once he finally hit his stride, his popularity as a cowboy lasted a good long time.

There was one problem, though. His newfound success coincided with the last days of World War II and Hollywood found herself short of handsome, capable leading men. Though the war ended only a few months later, the industry continued to feel the pinch as the slack took a while to catch up and return to any sense of normalcy. Allan still looked darned good in a tuxedo and had long since proven he was more than credible as a handsome, urbane leading man — even without a gunbelt and never having to shoot a single bad guy in the process. Since Republic had a few "light fare" scripts ready to go into production but almost no one to fit the

Allan in Gay Blades.

bill, Allan — under contract and physically available — was recruited to take on such forgettable films as *Gay Blades* (1946), *A Guy Could Change* (1946), and *Night Train to Memphis* (1946). More frustration for him. Allan feared he might be going backward on his career path.

Red Ryder, the serial, irrevocably saved him from that fate. Allan was selected from the Republic rosters to pick up on the already well-known characterization where actor Bill "Wild Bill" Elliott had left off. Elliott was being moved up in the Western movie ranks. Reports stated, "After searching the territory over the studio decided that Lane was the one man who would be able to get the job done."

Allan inherited the as-yet unfilmed scripts Elliott would have done, much like he had with the Don Barry scripts a year earlier. He also initially inherited Elliott's clothing — the black hat; a gray, seemingly ironed, cowboy shirt including arrow-designed pockets; and chaps. Somewhat pristine-looking duds for a guy who rode the dusty trails and got into all sorts of often messy work while getting rid of bad guys. Viewers didn't seem to mind such a minor detail. After the first *Red Ryder* picture, Allan got his own outfit, which he wore throughout the remainder of his time as the character. His pay was bumped up to $350 per week and ultimately,

Allan in a Red Ryder *promotional still.* PHOTO COURTESY THE COSTELLO FAMILY COLLECTION

as the series took root with him in the saddle, he began making more substantial money: $450 each and every week.

Allan needed his own horse since he was now playing the lead in an ongoing western serial as an identifiable continuing character. He had drastically changed profiles, from co-starring with beautiful ladies to co-starring with beautiful horses. There was one good thing about this: the horses didn't argue with him and were rarely as temperamental.

Allan as Red Ryder, man and horse. PHOTO COURTESY THE COSTELLO FAMILY COLLECTION

Thunder, Bill Elliott's horse, was already branded and well-identified with the *Red Ryder* product. In ways, Allan also inherited him...for a price. He was able to come to an agreement with Elliott to purchase Thunder, and once he brought him home, Allan renamed the horse Black Jack. Black Jack would ultimately become almost as much a celebrity as his owner.

With so much changing behind the scenes, the studio press machine kept Allan busy to ensure his name, his face, and that of his horse, continued to ride high in the memories of the ticket-buying fans.

When movies weren't being made, his bosses paired him with a variety of entertainment types in a whole host of publicity scenarios. Most often, his event audiences were made up of children. In June of that year,

Tommy Dorsey hosted 8,000 underprivileged children in three different theaters for the Fourth of July weekend. Allan, touted as " 'Red Ryder' of the screen," was a guest star, and he worked alongside the famous orchestra leader to make the children smile.

His side "career" as a comic book hero began the same year, also thanks to *Red Ryder*. The first comic book in which Allan was seen came out in

Allan plays Red Ryder for the first time.

December of 1946. Dell Publishing put him on the back cover of issue #41 in the form of *Red Ryder*. Under the *Red Ryder* mantle, his presence grew even more through the spring of 1948.

Santa Fe Uprising (1946), the first Allan Lane *Red Ryder* production, was in theaters in late November. This was filmed at the Iverson Ranch, and one review said of his work, "Allan Lane's portrayal of the rough riding, straight shooting marshal of Bitter Springs, New Mexico is excellent in his initial Red Ryder role..."

Republic didn't waste time in doing all they could to circulate their stars and make sure audiences stayed excited about each and every one of them. The studio wanted consumers to anxiously await the next, and the next, and the next serial installment, and then each new serial, not playing favorites for long with any one of their high-profile cowboy stars.

Out California Way (1946) was on the screen hot on the tail of Santa Fe Uprising. This wasn't a starring vehicle for Allan, in fact not much more than a walk-on amongst a group of other cowboy stars of the time, but it was an opportunity to be featured in the Western genre along-side a handful of the studio's bigger and better-known stars, including Monte Hale — the actual lead, along with Roy Rogers and Trigger and

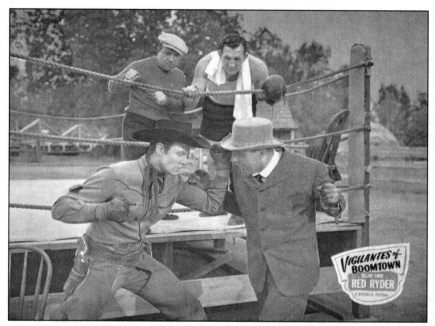

Allan as Red Ryder in Vigilantes of Boomtown, in the boxing scene.

others. Even young Robert "Bobby" Blake as Little Beaver, Red Ryder's sidekick, had a piece of the action, though he played a different character in this one.

Vigilantes of Boomtown (1947) had a lighthearted storyline and catered to Allan's sports ability. Though he was almost always stoic and a bit stiff in his characterization, there were moments of humor, particularly when he watched the sparring in the ring of the visiting boxer, Gentleman Jim Corbett. Standing to the side of the quickly-put-together ring, Allan, in the guise of Red Ryder, tried to mimic the boxer's moves. His efforts were almost childlike, and gave the impression of a man who wanted to be able to do what he saw the other doing so well. The story centered on a bout between Corbett and Bob Fitzsimmons, a match that did occur in real-life in Carson City, Nevada, in 1897.

Allan was thirty-eight years old. Despite his receding hairline, he was still striking-looking and gave off the impression of a man not to be messed with. His physique looked as solid as it had ten years earlier when he struggled to make it in those light drawing-room dramas. He still cut an impressive figure, and the idea of him as a cowboy hero wasn't in the least bit hard to believe.

Allan with Black Jack and his self-identified horse trailer. PHOTO COURTESY THE COSTELLO FAMILY COLLECTION

By the time Allan had completed a year's worth of installments in the *Red Ryder* series, and the end of his run as this comic book hero, he was making $700 per week. After so much time and effort trying to get there, Allan's wallet finally equaled his visibility in the industry. One article said of his portrayal of this already well-established character, "With each new *Red Ryder* role to his credit, Allan Lane becomes more convincing as the hard-hitting, quick-thinking hero..."

The last in the Allan Lane *Red Ryder* series hit the screens in the late summer of 1947. What had been an integral part of the appeal of this recurring storyline — the characterization of Little Beaver as Red's sidekick — had finally become an issue of concern. Bobby Blake was growing up, and that was a problem for the show's producers. Comic book characters were static, never aging.

The Powers That Be were forced to have a powwow to decide what to do next. Rather than put out a wide-reaching and intricate stage call for another young actor to take the part from the aging Blake, they chose a more drastic solution and ended the series. This allowed Blake to move on to more age-appropriate roles and the production to sidestep complications that may have arisen had the role, and the show, been kept alive.

Red Ryder *movie still with Allan, Bobby Blake as Little Beaver, and Martha Wentworth as The Duchess.* PHOTO COURTESY THE COSTELLO FAMILY COLLECTION

This way, they didn't have to worry over maintaining consistency amidst what had over the years become regular and expected characterizations.

The Little Beaver issue might not have mattered much if there hadn't been another, more basic, "housekeeping" concern. *Red Ryder* may have continued for any number of years if not for what was ultimately classified as a "clerical error." The official renewal date was missed by a few days by someone on the office staff. This important point had been checked annually with the copyright owner, and previous renewals had occurred without a glitch. This time, the oversight was quickly addressed. Except for one alteration, things would have gone on without a blip. The copyright owner granted the renewal but with one added condition: higher royalties. This wrinkle caused the studio to balk, and they refused to pay more. Despite a series of talks designed to come to an agreeable decision, nothing could be resolved.

A group pronouncement was made in the press to discontinue the series. Allan's stint as Red Ryder was over, through no fault of his own.

Allan in an action-packed scene as Rocky Lane. PHOTO COURTESY THE COSTELLO FAMILY COLLECTION

The last *Red Ryder* debuted in August. Once the comic book hero galloped off the screen into the annals of history, studio brass went into a number of behind-closed-door discussions, putting their heads together to figure out what they should do next with their now exceptionally-popular Western star. Republic had a marketable and profitable commodity in the guise of Allan Lane, and they needed to move fast to ensure they kept him on their roster.

Within three months, Allan was back in the movie saddle. Not only was he working but he had been given the title role in a brand created expressly for him. The new character was called Rocky Lane. *The Wild*

Frontier (1947), first in the *Rocky Lane* series, was in theaters around the country by October. Little did Allan Lane know then how this new characterization would affect his future.

No time was wasted. Republic's mistake became Allan's golden opportunity. Immediately after being handed his own recurring, starring vehicle, a press release was circulated to make sure fans knew he wasn't going any-

Allan and horse are simpatico as they chase the bad guys in another Rocky Lane *adventure.* PHOTO COURTESY THE COSTELLO FAMILY COLLECTION

where but up. "As each new picture in the Ryder series was released," it read in part, "Lane zoomed higher and higher and as a reward he has since been graduated to the famous 'Rocky' Lane series of super-action Westerns."

His paycheck increased in direct relationship to his elevated stature. Rocky Lane vehicles were seen as "box office smash hits." In each one, Allan consistently offered his audience exactly what they came to the theater to see: "ACTION in capital letters!" He could be counted on for a handful of "good fist fights, plenty of fast and fancy gunplay, and a good portion of hard riding thrown in..." He was even applauded for including "an element of suspense" in every Rocky Lane offering.

In *Allan "Rocky" Lane Republic's Action Ace*, authors Chuck Thornton and David Rothel give a good overview of how Republic financed their movies during this period. The studio put each new picture into one of four categories: Jubilee, the lowest budget group; Anniversary, second to the bottom; Deluxe, near the top; and Premiere, which received the highest budget of their output.

Allan with Black Jack and the trailer used to transport the horse to events.
PHOTO COURTESY THE COSTELLO FAMILY COLLECTION

Allan's *Rocky Lane* series was planned as a low-budget effort, with his pictures placed in the Jubilee category. Each one rarely rose above a $50,000 cost. Most were filmed at the Iverson Ranch not far out of Los Angeles in a rugged mountain terrain. These low-dollar releases kept the studio going. They saw to it that audiences would lay down their hard-earned dollar to see their action hero take care of the bad guys every time a new release hit the theater. That $50,000 put out to create each of Allan's pictures could almost certainly be relied on to bring in about $500,000 when the box office returns were counted.

Allan took advantage of the fact that really for the first time in his life, he had a solid income and could finally feel good about laying down roots.

Since he had purchased his "small ranch" he now found comfort in populating his homestead with what made him happiest: horses. He ultimately had no less than eighteen head of registered stock on his property, and he raised and trained horses as a sideline.

The studio made sure a new biography for Allan went out under their official letterhead. Even though the movie companies for which he worked had changed over the years, the information about him stayed basically the same. This time, the publicity department simply regurgitated details already distributed about Allan time and time again; most of which remained fabrications ever since they were first listed to his name.

Republic had a bona fide Western screen hero in Allan Lane, one who had taken fire with hungry serial-watching viewers. His bosses were not about to say anything of his background to counteract that all-important, and now popular, image. One article unintentionally explained the sometimes made-up story-building this way. "Hollywood always has had difficulty with its Western heroes. Most of them just don't conform. What they preach on the screen is not what they practice to the public's back."

Allan was said to grow into, and favor, this sort of editing of the original facts, both in front of the cameras and during his personal time. He began to live the life the press created for him long ago. "He goes in for the rough, tough, rugged, action-packed films with lots of shootin' and fightin' — the real he-man stuff that appeals to the red-blooded adventure loving audiences." Republic announced that the actor himself felt this kind of picture, with him as the Western hero, was "a great thing for the youngsters of the country" because they showed a "cowboy who sees that right always prevails."

On the screen, Allan's most successful characters were good to children, and they always represented what was right and true. He worshipped his horse, rode like the devil was at his heels, and publicly denounced unhealthy vices. "His tremendous following of fans thrills to Rocky's rugged gun fights, fist fights, and chases on his horse, Black Jack."

So then, that was that. Once Rocky came to be known as a sincere defender of justice and citizens who needed defending, this was where the character was solidified. This was where fact met fiction and forever after became Allan's history — right or wrong, or a combination of both.

Studio bosses were smart to embody Rocky's philosophy in the person of the actor who played him. Allan, it was said, was a "very determined young man. He knows what he wants and he fights to get it." That was followed up with a statement purportedly from Allan himself. "I learned a long time ago that this is the only way to get along in the world, and if

I have any basic message to the youngsters of this country it is just this — fight for what you think is right and I promise that you'll win out in the end. But be doggone sure you're right before you start to fight."

This is, for the most part, what he did — as a man and as an actor. Allan had never made any effort to change details the public believed to be true about his back-story. He stood behind those facts even more once "Rocky"

Allan and Black Jack riding hard and fast. PHOTO COURTESY THE COSTELLO FAMILY COLLECTION

had been added to his name. That one nickname was the part of his history that offered him a solid new identity all his own, a way to walk into a promising new future. This became the crucial part of the persona that began to surround him, day in and day out.

His new character's name was the result of a conversation Allan had with a producer who dictated he could not possibly carry his unique western brand on the shoulders of such a simple name as Allan. Though that name had served him well for all his professional years until this moment, the producer felt he now needed something which would cater more to his new image — a moniker that could easily become his surefire rocket to stardom.

This unnamed producer called him into his office one day and said, "Look, Allan, we need a nickname for your new series. You got one?"

Allan decided to play around with the guy before giving him a serious answer. He had been called Rocky in grade school, but had also been called something else, a handle based on the usual antics of young boys busting each other up in the school yard.

"Yeah," he answered the producer, "back home the folks did have a nickname for me."

"Well?" The guy was getting impatient with this game.

"Well, they used to call me Toothless!"

After the producer picked himself up off the floor, and Allan had a good laugh at his expense, he went on to admit to one other nickname. That is when he, and his alter ego, became forever entwined, from then on the two melding into one. That is when he became known as Allan "Rocky" Lane.

Alan in cowboy regalia for a special appearance and sporting fancy boots.
PHOTO COURTESY THE COSTELLO FAMILY COLLECTION

CHAPTER FIFTEEN

Rocky Lane
Rides the Range

Allan was now under a solidly binding contract to a studio — a studio which made him the star of his own series. Finally he had made the grade. He was leading the pack not only on the marquee — the name of Allan Lane had been there for a number of years already — but now including "Rocky," his name became synonymous with his character. He was still Allan but his onscreen double, Rocky, really carried the weight far more than he ever had on his own.

And he lived the life. Taking care of his family as always, he finally also began focusing on himself and what money and a richer lifestyle could do for him. In one such example, he regularly bought his boots from Abraham Rios, unofficially called "the bootmaker to the stars." Rios was a leather artisan in Texas who also supplied to the likes of Roy Rogers, Gene Autry, and Bill Elliott. Nothing Rios created cost less than $40, even at that time a hefty fee. Boots he made for the stars were on the higher end of the scale, in the neighborhood of $150 per pair.

By late in the year, Allan was being touted as "a cinema cowboy in the old time Western tradition of Tom Mix, Hoot Gibson, and William S. Hart." Yet he was different, since he was the only high-profile serial cowboy who did not play a guitar or sing. Many viewers appreciated his work even more for this reason. His pictures were said to offer more realism to the end product, with his focus on rescuing the distressed, fighting the good fight — figuratively and physically — and still wrapping it all up within a happy ending. Everything ultimately went well on the western front when Rocky Lane was around, and consumers came to expect exactly that from any Rocky picture.

He was overly particular about his presence onscreen and how he played his part. Many co-stars or guest stars would later berate his memory because of this. With the *Rocky Lane* series, Allan became a solid star, *the* star, for the first time in his already-long career, and he took every effort to stay that way.

In the Allan Lane section of Chuck Anderson's "The Old Corral" website, he tells a story from actor Harry Lauter. Lauter wore jeans for his part in one Rocky Lane feature. When Allan saw this, he ordered him to take off his pants because, as Lauter quoted Allan as saying, "I'm the only one who wears jeans on this set."

Allan's name was on the marquee. Finally. He had taken great pains to create an identifiable characterization in the persona of Rocky Lane, even going so far as to ensure he wore specific clothing every time he portrayed his alter-ego. While his real-life personal interaction skills may have been seriously lacking, his point was a valid one. Rocky dressed a certain way to set him apart as the head honcho in every screen moment. This might not have made him well-liked when the cameras stopped rolling but the sound bite example indicated how well he understood the concept of market branding years before that ever became a hot-button term.

The series had been intentionally designed in a creative "assembly line" fashion. Allan was under exclusive contract as the lead, which meant his name carried each and every picture. This put the pressure on him to do as good a job as he was capable of doing. The casts, producers, and directors were also in-house Republic employees, yet they went from one production to another. This gave them regular work and a decent income with little demand on their character delivery from one picture to the next. If a Rocky Lane picture didn't meet expectations, they would not be the ones who would suffer the end result.

Allan had eight features come out in his second year as Rocky, and there appeared to be no end to his growing professional success. But was there something wrong behind the scenes in his personal life? Two weeks after *Marshal of Amarillo* (1948) hit screens in July, a number of Allan's personal belongings were auctioned off at the Sherman Oaks Galleries on Ventura Boulevard. Among items up for sale was a first go-round of expensive pieces from his spacious, though considered "small," Encino ranch home. Wrought iron dining sets, a custom-built over eight-foot-long sofa, bric-a-brac, cut crystal, and other items were on the block under the direction of bonded and licensed auctioneer John Wallis.

Why was Allan lightening his load of personal possessions he had only recently amassed? Why was he paring down? An exact answer is unknown, but it appears he needed expendable income. Ready cash. He may have had an inkling of things to come or he may have been involved in a business deal requiring an immediate output of money. This mystery had only just begun. Time would tell the story.

A few months later, Allan's life appeared to be business-as-usual. He was part of a huge publicity effort produced for the debut of the California Bank on Hollywood Boulevard. On September 18, an article began, "Hollywood's dignified California Bank opened for business today." The premiere was called a "hoop-la," with the likes of Jack Benny, Jane Powell, Lassie, a few starlets, and "cowboy Allan 'Rocky' Lane" being part of the festivities. There were searchlights, free cocktails, and a lot of well-orchestrated funny business, all somewhat unique and press-worthy for the debut of such an otherwise serious business.

Marshall of Amarillo *as the lead on a double feature with Monte Hale's* South of Rio, *circa 1949.*

Jack Benny "lugged" in a striped mattress and proceeded to dump out a deposit of nickels and dimes. A pretty starlet named M'Liss McClure brought funds for her new bank account in the curled top of her stockings, and made a big deal of revealing the money. A stagecoach rolled up to the front door to let out more starlets, these ladies daintily carrying bags of gold dust, which were really bags of sand. Before they could get in the building, villains had to show up, of course, in an effort to rob these delicate damsels in distress.

Not about to happen, though, with the likes of Allan "Rocky" Lane on the scene. Rocky, as the required hero in the scenario, rode into town on his trusty steed, and he and Black Jack gallantly saved the day. Lassie was then able to bring in a bone to be deposited in a vault, and Jane Powell got into the act right after him.

Once the star-studded playtime was out of the way, serious partying got started. People mingled all around, from movie stars to bank presidents and everyone in between. The entire crowd got into the game, with free-flowing liquor and ham-and-turkey sandwiches served in the bank's "lush" restaurant below the business part of the building. A good time was had by all, including Allan.

About this same time, he once again became a comic book hero. Fawcett published *Rocky Lane Western #1* in May of 1949. This contin-ued throughout his onscreen life as Rocky Lane, with a few writers penning any number of stories about the Western hero. As the years wore on, various artists took on the job of drawing his face and figure with varying results. Some were spot on, others were poor representations. Western entertainment historian Boyd Majers called Allan one of "Fawcett Comics' biggest sellers and longest-running Western titles." Charlton, another publisher, took over the job in 1959 after Fawcett folded.

The first Rocky Lane *comic book cover.*

Even as he worked hard with no apparent end to his Western hero adventures, there remained a considerable amount of chatter about Allan's finances and how he spent his money. A newspaper article revealed he had a "rich horse...one of the wealthiest horses in pictures." Allan swore, maybe tongue-in-cheek, that the money all belonged to Black Jack and was not part of what he personally earned for each movie. His horse earned that money, not him. The article indicated how Allan, like Rudd Weatherwax, Lassie's owner, went to "fabulous lengths to maintain the fiction of independence between himself and his animal Black Jack's money in the bank under his own name." Again, like Lassie, separate accounts were diligently kept on Black Jack's earnings and expenses.

And Black Jack did have legitimate expenses. His saddles cost anywhere from $350 to $3000 — work saddles, everyday saddles, and even Sunday and parade saddles. Silver bits with his initials in gold. Fancy bridle straps and silver breast collars. "Day sheets, coolers, halters, and saddle blankets in every style available." And shoes? He had more shoes than a Hollywood beauty queen, getting new ones every two weeks, and many types, too: rubber shoes for personal appearances in hotel lobbies and theaters; steel shoes for rodeos and movie work; special shoes for slippery pavement and parades; oh, and racing shoes.

The article outlined the opulence of Black Jack's "bedroom," saying, "Who would dare call it a stall?" The space measured fourteen feet by fourteen feet and included a drinking fountain, a decomposed granite floor at all times covered with rye straw to a depth of two feet, and a radio, "since music seems to soothe him." The piece finished with the somewhat sarcastic comment, "No television, however, at this writing."

All this gave insight into part of what was consuming Allan's funds. As quick as the money was coming in, it was going right back out the doors — the stall door included. Other sizeable portions of his money were going to his mother, his sister, and even his cousins. Much of his wealth, however, was poured into his passion for horses. Not only did he ensure his personal steed was well-attended — a horse that literally carried him from picture to picture and kept him in business — but his passion for buying and training, and betting on, other equines had proved to be an expensive and financially draining pastime, too.

After all, as a Hollywood celebrity, Allan would be expected to have a clear-cut vice. His attraction to all-things-horses fit right in with his image, and no one was the wiser if his money was slowly dissipating as a result. He wasn't known to be much of a drinker, and he didn't do much smoking, either. He wasn't a wild-and-crazy womanizer despite his multiple marriages. His inability to cultivate and hold down a personal relationship had become well-known in the movie community. So instead of any of the usual and well-touted money-drainers, Allan Lane poured his free time, passion, and finances into horses.

An *Indianapolis Star* magazine article in November quoted Allan as saying, "I'm really just a very conventional fellow." While the comment's veracity might have been questionable, depending on anyone's personal definition of "conventional," Allan wasn't these days offering the press much in the way of off-camera antics, romantic or otherwise. His professional efforts were consumed predominantly by youngsters, and he was sincerely conscious of his audience. His screen character regarded "strong drink and tobacco as very unnecessary evils."

Allan, it went on to say, was the same at home as he was in his movies. If he was offered a cigarette or a cocktail, he reportedly would respond with a "polite, but firm, 'No, thanks.'" That didn't mean he never drank or had never smoked but he was aware of how what he did in private could easily become public information thanks to the always-hungry media. He fiercely protected his onscreen image and was cognizant of how what he did when he was on his own time affected the product he put out — the work that supported him. Whether this was a philosophical approach or a practical one, or possibly a combination, either way, Allan Lane had chosen a specific path to follow since he had become a brand name.

His public philosophy about life, often touted, was, "Fight with all your might, but be sure you're right before you fight." Allan was single-minded in what he thought to be right. Everyone knew he was opinionated. He was never afraid to fight for what he believed in, even when his beliefs might fly in the face of other people's opinions. But those types of fights were usually at the cost of professional relationships, and close friendships, not at the cost of his livelihood.

When someone would speak to him about his fans, he made it clear he did care about their opinions. He would say, "Gosh, aren't those kids wonderful? You know, I love every one of them!" Allan was thoroughly aware of his audience. He was conscious that his bread-and-butter came from him being able to relate to, and continue to satisfy, the young folks, and his interest came off as genuine. He seemed to truly care for those ticket-buyers — or at least the children of the ticket-buyers.

The uneven path of his previous years in movies was offered up as a point of discussion in one interview from this period. He told the reporter, "You could twist my arm, brother, and I wouldn't get back to wearin' a wing-collar and workin' on those hot stages." He was, it said, "in Westerns by choice." Having already been a straight leading man, he "could be again, for the offers of bigger pictures" still came his way. But the idea of having to work on an enclosed set was distasteful to him. Those "slow-moving drawing-room dramas" depressed him. Allan didn't do well in the long run being cooped up anywhere. He much preferred ranches and open ranges, and riding a horse is the path he would stay on to get him to his next paycheck.

"He complains that when stage doors are closed, and the lights begin using up all the oxygen, it gets so stuffy that his blood coagulates." The long hours in front of the hot cameras, with no action except for patter and pleasantries, had taken their toll in the earlier days and made him an unhappy man.

How much of this extensive article and interview was literal fact, and how much was a continuation of the legend created years earlier when he arrived in Hollywood, is not clear. He was also said to have cultivated a love of the outdoors "all the way back" in his farm days in Mishawaka.

Yet there is no indication Allan ever lived on a farm, in Mishawaka or anywhere else.

There was just enough nostalgic and easily believed background in this piece, however, and it was exactly what his fans wanted to hear. Working on that probably imaginary farm as a youngster, as the story went, "gave him both a profound respect for horseflesh and enough spending money

Saugus Rodeo.

to go to town on Saturday and marvel over the escapades of Tom Mix and 'Tony,' and William S. Hart and his great horse." Such images the concept brought about were enough to ensure young moviegoers of the day would continue to put down *their* money every Saturday afternoon to see *their* hero, Rocky Lane, ride the range and rescue the good people from the bad guys.

The article said Allan had initially been placed in pictures as a handsome leading-man type as the result of a misunderstanding. He reportedly attended a rodeo in Saugus, California. The Saugus Roundup started as a series of rodeos built on property known as the Baker Ranch and owned by Roy Baker. Those rodeos were initially a part of The Saugus Stadium, which had been built in the 1920s by cowboy star Tom Mix, who bought the property from Baker. Young hopefuls of the time, many of them actors, would enter the contests for the chance to win the purse.

Allan's story goes that while he sat atop a fence watching the riders, a movie director, Avery Edwards, spotted him and said, "Come to my office tomorrow morning. I think I can use you in my picture." Allan was excited, the reporter wrote, and wanted to make a good impression, so he borrowed a "city" suit from a friend, got his hair cut and had his shoes shined. When he showed up in the director's office in his city-slicker finery, his appearance led him to be signed as a leading man. A Hollywood-type actor — one "who had never ridden a horse" — was given the part of the cowpoke.

However Allan got his first big break, the real truth may never completely surface. There were inherent problems with the different stories, and there were a number of such stories. If anyone had bothered to research them at the time, the reality may have been more obvious. As a young man or at any time thereafter, it bears repeating that Allan Lane was never a farm boy and had never been a "Notre Dame" athlete. Being on the farm and being on the Notre Dame field were opposite ends of the spectrum. For Allan, the truth was somewhere in the middle and more than likely a lot less exciting in the minds of the studio's publicity departments.

So in the long run, Allan Lane — a created name for a created man, a name whose origin is still unknown but likely was handed to him by a studio executive — had rather easily become whatever anyone wanted to see in him at any given time. However it really happened, Allan was believable in his Western persona. So much of what he had been in the beginning was practically already long-forgotten. The cowboy persona stuck, and Allan happily rode with it.

He had won a popularity poll of "action-film fans" in 1946, taking first place. One reporter said of him, "He is at his ease on the screen only when his role calls for hard riding, fast shooting, and tough fighting." Allan himself remarked about his work, "I believe the folks like the pictures because they're in the old Mix and Hart tradition. Full of action, fights and chases."

The chance to "shed his fancy clothes" and often work outdoors suited him just fine. He had begun to genuinely live the part of a cowboy type in his personal world as well as in his professional life. All his clothes were styled along Western lines. "They're not fancy, though," he insisted.

Allan was often said to "speak Western jargon, leaving in his wake countless dropped 'g's' and frequent references to 'puttin' on the feed bag' and 'bein' in the bull pen.'" His niece, Pat, and other members of his family never recalled him speaking this way during personal get-togethers, so yet again this could have been part of his intentionally-created mystique.

Either that or he easily went back-and-forth between the two personas, depending on who he was with at any given time. He was, after all, an actor.

One detail circulated about him was not ever in question, though. He was definitely in deep with his horses. These creatures were, as the article indicated, "an integral part of his life." His ranch in the San Fernando Valley included "10 head of registered stock."

Allan in his element. PHOTO COURTESY THE COSTELLO FAMILY COLLECTION

Add to that, Black Jack's importance was non-negotiable, and the reporter indicated that visitors should not ask Rocky about the animal's worth to him. "Why, you might as well ask me the value of my sister," Allan would usually respond. In many ways, that said a lot of how highly he thought of his sister.

Black Jack, of Morgan blood, was insured at $20,000 — more than Allan carried on himself. While that might have seemed outrageous to the average individual, the horse was literally not only his good friend but also his cash cow, likely as important to fans in the final Rocky Lane product as he was himself.

An interview had been done as Allan completed *Sheriff of Wichita* (1949), part of his eight-a-year movie quota. For sixteen weeks out of his every year under contract, Allan lived and breathed as a cowboy of the Old West, so he might have been forgiven for also living like one in real life.

In this particular film, the script called for Allan to "perform a head-long slide," dropping and skating across the ground to escape a bad guy chasing him. Director R. G. Springsteen set up a camera to catch the action directly at ground level as Allan dove toward the lens. He went into the action with so much gusto he had to turn his head to the side at the last minute to ensure he did not get hit with the rim of the camera. This became a stock move for his Rocky character from that point on.

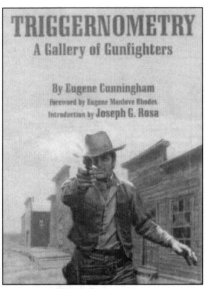

Triggernometry *by Eugene Cunningham.*

He told a story in that interview to illustrate his love of America's earlier western period. "Last night I dropped in at a bookstore, just browsin'," he said, "and spent 40 bucks on books about those days. One, just chock full of material we can use, was called '*Trigger-Nometry*'!" This title referred to the various ways of using a gun as well as different holsters and harnesses and how those moves would affect the treatment of a gun in the hands of a professional. Written in the 1930s, the author, Eugene Cunningham, had interviewed many people who had personally known many of the old west's most famous outlaws and those who chased them.

Allan's words, including "material we can use," showed he was always looking for ways to infuse his portrayal of Rocky with believability. He also revealed that he was included as a part of the growth of the Rocky Lane persona, and his input was viable.

Allan was effectively a method actor who believed in steeping himself in the period in which his character lived. He was a no-nonsense actor; still being recognized as a non-singing cowboy was a point in his favor in the type of product he put out. "There's no guitar-strumming, moon-light serenades, or singing of any kind in the Allan 'Rocky' Lane super action Republic westerns," one article explained happily. "Rocky goes in strictly for he-man stuff — fast chases and hard fighting with bare fists and blazing guns!" Just what all young boys wanted in their entertainment. Whether or not their cowboy could sing usually mattered little to them.

Since his was a recurring role — a role specifically created to cater to his particular persona — a desire to be as authentic as possible drove every little thing Allan did professionally. This made the intermingling of fact and fiction logical in how he lived his life when he was away from the

cameras. Allan, the man, had fast become a mirror of the character he portrayed as an actor in front of the world.

His time between pictures was spent training his horses, first and foremost. He also continued to make personal appearances, doing rodeos and Frontier Day celebrations as well as speaking to young people in a variety of scenarios. With "Rocky Lane In Person" emblazoned at the top, elaborate press packets were sent out to local theaters, businesses, and town officials to gently suggest how they might best promote Allan "Rocky" Lane's appearances in their area. Inside it told of what the readers would find. "Advance Stories, Personality Features, Interviews, Biographies, News Mats." All of this, mostly in the form of stock newspaper articles, was included to make it easy for any venue to pop in their name and the dates of the event and then send the information out to the eager public.

Ad for Rocky Lane appearances.
PHOTO COURTESY MR. BILL "PETE" PETERSON

Headline suggestions in these pieces included, "Remember The Kids," "Don't Overlook Radio," and "Work For City-Wide Newspaper Breaks." One of the suggested articles blared, "Rocky Lane Explains Kiss-less Films," showing that the studio wasn't averse to a bit of sensationalism to sell tickets. In answer to the question, "Why don't Western screen stars ever kiss the girl?" Rocky answered matter-of-factly, "Because it embarrasses the kids. The boys particularly are embarrassed by what they call 'mush stuff.'" The piece went on to explain Rocky's philosophical thoughts on this topic, all purportedly in his personal voice.

In the fall of 1948, concurrent with the release of *The Denver Kid*, Allan appeared in Long Beach as the special guest during "National Newspaper

Salute to Newspaper Boy Day

Allan (Rocky) Lane will salute in western style National Newspaper Boy week tomorrow, in a personal appearance at the State theater, where Long Beach newspaper boys will see a preview of a new Lane cactus thriller. He is shown with horse Blackjack receiving the invitation of a Long Beach delegation. From left, the boys are Dick Miller, Mack Mitchell, Lanny Rupp and Sam Holloway.

Allan smiling in a newspaper clipping as he chats with four boys chosen to represent "National Newspaper Boy Week"…and meet Rocky Lane.

Boy Week." The city would have received one of these press presentations ahead of time. With Rocky Lane as the hero of many a young boy, the kids were excited when he showed up in the flesh to salute them personally. They had the chance to preview what was called "a new Lane cactus thriller," and a number of them had pictures taken with him and Blackjack. This photo opportunity showed him receiving a newspaper from a happy group of four young men.

CHAPTER SIXTEEN

Allan 'Rocky' Lane, the Businessman

Allan's business side kept him always busy as an important part of the evolution of the Rocky Lane persona. He also conferred with publishers about his *Allan 'Rocky' Lane Comics*. This had fast become an important part of his income. In addition, he had a direct hand in the manufacture of products built upon Rocky Lane's ideology, and endorsements were a regular part of his world — and his bank account.

Allan "Rocky" Lane had fast become a corporate entity. He did what he needed to do to keep the money flowing. Another auction of his personal belongings slipped into the picture in July, with the same auction house at the helm. This had turned into an ongoing effort, somehow kept quiet and largely, but not totally, out of the press as each new auction came and went.

He had always been, first and foremost, a businessman. He had never been afraid of hard work, and from his earliest days had deeply understood the need to acquire the work and do the job in exchange for the paycheck. There was nothing out of the ordinary about how he would have figured out how to take a marketable character and be an active part of making that character profitable from many different directions.

And as always, Allan's family remained a part of his world. Reports claimed his parents lived with him in California. This wasn't actually true, not in the way it was indicated for public consumption. His parents were divorced and had been for years. They had spouses of their own, or had had spouses of their own, and though those relationships had difficult times, not once had Bill Albershart and Allan's mother ever gone back to each other.

His mother remained with her husband, Will, even though they were officially divorced. There was a trailer at the back of Eva and Billy's property. Anne lived in the house with her sister and Billy. By the early 1940s, also living there were Will's middle son, Tom Costello; his wife, Jennie; their young daughter, Gerri; and newborn baby, Pat. Anne spent a great majority of her time doting on the new babies, and during Pat's first year of life, 1943, she barely ever let her out of her sight. Anne, who became known as Gramanne to the Costello kids at her choosing,

Left: *Allan reviewing film content behind the scenes.* Right: *Little Cheryl Rogers and her father, Roy.*

remained dedicated to her grandchildren — *her* grandchildren — for the rest of her life. And they were dedicated to her.

On the other side of the family dynamic, these kids knew nothing about Bill Albershart, where he lived in California, or how he lived. Their grandfather, Will Costello, lived out back of the house in the trailer. As usual, the facts of Allan's life were skewered to best fit his press needs. He did, of course, live in California, as did both parents, but he hadn't physically lived with the two of them in the same home since he'd been a young boy.

A month or so after *Bandit King of Texas* (1949) was released in the summer of 1949, Allan learned of a young lady who had a serious crush on him. Her name was Cheryl, she was only nine years old, and she was the daughter of Roy Rogers. This amused Roy tremendously, and since he and Allan were well-acquainted and had worked together, Roy decided to give his little girl a treat. He arranged for Allan to come to dinner — an evening that, by all accounts, thrilled the both of them.

Once introductions were behind them and dinner had come and gone, photos were taken with Cheryl and Allan together. All went well, and the star-struck little girl was delighted, as was Allan, who had thoroughly enjoyed himself.

Yet days later, as soon as she had a chance to view the photos, Cheryl was clearly displeased. One of the pictures had to be destroyed, she told her father.

"Why?" Roy was surprised at her vehemence. He assumed she was having a moment of little girl vanity.

"Because," as the story went, Cheryl replied firmly, "Rocky's eyes are half-closed and he doesn't look his best!"

There was also a visit to the zoo, which created a fun-filled day for Cheryl and Rocky, and they were now good friends.

An effort to bring *Red Ryder* to the small screen began as early as 1949. Republic Pictures wanted to re-release Allan's version of the series while, about the same time, Equity Pictures, also known as Eagle-Lion Films, was trying to debut a new *Red Ryder*, a "series in color" starring Jim Bannon. Equity/Eagle-Lion had come into being around 1919 as a producing and distribution company, and was active into the '20s. Revising their efforts in the late '30s, they returned in the late '40s as a viable production company.

Their work was probably best known under the Eagle-Lion banner. In May of 1949, Hollywood columnist Erskine Johnson was reporting news of a legal battle, naming Equity and Republic and pitting Allan against Jim Bannon. "Legal fireworks coming up over two Red Ryders on the screen," he wrote. The story went that Republic wanted to "reissue its old series starring Allan Lane." Equity was going to bat with Jim Bannon as the star. Johnson's column stated that both companies were "talking to attorneys." Jim Bannon's side ultimately won the battle, at least in the short run. He did four *Red Ryder* installments in this fashion.

That slight setback didn't harm Allan's career in any way. He was riding high as Rocky Lane, and even though the re-issue of his *Red Ryder* persona would have added to his repertoire, the lack didn't take away in any fashion from all the new work he put out. In July, a newspaper article claimed he was "fast becoming one of America's favorite cowboy stars."

The untold saga behind Allan's complicated finances came back to the forefront in early 1950, when newspaper ads appeared again, announcing an "Important Auction Sale." At least three auctions were held, with a few of them being two-day affairs. The items up for grabs were expensive goods from Allan's home that had not sold a few years before — in his first effort to bring in quick cash. From late January through March, notices were made about the sale of well-crafted, sometimes handmade furniture, china, and other personal and easily identifiable goods.

A brand new official studio biography came out for Allan in early 1950. Republic felt they had a winner on their hands with the *Rocky Lane* series, and they were intent on getting as much leverage out of the actor in as many arenas as they could create. Little new detail was revealed about the man behind the character, and what was shared was, as usual, barely more than a rehashing of old information.

Depending on when something had been written about him over the years, he had either gained or lost a few inches in this particular iteration. He was said to be six-feet-two-inches. A few reports claimed he was only six feet. Many others would say he was "well over six feet." His niece, Pat, believes he topped off more toward six-feet-three-inches. His weight almost always stayed the same in these reports, listed at 195 pounds. An important fact since a fast-riding, bad-guy-chasing cowboy had to stay lean to be able to do his job.

What is most interesting is what was not included; Allan's year of birth was not listed. The studio did not care to put direct focus on the fact that one of their highest-riding cowboy stars of the New Year was already over forty years old.

A solid determination to rebrand him was evident in every written word. Once again, how he was addressed in public became crucial to his continuing success, and he was being seen more and more as simply Rocky Lane, "as he prefers to be called." By design, little attention was paid to the "Allan" part except where his "legal" name was indicated to be Allan Lane, though he had never officially changed that name from Harry Albershart. This was a minor detail that seemingly did not deserve a mention. A cowboy called Harry Albershart would have never fit the bill.

His metamorphosis from a face and name standing out in the crowd, to a character, only the character, a larger-than-life living and breathing hero from a comic strip, à la *Red Ryder*, had solidified. "As a reward" for his success as *Red Ryder*, the piece declared, when the character "zoomed higher and higher" under the actor's interpretation, he was "graduated to the famous 'Rocky' Lane series."

Allan had entered the part of his life where he would rarely ever again be publicly known as himself. Instead, he would take on different characterizations, and as the man behind the image he would largely come to represent only that persona he portrayed onscreen. Living the role turned into the norm for him.

Allan was now spending most of his free time betting on horses at Santa Anita and other tracks along the southern California coast as well as in Mexico. He was at the track with his own home-bred and trained steeds in 1951. But behind the scenes, he still had a void in his life. The horses could only keep him company for so long. They did nothing to help him stay warm in the evenings. He had a dog named Flip Jack but he, also, didn't take the place of human interaction.

Allan was sadly alone. He was finally doing well professionally, with Rocky Lane prominent on the Saturday afternoon movie screens. Yet there was no intimate relationship in his life, no one with whom he could share his success — a success he'd been reaching toward for over twenty years.

Allan filled that need for personal contact with his mother, sister, cousins, aunts, and nieces and nephews. They were there for him, and he for them. Allan had become a member of the Costello family at the age of fifteen, and though it took time for him to feel comfortable with the new structure, he ultimately embraced the Costellos as his people.

For his mother, there had never been a "step-family" feel to this connection. Will's children had become her children soon after the two of them said, "I do." His sons called her "Mother" from the get-go and in that union, Allan gained three brothers. When those boys grew up and had children of their own, he naturally considered himself their uncle, as he would if he shared their blood.

The family had gelled well, and by this time in Allan's life, twenty-five or so years later, he acted as any uncle would with his nieces and nephews. By all accounts, he cared for them dearly, and whenever they were all together he was in the thick of it with them. It was as if they were his "kids" since he had none of his own.

The Costello children looked up to their Uncle Harry — they felt special because they called him that but everyone else called him Rocky. He was famous, and that alone tickled them. Uncle Harry was a movie star seen by lots and lots of people on the big screen, yet when he was with the family, he was one of them.

His niece, Pat, said friends in school were aware her uncle was the cowboy named "Rocky Lane." Show-and-tell was a fun time for any one of them after Uncle Harry had come by for a visit and left them with a gift or a remembered experience. Just one of many such souvenirs was a personally signed photo each kid received during one family get-together. He never came to visit empty-handed.

Family gatherings were almost always at Gramanne's or, in earlier times when they were together, at Aunt Eva's home. Be it Thanksgiving,

Allan taught his young fox terrier, Flip Jack, many cute tricks. PHOTO FROM SCREEN GUIDE AND COURTESY TINSLEY YARBROUGH

or Christmas, or Gramanne's birthday, the large family came together to celebrate, and the kids — as well as his mother and the rest of the adults — waited expectantly for Uncle Harry to arrive. There were times when he couldn't be there. His schedule was busy and the family understood. On those occasions, even though he wasn't physically present, they would get a call from him and he would chat with the children, or he would send a special message to everyone through Gramanne.

Pat told of a specific Thanksgiving at Gramanne's house. Uncle Harry walked in the door and the kids marveled at how tall he was. There were ceiling beams in the dining room, and Pat recalled how his hat touched the beams as he made his way around the room. Laughing, she said, "I thought he was the tallest man who ever walked."

They had a cousin named Ricky, similar in age to her. Allan started clowning around that holiday with Ricky. There was always a great deal of food at Gramanne's house during these festivities, especially on Thanksgiving. Pies were the cornerstone of the meal, and she was known

Allan signed this photo, "To Aunt Eva — With love. Me & Black Jack."

as the queen of pie makers. She painstakingly taught her granddaughters the art of creating the most beautiful and the most delicious, and there was never a holiday without everyone in the house clamoring for multiple helpings of Gramanne's pies.

This day, Allan caught sight of the whipped cream can sitting to the side, just waiting to be the topping for the pumpkin pie. He casually pulled

Allan posing near his pool, with his home in the immediate background. PHOTO FROM SCREEN GUIDE AND COURTESY TINSLEY YARBROUGH

young Ricky to him and then suddenly grabbed hold of the whipped cream canister in his other hand.

Then the games began. As Allan took the can and sprayed whipped cream into Ricky's mouth, the boy screamed, squirmed and giggled. The rest of the kids got into the act, and a sea of white foam and laughter ended up all over the place. In the middle of all of these yelling, giggling children, full of sticky whipped cream everywhere, was the previously spotless and well-heeled Allan "Rocky" Lane. He, as the instigator, was now a mess as well.

Pat said he rarely missed a chance to get silly with the young kids at a family gathering, whatever the potential fun might be between them. At home, he was always just "Uncle Harry" to each and every one of them.

Behind the scenes between work efforts, he continued his publicly-known but rarely publicized generosity with children. Allan's ranch property included a pool. An article in the February 1951 issue of *Screen Guide* magazine included a photo of him kneeling at pool's edge. The copy indicated that twice a week Allan opened up his back yard for the enjoyment of a "horde of children"…along with their parents or "other responsible grownups."

In the public eye, he was number eight of the "Top Ten Cowboy Stars" in the country, according to a *Motion Picture Herald* poll. Allan's *Rocky Lane* series was going strong in 1952. By all public accounts, he had become a bona fide cowboy star. While Allan was riding high, an Associated Press article by Bob Thomas came out in July, in his "About Hollywood" column. The piece featured Gene Autry bemoaning the slow death of the Western movie genre. Autry candidly stated Westerns were in a slump ever since big-budget movies starring the A-list crowd, expensive stars such as Clark Gable, Gregory Peck, and John Wayne had become popular.

In other ways, though, Autry thought this turn of events was good for program Westerns, the sort in which he not only starred but also produced. He brought Allan into the mix when he stated, "Now there are only four regular series — myself at Columbia, Rex Allen and Rocky Lane at Republic and Johnny Mack Brown at Monogram."

So far, Allan had survived the changeover in Western genre styling. Whether that would last or it was only a matter of time was anyone's guess. There was a clash of the old and the new brewing in Hollywood. Allan remained solidly ingrained with his own series. That kept him picking up a paycheck amidst a suspected industry-wide salary cut for actors and writers and other movie professionals. Yet, as he'd learned time and time again, success today did not mean success tomorrow.

Nunnally Johnson, a well-respected moviemaker and screenwriter, was considered a true Hollywood insider, reported to know almost everything going on in town. He would write letters to others in-the-know, many of them intimate friends, and they would share their opinions on the comings and goings of their business. In May, he reported that Twentieth Century-Fox was at the helm of a town-wide, growing studio salary scare. Executives were slashing pay across the board, giving employees but a few lukewarm options as to how they would prefer to take their medicine. This was seen as a bullying tactic.

"The town's sweating," he wrote, "and the guilds are all conferring day and night" about the possibility this treatment of studio personnel would soon go from studio to studio like a quick-moving disease. Warner Bros. had made serious, and similar, noises the year before, but this time it seemed to take root. Republic wasn't mentioned specifically, yet the industry in general was in the midst of full-tilt growing pains, and almost everyone kept one eye on their paycheck and the other on industry trends.

This may have been why Allan, always vigilant as to how he would make his next dollar, kept his focus looking ahead to secure his living. Even with his professional world wrapped up in his *Rocky Lane* persona, there is reason to believe he saw the writing on the wall early on and lent his name out as a publicist to add a few dollars to his wallet. With little more than a slight name change, he could stay connected to the entertainment world while not standing in front of a single camera.

Working as Alan Lane & Associates, intentionally utilizing a different spelling as he had done at different times in his past, he did his magic to promote others in the business as early as January. One client was the California Television Realtors Association, which had a fifteen-minute airing on KTTV. His company secured them a fifty-two-week spot. Allan would soon have more dealings, once again as an actor, with KTTV.

This would not have been a conflict of interest, especially since he worked only part of that year churning out his TV series. The rest of the year, he still needed an income to support his lifestyle and other business and recreational ventures — namely his horses. He had an extensive background in promotions, and he intimately knew the ins-and-outs of advertising. His history proved how he was able to quickly move between personas whenever he needed to do so. He also brought in an income by continuing public appearances as Rocky Lane. His comic book and product lines rounded out his earning potential.

As his expenses grew, Allan upped efforts to meet his financial challenges. He was not a man to stand idle for any length of time. He didn't shirk his responsibilities, either.

There were four *Rocky Lane* movies released in 1953. At least the first one, *Marshal of Cedar Rock*, had been made in the summer of 1952. Allan was by that time well-established and feeling comfortable in his place as the lead actor on set. The crew had arrived ahead of the cast on location in the Burro Flats area of California's Simi Hills. They set up shop and when Allan and the rest of the bunch showed up, all seemed perfect. The weather looked as if it would cooperate. Yet three days into production, a storm hit, starting out as a sand storm and, by the time it finished, there were three inches of snow on the ground. All work halted for a week to allow the normally calm area to return to normal, and get work back in gear.

Local kids would gather after school, excited to sit on the periphery and catch a glimpse of Rocky Lane at work. The story went that usually they were well-behaved, thrilled at the chance to be there. This particular day, Allan had a scene where he posed as a cowhand, leaving his marshal's

Rocky Lane at it again in Marshal of Cedar Rock, *with Phyllis Coates looking on.*

duds — which included a shiny badge — in his trailer. After he completed that bit, he went back to change into his marshal's outfit only to find his all-important badge was missing.

He had a good idea where the item had gone. He stepped out of his trailer and calmly approached the eager youngsters. Allan explained how crucial that badge was to the entire movie and thought out loud how he certainly must have lost it. He asked if the kids would help him search amongst the surrounding rocks and bushes. Only a few minutes later, one young man "found" the shiny silver badge and returned it to Rocky. He thanked the boy and went on with work.

At the end of the day's efforts, Allan located the boy and gave him the badge. It wasn't really that important to the production in the long run — he had them made by the bagful because they tarnished quickly and easily.

The child was delighted and, of course, made sure all his friends knew what their hero had given him. The following day, there were more kids than usual hanging around, waiting to watch Rocky at work, and each let him know they wanted a badge of their own. He pulled out an extra bag, handing out badges to each kid there that day.

Another incident on the set of *Marshal of Cedar Rock* gave insight into Allan's behind-the-scenes interactions. His female costar, Phyllis Coates, happened to share that her real name was Gypsie Ann Stell. This must have tickled his funnybone, and the next day, he presented her with a gift. He gave her a nicely wrapped package and when she opened the box, she found a large square of shiny black chiffon, more than perfect for use in a fancy show by a burlesque queen. Everyone, including Phyllis, had a good-natured laugh.

El Paso Stampede *theater poster.*

El Paso Stampede (1953) was Allan's last heroic trip as Rocky Lane riding off into the sunset on his horse, Black Jack, and it hit screens in early September. The movie serial Western was facing a disastrously-waning audience as TV soared in popularity, collecting most of the viewer loyalty. It was so much easier to be entertained in the privacy of one's home than it was to make the greater effort to go to the theater. Expense was also a big factor. The cost of putting a television set in the house — even with popcorn and soda thrown in for each program — in no way compared to the greater amount of pocket change it took to see another and yet another movie on the big screen every weekend.

Many issues came together at once to force the core of Allan's professional existence — the serial — into becoming a thing-of-his-past. The biggest was Allan's contract with Republic, which came to an end in May of 1953 as a result of the waning interest in the product. Rocky Lane, along with the B-movie matinee serial, had become passé, for the most part replaced by the more advanced television entertainment.

As a result, Allan's by-this-time $700-a-week paycheck went dry. He was suddenly a free agent for the first time in a decade. Despite the demise of his series, that year he was, for the second time in his career, listed in the *Motion Picture Herald* "Top Ten" cowboy stars. This time, he was fifth on the roster.

Such recognition didn't stop him from, almost overnight, disappearing from recurring public view, even though his catalogue of movies was still seen regularly on late night TV. His early films and serials were repeat fare for anyone who checked their TV guide, but he was no longer a current commodity. While royalties continued to come his way for the large body of work he had amassed over the years, as well as comic books and product lines, that didn't help much to keep his name in the limelight.

Allan was once again in the same position he had so disliked years before: he needed to go looking for regular work. The difference now...he had expenses he hadn't even dreamed of in those earlier days.

CHAPTER SEVENTEEN

A Horse Is A Horse — And Allan's Best Friend

Race tracks had long since become Allan's second home. He was a horseman, not so much in the riding aspect but more as a businessman. He knew a good horse when he saw one, and he deeply understood the animals. Buying and selling, and training racehorses was an occupation as well as an expensive hobby. Without regular movie work to keep him busy, horses grew more important to his sense of self. Training them helped financially support his sideline: spending leisure time at the tracks.

In early December of 1953, his name resurfaced publicly, this time without "Rocky" attached. Without being so identified anymore, his days as a known quantity under the name of Allan Lane were falling behind him. Sadly, that meant any new work he did was often overlooked. Allan found himself back on TV, now for a local and limited audience. Of all things, he hosted a game show called *Cut The Film*, which aired at the beginning of the month. The show was seen in the Long Beach, California, area on KHJ, Channel 9.

Allan had never been identified with such a genre, but with his recently high visibility profile, as well as his long history within the movie industry, his presence added believability to the concept. *Cut The Film* offered prizes to competing viewers. The concept was a unique one. The show ran film clips dating from the 1900s to the current year. As clips were shown, calls were made on-air to known registered viewers, and a question was asked about the clip on-air. Each show included a 'mystery clip' jackpot, worth more than all the others.

The show was on weekly during the month of December, after which time it disappeared without obvious explanation. Whether it had been intended only as a limited release or it ended because the concept wasn't embraced by the public is unknown. Whatever the reason, Allan's career as a game show host ended nearly as soon as it started.

He continued to emcee parades, loan himself out to rodeos, and do a considerable number of other public appearances throughout the year. Still a crowd pleaser, in 1953 Allan traveled to North Carolina to appear at the Carolina Theater in Rocky Mount. It was clear, based on a few newspaper announcements that little had been done to promote his appearance. Now that he no longer had a studio publicity department to back him up, he took what he got. The article was long but included almost nothing not already spewed out in countless press releases from his many years of steady work as both *Red Ryder* and *Rocky Lane*. The piece did state, however, that Allan's popular series work was still being shown "on television all over the country."

He also rode in the Carolina Carillon Christmas Parade that year in Columbia, South Carolina. Allan was decked out in his best western regalia and looked every inch his confident *Rocky Lane* self. There must have been an attraction to the Carolinas for Allan that year, since these two events hit within a short two-week spread. While he may have gone home to California between them, chances are he hung around town between appearances — maybe buying horses and visiting local race tracks.

All this work piggybacked onto his previous movie personas yet it did not do much in the way of paying his bills. Passive promotion seemed to be a better use of his time and finances, and he focused on what he could do from home. Even if unintentional, that which had not long ago been his enemy — television — suddenly became his key promotional vehicle.

Southern California TV programmers took advantage of Allan's local residence. KRON-TV's Owl Theater, which presented late-night movie showings, re-released *Gay Blades*, made in late 1945 and originally aired in January of 1946. This was a cut-and-paste version, trimmed down to fifty-three minutes to fit TV's commercial needs. That the plot had a similar flavor to Allan's actual biography — his character was a New York hockey player approached by a Hollywood talent scout — likely had something to do with its choice as a solid representation of him and his earlier work. *A Guy Could Change*, one of Allan's 1946 films, also made its way into KRON's late night schedule.

Movieland Matinee, an afternoon film presentation on KTTV, showed a selection of Allan's early films. The host was a man named Ed Reimers, who had recently become a television and commercial announcer, narrator, and reporter. He would go on to work as an actor in a few minor roles, while mostly as an often-heard voice on a number of television shows in the late 1950s and into the 1960s. *Call of the South Seas* was one of their Allan Lane movie offerings. Under the guise of Alan Lane & Associates, Allan had done publicity for California Television Realtors Association only a year or so before, promoting the organization on KTTV.

All of this put royalties into Allan's pockets. With the replays of his series work and earlier big-screen movies, he still had regular income. Money was flowing, though nothing in comparison to what he had known just a few years earlier.

Allan was lonely. He called women "the most wonderful and necessary creations the heavens ever produced" but had spent his most successful years by himself, with no special lady with whom he could share the joy of those good times. Now he was feeling a slow erosion of his world, causing him to wonder what good all that success had done for him.

He was once again staring into a future of financial and professional struggle, and doing so with no one to help bear the burden. Allan had built his most successful career path on his ability to assume a progression of characters. As far as his public was concerned, he had become those characters. The majority of actors made a career out of playing different characters in each new effort, allowing them to hold onto their private persona when not on camera.

With *Red Ryder*, and then even more as *Rocky Lane*, Allan had become an actor living inside an actor, inside a private man. Once those fictional but financially and professionally life-giving cowboys were no longer part of his daily existence, his professional world and his private world began to crumble, and the wallet started to empty at a faster pace than ever before.

Somewhere around February of 1954, Allan met and married a sweet-looking petite lady with dark hair and olive skin. Her name was Emma Raimondo. Emma had skated in the 1939 Ice Capades, leading her into brief appearances in a few movies. From 1945–1947, she was in three films, working under the name of Toni Raimando, all of which were uncredited.

Any discussion over how she and Allan got together would be nothing more than conjecture, since little is known of her life after her movie appearances and before the pair married. She resided in Los Angeles with her parents when she attempted her movie career, and then she moved to Hermosa Beach. She lived under her maiden name, and no other marriage record prior to her union with Allan has been located. In 1953, she was a part of a group called The Sandpipers, a social organization that served to better the surrounding community. Emma seemed to be gentle, well-liked, and productive.

Allan's niece Pat remembered meeting Emma. She said she was small and very pretty. She wore her long hair pulled back in a bun, and Pat said Allan's family loved her. She was "the nicest lady," and seemed truly interested in Allan's family and the people who were important to her new husband.

Three or so months after the union was made official, the family learned the marriage was over. Everyone was devastated. The split genuinely upset Allan's mother. No one knew why he and Emma split. The state of California required a legal separation a year prior to granting a final divorce.

There was one unusual insight into the dissolution of their union: Allan filed for the divorce, not Emma. She was a practicing Catholic, and one supposition was

Emma Raimondo in younger years.

that Allan took the action to save her the need to do so, seeing to it she would not endanger her religious world any further. This would seem to insinuate their separation was amicable. Maybe even bittersweet. One of her nephews said later in her life, after she remarried and had children, she no longer took communion in church because of her failed marriage. She had kept pictures of Allan and a copy of their divorce document for over fifty years, found after her death under linens in one of her closets.

A few months after his fourth marriage ended, on July 30, 1954, a quarter-sized ad appeared in the *Los Angeles Times* advertising a "2 NIGHT AUCTION EVENT" beginning, both nights, "promptly at 8 PM." This "event" was put on by the Sherman Oaks Auction Galleries, again with John Wallis, Auctioneer, at the helm. This public sale, based on the presentation of the ad itself, meant serious business. Included was a clear headshot of Allan "Rocky" Lane in full cowboy attire. In part, it read, "The entire contents of 'Rocky' Lane's beautiful Encino estate will be offered at public auction…" The remainder of the ad went on to list a dozen or so of the items up for sale, some of which had been detailed in previous but smaller auction ads in earlier years. Those advertisements had not featured his face, but clearly identified his unique possessions.

Allan had such items as a "console spinet piano," a "luxurious custom built 8'6" sofa," a "dinner and crystal service for 12," and many other expensive and well-appointed pieces from his personal collection. The

. . . JUNE BREAKFAST Chairman Dorothy Nowack at the microphone wearing a 1900 bathing suit. With her are left to right Emma Raimondo, and Dottie Busby, co-chairman.

Emma, far left, as part of a Sandpiper event, not long before she and Allan married.

advertisement ended with, "The furnishings are so handsome they beggar description — and space does not allow for full enumeration."

In other words, Allan "Rocky" Lane had lived well, at least for a while, and something had to change now that the bottom had fallen out of his money-making machine. The intent was to sell his home down to the bare walls. Allan needed money, and this time there were no limits placed on what was to sell.

Exactly two weeks to the day later, another ad was in the same newspaper, this time a bit smaller but no less intentional. Allan's name was boldly identified, and quite a number of the same items from the previous sale, as well as from sales in earlier years, were itemized. This ad said,

"Many other fine items too numerous to mention…on exhibition to sale time." Included were, "Lots of leather items, Venetian crystal, copper, brass, china, figurines." These and other pieces mentioned seemed to indicate he had had so much to start with that it took multiple auctions to list it all. Simply the recitation of belongings painted a picture of a life behind-the-scenes few knew Allan Lane had lived.

Los Angeles Times *ad announcing the "Sale of the Year" as a "2 Night Auction Event" for the entire contents of Rocky Lane's Encino estate.*

This was the beginning of yet another difficult time in Allan's life. He was no longer an actor on top of the heap. In fact, acting roles became few and far between and he was forced, yet again, to recreate his world. He began to call himself a businessman rather than an actor, and associated with a local and recently expanded iconic chain of department stores named Nash's. The Nash family was said to support the local general arts community. The alliance with Allan's name, which still carried punch, had the chance to benefit them.

One of those stores was near his new home, where he had moved from his "beautiful Encino estate." It is assumed he sold the ranch after he was able to divest himself of as many expensive belongings as possible. He took up residence in an apartment above a storefront on 39 West Colorado Boulevard in Pasadena, an extraordinary let-down from his previous digs. The ranch had meant security, but that period of his life was over. Apartment-living would again become his norm, and he would live in a succession of rentals for the rest of his life.

Allan still got a few chances to act and he did so whenever the opportunity arose. Good roles were few and far between, but he had an agent who actively sought work for him. Daniel "Danny" Winkler was well-known amongst the Hollywood set. He had been Dale Evans's representative prior to her association with, and marriage to, Roy Rogers. Danny also coproduced an episode of the *Roy Rogers Show* titled "A Slip of the Gun."

Danny had been in and around Hollywood and actors since the early 1930s. He managed the Trocadero night club in 1935, in between stints as an actors' spokesperson, so he was more than aware of the social scene and the way in which the business operated, both on and off screen. By 1940, Danny was not only managing such careers, he was intimately associated with at least one of these stars. He married actress Jean Rogers in 1941, divorced her about year later, and they remarried in 1943.

Jean Rogers was the female lead in the *Ace Drummond* short series in 1936, and became a hit soon thereafter in *Flash Gordon* (1936) as well as the 1938 Flash Gordon film, *Flash Gordon's Trip To Mars*. She had been in Hollywood for awhile, and by the early 1940s had retired for a few years to have a baby. Danny was with RKO Studios in those days as a "special contacts man."

Not long after her return to the screen, Jean was cast in a movie with Allan. *Gay Blades* in 1946 had her co-starring as his female lead. Whether or not Allan had known Winkler prior to this isn't certain, but he and Winkler ran in similar circles, dated some of the same women in the earlier days, and ultimately, just a handful or so years after Allan was in a movie with his wife, Danny Winkler was his agent. By then, Jean had permanently retired from the screen to raise their daughter.

Allan rattled around, taking on bit parts and doing promotional work using his business persona. In early 1955, he was a part of a few documentary shorts made by Ralph Staub — a director, producer, writer, and occasional actor mostly in his own work. Ralph is best known for his

Screen Shots series, which he began in 1930 and carried on into the mid-1950s. Allan was in a segment that aired in early February, titled *Pennies From Hollywood.* With him were many of Ralph's usual suspects, including Jack Benny, George Burns, Irene Dunn, and Loretta Young.

In May, Ralph released another, this one called *Hollywood Beauty*, and again featuring George Burns and Jack Benny, along with Bob Hope, Allan, Ralph, and other well-known folks. Film footage of the bank opening Allan had done years earlier was included, and this is where he entered the picture. His input into these *Screen Shots* was minimal. He did whatever he could, whenever he had a chance, to make ends meet and keep up with his hobby and the horses, and he continued to take care of his family's needs.

Allan had withstood a difficult relationship with his father ever since childhood. Whether money and family support had anything to do with the strain between them is speculation, but he did hold a grudge against the older man for the separation between his parents, and the difficulties his mother faced in those earlier years.

In early 1955, Allan's dad became ill, going through a violent personality change and mood disorder. He quickly became unmanageable, and doctors believed he was having mini-strokes. He and Allan were not on speaking terms on April 30, 1955, when William Herman Albershart died of a stroke. His obituary mentioned not a single word about his son's fame. The only indication of his children were their names — a daughter, Mrs. Helen Hower; and a son, Harry Albershart; as if the actor, Allan Lane, hadn't existed for him.

WILLIAM H. ALBERSHART

Funeral Services for William H. Albershart, 79, retired rancher and a resident of Southern California for the last 49 years, will be conducted at 11 a.m. tomorrow in the chapel of Edwards Bros. Colonial Mortuary, 1000 Venice Blvd. Interment will follow at Inglewood Park Cemetery. Mr. Albershart, who lived at [?]19 S. Alvarado St. and died Friday, leaves his widow, Mrs. Mame Albershart, a daughter, Mrs. Helen Hower, and a son, Harry Albershart (aka Allan Lane).

The obituary claimed Allan's dad had been a "resident of southern California for the past 49 years." However, fact from numerous South Bend, Indiana City Directories show he continued to live there as late as 1932. He was said to be a "retired rancher." Since he had always been listed as a "laborer" or "salesman" or "distributor," most often for the Mishawaka Woolen Manufacturing Company, it's curious as to how he came to be a rancher. He never owned any property of note. Funeral services for Bill were held on May 4 and he was buried in Inglewood cemetery, a family plot bought presumably by Anne Costello years earlier, though family believe Allan may have financed those gravesites.

Early studio photograph of Helen dedicated, "With love to my Dear Father from Helen." PHOTO COURTESY THE COSTELLO FAMILY COLLECTION

That Bill Albershart's children weren't in attendance at his funeral may have been forgivable, since not two weeks later, on May 16, Allan's sister Helen, aka Mrs. Helen Hower, passed away from a long battle with breast cancer. She was only two years older than her brother, and they had been close. As they became adults and their lives moved in vastly different directions, they saw each other at family functions, on holidays, and when stolen time would allow. No family feud between brother and sister. Allan had been there for his sister, especially financially, throughout her life.

Helen had been Allan's only living sibling, the one individual who knew the truth of their early beginnings. She had shared that life with him, and together they overcame a great deal of hardship. Allan was affected by the death of his father, and he handled it by himself. But he felt a heavy loss at his sister's passing, and his grief was shared by his mother and the entire Costello family.

Helen lived as a Catholic in her early adult years, and despite her separation from the Church for a few years, she was buried as a Catholic. A rosary was recited at the Church of the Holy Name in Los Angeles, the night before she was laid to rest. The next morning, a Requiem Mass was held. She was survived by her husband, her mother, and, as her obituary stated, "four brothers."

This attested to how close the Costello family unit was with Allan's mother, and the children she bore naturally. They had long before stopped being anything even remotely considered a "step family." Helen's niece, Pat, said Helen had been a "beautiful," petite woman, sweet. Her death devastated her mother, Anne, who had taken care of her, along with other family members, through to her last days.

The large heaping of difficult personal news did not slow down for Allan that spring. He and Emma had been legally separated the entire prior year. Ten days after his sister's death and less than a month after his father had passed away, Allan Lane's divorce from Emma Raimondo became official. He had married her under the name of Harry Albershart, but no matter what name he used, he was once again a single man, this time at the age of forty-six.

CHAPTER EIGHTEEN

Looking Into The Future

Allan had been out of the direct limelight for a few years. He had been working but not in front of the camera, when the chance to revive *Red Ryder* (1956) came his way. He wasn't destitute — he still had income from his years in front of a camera, earlier *Red Ryder* serial work and the self-titled *Rocky Lane* series. His comic books had taken on a life of their own, and that in addition to product connections of various types brought in residuals.

As well, he was seen on TV, mostly in reruns of early movies played in late night double features. Still, Allan Lane had not done anything new on TV or in the movies in a long time. He was aware, as were all well-known "B" cowboy actors of a certain era that his period on the movie screen was fast disappearing. Serials had become a lost art. Allan had to get with the times or be completely forgotten.

He chose to get with the times. The new opportunity was offered by Red Ryder Productions, which had become an enterprise unto itself. On July 12, 1955, the *Los Angeles Times* reported, "Gene Autry's Flying A Productions launches still another western series today when the new *Red Ryder* series goes before the cameras on location at Lone Pine." The article continued, "Alan [sic] (Rocky) Lane, who made quite a few *Red Ryders*..." would have the starring role.

In late June, Fred Harman, creator of *Red Ryder*, had signed a contract with Autry for "programs to be produced by CBS," paving the way for Allan to once again step in as *Red Ryder*. Television was all the rage, and while youngsters stilled loved their Westerns, they now often stayed home and watched their own small screens rather than go out to the movies to get their fix. Gene Autry had proven that moving from films to TV was a viable way to do business. Allan followed in his footsteps, and Gene Autry's Flying A Productions became his business partner.

This new *Red Ryder* had troubles from the get-go. Though the character had had repeated lives, none had been in this medium. There were many meetings held to iron out details of the new ground, and rights to produce and exhibit *Red Ryder* on television had to be secured.

Money to make all this happen was a big concern. Allan wanted the series to be successful. This could be his ticket back into regular visibility, giving him an entirely new medium in which to work as well as a new audience. Even though he'd done little TV, he had been in the enter-

Sally Fraser in 1956, the year after the Red Ryder *TV pilot was made.*

tainment business over half his life and knew the industry. Ignoring his growing financial concerns, he put up money to help ensure the success of this *Red Ryder* and in return, he expected residuals and executive creative rights.

A deal was secured and the show went into production. Copyright on the final product indicates programming completed in 1955. These works didn't take long to film, and the show was likely made late that year. By early the next year, the pilot, "Gun Trouble Valley," was in the can and ready for the viewing public to enjoy.

The star was "Rocky Lane," not Allan "Rocky" Lane. Other regulars were a young actor named Louis Lettieri who played Little Beaver, and character actress Elizabeth "Lizz" Slifer as The Duchess. Recurring roles went to James Best and Sally Fraser as a couple in love and about to be married. They were expected to be seen in future episodes. Sally Fraser had no idea at the time she was filming a pilot. "My understanding was that it was [already] a TV show," she explained.

A "pilot" was considered a single-effort episode made by a producer, or a group of producers, in a desire to ultimately create an ongoing series. The episode was then pitched to a network. If the network liked what they saw, they requested changes or, if good as it was, the pilot was aired to gauge

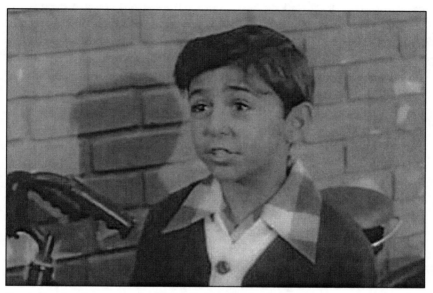

Louis Lettieri in a scene from The Public Defender *around the same time he played Little Beaver with Allan in the TV pilot for* Red Ryder.

audience response. As follow-up to positive viewer ratings, additional episodes were created. As long as the show had good ratings, the network requested more and a series was officially born.

Sally said Allan was "very pleasant to work with, business-like." She thought their work was well done, better than most such shows. She worked a lot then and felt the entire operation was professional. Everyone "fell into a 'get-it-done' groove" and quality was top-notch.

Lou Lettieri was a young boy when the opportunity came to play the by-now well-known character, Little Beaver. He was a busy child actor, in front of a camera a handful of years already with a host of credits behind him. His recollection of Allan Lane matched Sally Fraser's: professional, pleasant, and likeable. Neither recalled him as a social man.

Needless chatter still wasn't much to his liking. Allan was all about business, getting the job done, and making sure it was done to the best of everyone's ability. He was older than during his first *Red Ryder* efforts but had no fewer expectations. If his name was on the bill, he demanded the best out of everyone who signed on with him. And since this time his name was not only on the bill but also part of the production credits, he was especially concerned over end results. His money was on the line.

Allan continued to be at the top of his game and effortlessly stepped back into the role of Red Ryder. His performance was possibly even stronger than it had been ten years earlier. Interaction with the other characters appeared easygoing and believable, even gentle when he did scenes with his aunt and Little Beaver. He was in his mid-forties, yet despite the added years, a receding hairline, and possibly a very few more pounds, he was still fast on the draw with his gun and able with little physical effort to pull off the most demanding physical scenes.

A few times, as Red Ryder jumped on his horse to follow the bad guys, a deep voice came from nowhere. Without connection to the script, the voice boomed, "R-r-roll Thunder," in somewhat the same fashion as 'Hi Ho Silver' had been delivered in *The Lone Ranger* series.

The story of the demise of this *Red Ryder*, as it is known, indicates there were time-slot issues when it came to the point of getting the new show regularly on the air. Whether or not that was the only reason is not known. It is known, however, that network executives couldn't agree with the production staff and the entire effort was shelved. *Red Ryder*, the TV show, was dead before it had a chance to gain a viewing audience.

This experience caused deeper issues for Allan and his pocketbook, and it made him less inclined to put out much effort in the industry anymore. He'd sunk money into the TV version — money that had not shown a profit — and, even more so, it proved to be a loss for him in every way. He needed to find something else to sustain him.

The issue wasn't that Allan didn't get work but the work he found in no way compared to the efforts of his heyday. Allan Lane may have been a "B" Western actor but he had been a star in his genre, and for years his name on a marquee meant something. He had been a draw for many Saturday afternoon matinees, putting out consistently well-done work. Yet here he was now with no regular paycheck and nothing that carried his name any distance.

When all else failed him, Allan was still popular on the cowboy parade route. In May of 1955, he rode in a grand procession for an audience of 45,000 people. This was the Monrovia Day Roundup and Allan led the festivities, touted as "motion picture actor and grand marshal." There was a breakfast and luncheon, and an official barbecue staged by the Monrovia

Mounted Police. The parade route was listed in detail, with a total of 135 floats, bands, majorettes, and riders. A "Roundup Queen" and her court presided over the day's events. A quick in-and-out and only twenty-five or so miles from his home gave Allan no more than a bit of pocket change, but it kept his face and name in the press just a bit longer.

Away from the entertainment world, he did work as a hotel manager

Allan in the Winner's Circle at Caliente with horse, Black Duke, Glen Lasswell, the jockey, and well-wishers and friends. PHOTO COURTESY THE COSTELLO FAMILY COLLECTION

and leasing agent. In exchange, he received room and board for as long as he kept the job. There is evidence he did so starting in late 1955 and off-and-on for a few years.

One thing that didn't change for Allan was his love of horses, a blatantly obvious fact for anyone who knew him and his almost sixth-sense connection with equines. He continued to buy and train them, and in 1956 on New Year's Day, one of Allan's horses, Black Duke, won a race at Caliente.

The jockey was Glen Lasswell, a twenty-three-year-old hot shot known to be brash and who managed to occasionally get into trouble — but he knew how to win, and he won often. Allan posed for a photograph taken by official track photographer Frank Preciado. With him was Black Duke, jockey Glen Lasswell, and a host of well-wishers. Allan looked like a proud father.

About three weeks later, he was in the Winner's Circle again with another horse, Brulea. The jockey this time was named Fields, and the day was another bright one at Caliente. More official photographs —

Allan in the Winner's Circle at Caliente once again, this time with a horse named Brulea. PHOTO COURTESY THE COSTELLO FAMILY COLLECTION

including the horse with Allan, the jockey, groomsmen and friends. Allan knew his horses, and his horses knew him. Theirs was a deeply symbiotic relationship.

That year, 1956, could have been named "The Year of the Horse" for Allan. He usually did well with those he trained and ran. If he didn't win, he usually placed. The purse would for the most part go right back into the next horse, and the next, whether it was for training or for betting.

Allan and his stepbrother, Justin Costello, were kindred spirits. They found enjoyment and relaxation at the track and often went together for dinner, drinks, and the races. Justin, according to his niece and nephew, had an addiction to "playing the ponies," and when he and Allan got together, they drew out the recklessness in each other. They had in common betting on the horses, enjoying cocktails, and chasing pretty women. Enough to solidify their brotherhood.

In March, he again hit it big with another of his horses, this one named Timbuktu. The race was held at Tanforan, and Timbuktu's trainer was a man named Howard Long. Allan had partnered with Howard for this one, and the race paid off for all involved.

Allan in the Winner's Circle with horse, Timbuktu, along with trainer, Howard Long. PHOTO COURTESY THE COSTELLO FAMILY COLLECTION

The New Year of 1957 dawned. Whether times were easy or hard, Allan refused to be held down for long, and he never stopped working. The advertising agency that recently carried his name with a slightly altered spelling seemed to pick up steam the longer he stayed away from acting. He kept a number of irons in the fire, and as the visible head for that agency, it is believed Allan became involved in the creation of what was called "closed-circuit TV" stations, an early predecessor to pay-per-view. This was a fledgling industry, really a dream for the most part, but those who believed in Pay TV believed wholeheartedly.

One of the few companies in this new market, Trans-Community Television Network, was headquartered in Beverly Hills and owned by Jerome Doff. Doff had been an actor's agent before he became a lawyer. He began efforts in 1956 to bring selective, and subscription, television to a small market in Cedar City, Utah. His plan would give residents an opportunity to watch what they wanted, when they wanted, if only on a small scale. Doff worked out a deal with NBC and ABC, and the effort looked promising.

Enter Alan Lane. His earliest press notices spelled his name as Allan Lane before dropping one "l." Both as an advertising man and an actor with a recently big audience, no matter how the name was spelled, Allan was a good catch for Doff. He was intrigued by the concept and believed in future potential. Doff named him Vice President, and Allan utilized his long-honed skills as an advertising professional. The product may have changed but his skillset had not. He still had the talents he used as a New York City ad man in the mid-1930s.

Trans-Community Television Network folded into a new company, Skiatron, named after a particular type of tube used in the transmission of data — an early form of computer. The president was a slick salesman from way back in the movie world named Matty, or Matthew, Fox. Fox was smart. Very smart. A man of ideas. Only a few years earlier, he was Vice President of Universal Pictures. He had developed the soap bubble pipe for children, cornered the market on 3-D glasses, and now he championed pay-per-view TV. In recent years, he had created a company that procured older films for reissue on television. Matty Fox was all over the new world of television entertainment.

Jerome Doff was initially the Vice President of Operations but by late 1957, he'd left that position and Allan was in the seat. Being behind-the-scenes in early television innovation seemed natural for him. He had been in on the end of silent films and the beginning of talkies, and now Skiatron offered him a chance to utilize his vast entertainment experience in a business atmosphere. He set up shop and went to work.

Skiatron put him in front of the cameras as a talking head. Allan believed in the future of this new technology, and he vigorously promoted Skiatron's efforts on panel show debates, making an argument for moving forward in this new medium. From there, he took on additional venues — on television, speaking to the press at release events, or standing at a conference podium.

In February of the following year, Allan was a "headline speaker" at the Western Radio & Television Conference in San Francisco. As an actor he was used to learning his script and playing his role. He was well-skilled in how to perform the part and elicit, as well as influence, a response, proving to be an excellent choice as a spokesman to promote the brave new world of Pay TV services. After he gave his speech, he was part of a panel discussion on the future of television.

In the earlier world of entertainment, Allan became known for playing a fictional cowboy figure and had walked, talked, and even breathed the role. Yet the figures of *Red Ryder* and *Rocky Lane* weren't realistic versions of how he looked when he was out of character. His Old West garb with a ten-gallon hat on his head, often on a fast-moving horse, made it relatively easy to mask his appearance as he aged.

Allan in a suit and without his hairpiece at some point in the late 1950s or early 1960s. PHOTO COURTESY THE COSTELLO FAMILY COLLECTION

When he promoted Skiatron's newfangled Pay TV ideas, he was no longer *Rocky Lane* or any other fictional character. People who saw him in a suit and tie, with a receding hairline or a hairpiece, and often glasses, seated at a desk or speaking in front of an audience interested in the future of television, could easily be forgiven for not recognizing him.

A big draw for Allan, in addition to the chance to be on the cutting edge and redeem his name and image, was the chance to promote baseball in the homes of masses of eager fans. After the 1957 season, the New York Giants moved to San Francisco. Owner Horace Stoneham believed in the Pay TV concept, and he signed an exclusive agreement with Skiatron to carry their games to paying customers. Skiatron guaranteed Stoneham about $12,500.00 a game — a considerable amount more than they could make in the traditional fashion.

Unfortunately, Matty Fox made promises he could not yet deliver. The technology, in the hands of his or any other company, wasn't yet ready to be implemented. Matty was a visionary and he was sure they were on the verge. Rather than explain the difficulties, he promised Stoneham — in front of Congressional hearings — that he could have San Francisco wired for the service for less than six million dollars. He could do Los Angeles, he promised, for double that amount. Matty boldly told the committee, as well as anyone else who'd listen, that pay television was the coming thing.

His pitch had impact. Stocks raised, with Skiatron being one of the five most active that day on the American Stock Exchange. The next day, the Los Angeles City Council bought into his presentation and approved Skiatron's bid to wire the city. The Giants' owner had purchased a large block of the company's publicly traded stock. Everything was a match made in Heaven.

Thousands of miles of ground needed to be broken and prepared for Matty Fox's dream to become reality. He had built his dream much on the backs, and pocketbooks, of others. Ultimately his continuing inability to deliver led to his downfall, as well as the downfall of others. History has proven his ideas were innovative, but he was ahead of his time and utilized shady business tactics in the process.

Allan as well as his money may have been caught up in the furor. This might help explain part of his earlier financial mysteries. His involvement in the Pay TV movement appears to have started in the second half of 1948 when he began to sell off property. He well may have needed ready cash as a hefty investment in what he hoped would become an innovative and exciting way to change the course of entertainment media. Allan had been in the industry since the dawn of the talkies. He knew how Hollywood worked from the inside-out. He believed his investments of money and name would be an important contribution to the evolution of this medium.

An article overview by Lewis Bagwell on Allan's extensive career came out that spring, covering from his early days all the way into completion of the *Rocky Lane* series. Bagwell seemed determined to revive Allan's elevated Western star status and get the public to bring him back to the screen on a regular basis. His piece finished with, "Perhaps some bright, young TV producer will be wise enough to star Rocky Lane in a TV Western series. Rocky is the kind of personality that never wears out and his handsome features would be a welcome format to the TV screens." It then advised readers to "write to ABC, CBS, AND NBC, if you are interested in seeing more of Allan 'Rocky' Lane…"

It was a noble, well-placed effort that did not hit its desired mark.

While Alan Lane worked behind the scenes to further the evolution of television, Allan Lane still found occasional work in front of the camera. *Gunsmoke* haphazardly cast him a number of times in the next few years, starting in February of 1958. In "Texas Cowboys," he played trail boss Kin

Talley, a difficult, headstrong man who led what storyline previews called "a roistering horde of Texas cowboys." In this guest-starring role, Allan proved even a few years after his heyday's demise he was still a recognizable actor on the Western front.

One role for which Allan became well-remembered in post-*Rocky Lane* years was, somewhat surprisingly, set in modern day. He did not

Allan headlining a California parade with children behind him. PHOTO COURTESY THE COSTELLO FAMILY COLLECTION

wear a gun belt or ride a horse in an *Alfred Hitchcock Presents* offering titled, "Lamb to the Slaughter" (1958). He wasn't on the screen long, and didn't expend any extraordinary physical energy even though he gave the part his all. The role brought his acting capabilities to the forefront, and the segment has become one of the most talked-about of the entire Hitchcock TV series.

Barbara Bel Geddes and Allan in their last live scene together in "Lamb to the Slaughter," an episode of Alfred Hitchcock Presents.

Allan played Police Chief Patrick Maloney. His pregnant, sweet, and overly obedient wife, Barbara Bel Geddes, watched for his car in the driveway one evening as she made everything special for his return from a grueling day's work. Allan's acting chops were encapsulated in the opening scene, where he played his part perfectly — surly, uncommunicative, and downright nasty to his lovely wife. She desperately attempted to get him to tell her what was wrong. Finally, ordering her to sit down, he bluntly told her he was leaving her for another woman. His tone was nearly conversational yet his words shocked his unsuspecting wife.

As Allan, in the guise of Maloney, went through a short laundry list of how this would go forward and what he would do — he made it sound as if he were doing her a favor by filing for the divorce and ensuring she had all rights to the baby as well as seeing she had enough money to live on — the look on her face remained incredulous.

Interaction between the two was intense. Barbara and Allan made the situation perfectly believable. Every effort to see reason was played out on her end. She forced a kiss on him. After he declared his intention to leave, the emotions going through her head were palpable. Finally, she did the only thing she could think of to stop him. She killed him by whacking him on the head with the frozen leg of lamb she had intended to serve him for dinner.

All of this within about five minutes into the storyline.

Not a lot for him to go on but Allan infused the scene with believability. One reviewer stated he played the part with "cold effectiveness and a dour temperament." The four women who were married to him before this acting job, as well as many who'd worked with him over the years, shouldn't have been surprised — it was excellent casting. His marriage woes were never reportedly connected to infidelity, yet his version of this husband was every inch an outstanding performance. He stayed on the scene another third of the segment, flat-out on the floor as a dead man.

Allan picked up another role that year in the twenty-ninth episode of the first season of what would become an iconic TV western, *Wagon Train*. In "The Daniel Barrister Story (1958)," he had a small but pivotal part as opinionated Sam Miller, one of the family men on Major Seth Adams's train. Allan's character was rough, determined to do things his way. When a deeply religious man with an injured wife refused to bring in a doctor to help her though she begged for medical attention, Sam Miller was more than willing to force the issue.

Each instance of Allan's screen presence at this point in his career, limited though they had become, seemed to be a reflection of his personality. Did casting directors and TV executives typecast him, or did they utilize his traits to strengthen these roles? Possibly a combination of both.

The Saga of Hemp Brown (1958) was Allan's only movie appearance of the year, and one of the last of his career. He played the Sheriff, somewhat of an uneventful bit considering the line-up of movies in which he had starred and carried the weight of the entire picture. This one starred Rory Calhoun. Though Allan and Rory were only three years apart in age, Rory started acting fifteen years later. He was barely mid-career at this point, while Allan was in his waning years.

He worked regularly that year, though the parts weren't major. Shows in which he appeared came out one right after the other, with usually only a few days in between. He likely went from set to set during the taping of these episodes, with his work requiring a day or so of his time, or less, each time. Behind the scenes, he still did his part for Skiatron. The two personas never came together or got in the way of the other.

The end of this same year would introduce Allan to the horse that would ensure his place in television history for generations to come.

CHAPTER NINETEEN

Mister Ed and The Other Horses in Allan's Life

According to Alan Young's book, *Mister Ed and Me*, he was first approached in 1952 by veteran Hollywood director Hal Lubin to be a part of a television show that would star him, if he'd take the part, and...a talking horse. Alan had just received two Emmys for his self-titled show and he was doing well. However, as he put it, "...writing and starring in a live weekly television show was a draining experience."

Alan had gone to Hal first, hoping he might direct his show on film. Hal wasn't interested but countered with his offer. He explained the idea to Alan, who saw the concept "as exciting as a damp beach." He wasn't thrilled about sharing the top billing with a horse, either. As he explained it, "I was a comedian. I worked alone. I had a hit show on my hands." All around, Alan Young had no interest early on in being a part of Hal Lubin's TV show about a talking horse.

Fast forward six years. It was late 1958, and Hal had gone ahead with his idea, creating a pilot film titled *The Wonderful World of Wilbur Pope*. He found another actor to take on the starring human role. Seasoned actor Scott McKay happily accepted the part and, along with little-known actress Sandra White, they played Wilbur and Carlotta Pope, the married couple at the core of the storyline.

But this was a show about a talking horse, and to be successful, they had to have a talking horse. After Chill Wills turned down the part, Allan Lane snagged the role of the horse — or at least, the horse's voice. Chill Wills had been the voice of *Francis the Talking Mule* (1950), the first well-known success of this genre, produced for the big screen by Hal Lubin. Along with TV producer Al Simon, Hal got George Burns to put up the finances via his company, McCadden Enterprises. "Nearly everybody who saw the film liked it. George

Burns thought it one of the funniest TV comedies he had ever seen," according to Alan Young.

The early effort, however, never went anywhere, and history seemed doomed to repeat itself in Allan's professional life. Good thing he still had his behind-the-scenes work. He had left Skiatron and become the General Manager for Video Recording Tape Center in Los Angeles. No

Left: *Alan Young in an earlier studio photo.* Right: *Allan in a headshot taken about the same time as he guest-starred on a segment of* Mike Hammer.
PHOTO COURTESY WILLIAM "PETE" PETERSON

one seemed to want *The Wonderful World of Wilbur Pope* anyway. It failed to pique the interest of any of the networks and was dead on arrival.

So in February of 1959, while Hal Lubin and his team were working overtime to find a home for the talking horse project, Allan took on a guest role in the *Mike Hammer* series. In the seventh episode of the second season, "Husbands Are Bad Luck," he played Lefty Jones, a sleazy rodeo performer trying to hit pay dirt via his ex-wife who would soon marry a wealthy man from a prominent family. She didn't want her soon-to-be new husband's family to learn of her shady past, and Lefty knew he could get her to do whatever he wanted to make him stay quiet. But when he was killed barely halfway through the episode — which had become Allan's professional modus operandi, it seemed — the murder was pinned on her, and her troubles really began.

This character was not a nice one. Allan's role was unappealing in almost every direction. He looked good — still attractive and trim-figured — but that in no way took away from the truth that Lefty Jones was a woman-beater. This was the late 1950s. Such behavior, while never acceptable, had not yet been brought into the limelight as the horrible crime it really was. Men who acted as such were despicable, and that was the end of that. Allan's character was in all ways despicable, and he played him to the hilt.

The next year, Allan again started picking up regularly occurring guest roles. In *Hell Bent For Leather* (1960), he had a far-down-the-cast part as a character known only as Kelsey. This was a Universal production starring Audie Murphy. Allan's inclusion, along with Bob Steele, was used for the most part as an "old-timer's" cameo.

Allan was only a few years older than Audie. They knew each other from the earlier years at Les Hilton's ranch but had little in common these days, except they both owned and raised thoroughbred horses. Audie became a rancher. Allan was a horse trainer. Both had their heyday in other arenas — Audie as a war hero and Allan as a celluloid cowboy hero. Both men had bad tempers, turbulent married lives, and financial woes. One was said to have clear-cut, visible reasons for his difficult behavior — his war experience — the other — Allan — did not.

He rolled right out of that into an episode of Wayde Preston's *Colt .45*. In late January, the episode in which he played was titled "Arizona Anderson (1960)," part of the third season. He along with Don "Red" Barry — both considered old-timers — did their part in supporting roles, playing outlaws who wanted a share of government funds stolen by the title character.

There was a two-time appearance as historical western figure Johnny Ringo in *Walt Disney's Wonderful World of Color* episodes, "Texas John Slaughter: Kentucky Gunslick" (1960) and "Texas John Slaughter: Geronimo's Revenge" (1960). The true-life figure, Ringo, was loosely related to Jesse James through an aunt's marriage, and he ended up with his own place in history. These episodes came out in succession, and represented the sum total of Allan's professional connection with Walt Disney.

Allan Lane was deeply tied into the Western genre. Whatever anyone thought of him as a man, as an actor he had proven his ability. Studio folks and audiences alike remembered him as a cowboy, one who rode hard, always wore boots and big hats, and in the end, fought against, or for, justice.

His appearance in any one of TV's popular westerns was a nod to the early days, intentional or otherwise. The viewing public knew it, the studio executives knew it, and he knew it. Allan was more than aware he was able to secure these roles, small and brief as they were, because he was now only an image of the man he had been all those years ago. His heyday had been over ten years earlier and now he was playing his swan song.

He continued to most often stand on the side of the law on camera. In March, he again played a sheriff, Sheriff Brady in "Death of An Outlaw" (1960) on *Bronco*. This was a starring vehicle for handsome Ty Hardin and the series aired from 1958–1962.

In May, a second appearance on *Colt .45* had Allan playing the mayor of a western town in "Trial By Rope" (1960). He was little more than a prop for the law-abiding side of the storyline that had Colt investigating a ranch hand's murder.

Allan made the rounds of just about every popular Western TV show of the day. He was seen on *Lawman*, starring Peter Brown and John Russell. "The Payment" (1960) told of a reformed gunman who wanted to make amends with the widow of the first man he killed. Along the way, a bad guy and two sidekicks challenged him. Allan played Joe Hoyt, the head bad guy. Guest-starring in one western after another and interpreting characters from both sides of justice, Allan kept going the distance, though few people noticed anymore.

He closed out his 1960 resumé with a role in *Bonanza* in "The Blood Line" (1960). The entire story was built around the son of a solid-townsman-gone-bad. The son had not been raised by his father and when he came to town for a visit, he learned his dad had just been shot to death by none other than the upstanding Ben Cartwright. The young man vowed to avenge the death, with little more to spur him on than the memory of his father.

The storyline was touching, but if viewer's blinked, they missed Allan Lane in the pivotal role of Luke Grayson, the boy's dad. He believably played a belligerent drunk who had long ago seen much better days. That he was onscreen for less than five minutes didn't dampen Allan's gusto in taking on the character. He managed to imbue Luke Grayson with a sense of forlorn sadness for the man he could have been.

In 1960, *Los Angeles Times* movie and TV critic Hal Humphrey, in his "Viewing TV" column brought to light a new television effort in the works under Hal Lubin's direction. Humphrey's column was titled, "Talking Horses?" and it started off with an animated quote from Hal.

"They say they want something new. Well, I got something new — a talking horse. But now they're afraid nobody will believe it. I say, who needs to believe it? Then I remind them about Jackie Cooper's old *People's Choice* series with Cleo the talking dog. You know what their answer is to that? 'Yeah, but the dog's lips don't move.' Is that an answer?"

The piece went on to talk about Hal's ongoing efforts to bring to the

Allan as Luke Grayson in the opening scene from Bonanza's *"The Blood Line."*

small screen a story about a talking horse. There were few people who knew much worth mentioning of Hal's earlier attempts to get this project on the screen. That he wanted to revive the project received little attention as it was. The renewed interest in making *The Wonderful World of Wilbur Pope* into a recurring television show was being greeted with lukewarm attention, at best.

None of the networks had been interested. No one had bought the original concept or the presentation. But it was now 1960, more than half a dozen years later, and Hal Lubin had not given up. He managed to get George Burns to buy in as the producer at the beginning, and if Hal could find a way to revamp the original, he was willing to stay on.

The Wonderful World of Wilbur Pope had been filmed at General Services Studios on Las Palmas Avenue in Hollywood. George Nasser, the studio's owner, felt the short film would be good for audiences in theaters he owned. He asked television director-producer Al Simon if he would review the pilot and give his opinion. Al liked the concept but felt changes were necessary. A new, better-looking horse. A storyline revolving around that horse. Edits were needed all-around. George Burns agreed. Al Simon had been the President of Filmways Television before he moved to Burns's McCadden Productions.

As the primary money person backing the project, George Burns's opinion held a lot of clout, and so *The Wonderful World of Wilbur Pope* went back to the drawing board. Hal Lubin was introduced to television director-producer Al Simon, and things began to look up. Filmways, McCadden Productions, and Lubin Pictures entered into a deal to make this work. After changes were made and edits creatively applied, another try was made to sell the show.

George Burns was one of MCA's, Music Corporation of America, top clients. The agency had been the initial sales agent. Still not enthusiastic, MCA nonetheless agreed to give the show another go and presented it to D'Arcy Advertising Agency and one of their account executives, Steve Mudge. D'Arcy had built their television advertising much on the concept of sponsorship. They started early on with Coca-Cola, and Steve knew it could work again, so he decided to pitch the show to the Studebaker Corporation, one of his accounts. Studebaker was small but well-respected. Coincidently, or not, the company was headquartered in South Bend, Indiana, Allan Lane's home base.

Studebaker was at the time trying to find a marketing vehicle with which they could go head-to-head against Detroit's "Big Three" car makers. Timing was everything, and they decided their new Avanti could be the perfect advertising ploy, along with this innovative new show, to put them ahead of the game with their bigger competitors. But how to go about making this work with Studebaker's small advertising budget?

Steve Mudge was a smart man. He devised a crafty marketing plan by which Studebaker would be the only sponsor for the newly retooled *Mister Ed* show. He had the company come together with dealerships across the country to bring financing up to par to make the entire effort work. If dealers would throw in $25 each time they sold a car, Studebaker would match that.

Behind the scenes of the marketing effort, show production was in gear. The cast was being assembled and almost all of the main characters had been retooled. Initially, little was said about the addition of Alan Young, who agreed to come onboard in April when the idea of taking it to TV became serious. He was optioned to jump into the part previously in the hands of Scott McKay, and young, new-to-the-screen Connie Hines took on the role of the wife. Why there had been a cast change has never been publicly discussed.

Young recently said he had no idea how Allan Lane snagged the part of Mister Ed's voice for the original pilot, but he knew "Rocky," as he called him, had not been intended to take the part for the TV show. Alan said executives felt Allan was not "glamorous" enough. He was difficult and people thought he kept to himself too much. Executives wanted to replace him going into the TV version, so they auditioned a number of actors to take over the part.

In the long run, not a single one could match the timbre and richness of Allan's voice, and he was retained. That the actor behind the voice was contractually never mentioned or seen on the screen may have ended up proving Allan had been, all along, the perfect match for the job. His lack of "glamour," and his determination to keep to himself, became positive qualities that supported the role.

Alan Young, well-known to easily handle a live audience and good at improvisation, was asked to go on the road to sell the show. He would accompany screenings of the new effort, now being called simply *Mister Ed*, and convince Studebaker dealers their support would help sell cars, and they would become a part of entertainment history. Alan agreed, and in each city, he made an entertaining pitch for the marriage of *Mister Ed* and Studebaker. The shortened pilot was shown time and time again. And Steve Mudge, at the end of each pitch and showing, hit dealers with the closer. "How many want to buy this show?"

Steve Mudge, Alan Young, and everyone in the background were successful in city after city. The dealers went home pumped up and bought time slots on their local stations. The idea turned out to be a booming success, creating more syndicated stations for *Mister Ed* than they would have had if any of the networks would have taken them on in the first place.

While all this fancy salesmanship was going on, not a soul breathed a word about the complicated necessity for an actor behind-the-camera to give that horse life in the form of a speaking voice. Allan had done the earlier job and now had been re-hired to continue in the revised version. He, like his human co-star Alan Young, wasn't thrilled about playing second, or even third, fiddle to a horse, but it was regular work and he wasn't going to turn down the opportunity.

This makes one wonder if Allan demanded no credit even at the earliest inception of the show, back in its *The Wonderful World of Wilbur Pope* days, or if Hal Lubin and Al Simon, once there was hope of it going somewhere, had been gun-shy over discussing any secrets to the point of excluding the actor from any early credit. There was no press. Voicing the part of *Mister Ed* had initially been, for Allan, literally just another paycheck. He had previously done many bits that never went anywhere and after a few years of this pilot lying dormant and seemingly forgotten in a vault somewhere, at the beginning he had little worry over being "found out." Now it looked as if *Mister Ed* would be seen every week on television and Allan remained leery of what the whole effort would mean to his career, for better or for worse. This may have been part of why people around him felt he carried a chip on his shoulder.

Just about no one has ever said anything about the need for an actor to create the horse's voice or overall difficulties in putting together such a production. Allan's name has never been mentioned in any of the rare and brief bits of how the initial pilot came to be, or the execution of the final product. Most executives seemed more than willing, in fact they were delighted, to let his involvement stay hidden from the public once Allan made it clear he did not want to be officially credited for his part in the show.

So his part in the renewed project remained safely without notice. Hal Lubin wasn't naming him, and early-on no one else seemed to care about *The Wonderful World of Wilbur Pope* as a pilot, *Mister Ed* as a viable TV show, or about who was the voice behind that silly talking horse. All that was said about the matter was, "The horse is no problem. Lubin has a contraption that will make any horse a talking horse."

As easy as that. Becoming *Mister Ed*'s voice meant so little to Allan that he continued to look for other work long after he learned there was a plan to resurrect the original show with changes. He had no reason to believe he should stop job-shopping despite the new gig. He understood that if by chance the show succeeded, he would become *Mister Ed* in the eyes of Hollywood, and that truly embarrassed him. He wasn't sure how he should react. Allan needed the work, though, and he decided it wise not to make any waves. Yet.

If he could get something else more solid, and more respectable considering his long history in the industry, he would be in a better position to make such choices. Unfortunately, he was successful only in garnering bit parts with little credit. In many ways this period reflected back to the beginning of his career. Allan was getting roles here and there but nothing that would support him. His appearance in any one TV show would prove to mean little to the final product. There was a lot of, "Allan Who?" going around again, and he knew it.

Beyond the workplace, Allan continued to hedge his bets, literally, at the racetrack. In 1960, he picked up season credentials at Santa Anita Race Track, which allowed him entrance to the grandstand box area. He was identified as a "horseman" and given valid entrance at will. Allan obviously had enough money to keep him in good standing at the racetrack.

He did do one thing that reflected his confidence about his new television job. The *Mister Ed* paycheck proved to be better than any he'd had in a while. In January of 1961, in concurrence with his new gig, business trade magazines announced that Alan Lane, General Manager of Video Recording Tape Center, had been replaced by a new executive. Allan Lane, now the voice of *Mister Ed* (1961), returned to full-time work, once again leaving the business world for the entertainment industry.

CHAPTER TWENTY

Allan's Unintended Legacy

Allan Lane's story cannot be told without a lengthy mention of his good friend Les Hilton. Though Les was a few years older, he and Allan were of similar ages. They were Midwesterners, both learned early the meaning of a working man's salary, and had responsibility for ensuring their family stayed fed and clothed. Les had little more than a grade school education, possibly also Allan, yet they were both businessmen. Both were wunderkinds with horses. Les and Allan knew how to work animals with kindness and respect.

Loretta Kemsley, whose father trained animals for the Selig Zoo, was one of Les's neighbors. Les Hilton lived in North Hollywood on Saticoy Street at the time. Her parents bought their nearby property in 1947 for $6,000, and the homesteads were comparable in size. She was only two years old when she moved in, growing up in an idyllic setting for a young woman who was herself an animal lover.

"Most of Les' friends were cowboys, some of them stars like Audie Murphy, others just ordinary cowboys." Jessie James — a man with a famous name who owned a cattle ranch in the Valley — Les, and Murphy spent a lot of time together. "Audie, Jessie and Les were good friends with no distinction between them based on stardom. Same for our other neighbors, many of which were cowboys doing what they loved most."

According to Loretta, known as Lore, Les was well-known in the industry long before *Mister Ed* was dreamed up. He found work where he could over the years, supporting family members off-and-on. He had a large bunch of siblings, and after his parents died, Les became more of a father, ensuring they were never in need.

His personal story was similar to Allan's. Though there was a rumor Les was married years before — an early United States census listing indicated a wife — during his cowboy ranching days he was single, and to the best of anyone's knowledge, he had no children.

His career as a movie horse trainer appears to have started in the late 1930s, after he found his way to the movie industry after the mid-1930s. There are stories that he went to Hollywood because of an association with Will Rogers. Both men were from Oklahoma and they may have known each other there. However he came to move westward, Les Hilton ultimately well knew all the major and minor movie cowboys, and they knew him. Even the wannabes were acquainted with Les Hilton.

These men were amongst a group of friends who found a place to congregate at Les Hilton's ranch. Allan Lane was part of that bunch. So was Lore, even as a teenager. There were no pretensions amongst the movie folks. As she explained:

> *There wasn't a distinc-*
> *tion in those days with a two*
> *tiered society among us, with*
> *stars being catered to like they*
> *are today. They were just regu-*
> *lar people, both in the way they*
> *acted and the way we interacted*
> *with them. For instance, I was*
> *an adult before I realized that*
> *the nice man who rode the palo-*
> *mino mule and stopped by every*
> *so often on Sunday mornings*
> *was someone more than just a*
> *nice man. He was Noah Beery.*

Loretta "Lore" Kemsley in 1954 with Dick Jones on the set of the Buffalo Bill, Jr *series, a companion to* Annie Oakley. *Lore doubled for Nancy Gilbert who played Buffalo Bill's little sister.* PHOTO COURTESY LORETTA KEMSLEY

Audie Murphy provoked a specific recollection. "Audie Murphy wasn't the movie star, war hero," Lore said. "He was that gorgeous friend of Les' who flirted with us and drove a strange looking pickup called an El Camino."

Even Jay Silverheels lived nearby. Movie stables surrounded the ranches. These were the people with whom Allan spent time since he was often at Les's home, bunking there on regular occasions. They were horse people who understood these animals and were deeply in tune as a result of that bond. Lore explained, "It was the kind of neighborhood where Allan Lane would feel right at home and be treated like just one of the guys." About Les's relationship with Allan, "It is likely he knew Allan long before *Mister Ed.*"

Les trained the horse who ultimately became *the* Mister Ed. Lore explained his home set-up, "Les' barn was a single shed row (one line of stalls with a wide covered aisle) painted white." She elaborated, saying Ed's private trailer, with his name emblazoned across it, stood in front of the barn. There were two horse stalls, including Mister Ed's stand-in, Pumpkin. Les rarely trailered Mister Ed.

Mister Ed was kept in a stall with a duplicate front to the stall used on the TV set. When they had visitors, he showed off, doing his usual onscreen tricks — using the pencil to dial the phone, "talking" into the receiver, and any number of other stunts for which he was known. He loved attention, Lore explained. If a visitor stopped to see Pumpkin first, whose stall was next to Ed's, Mister Ed would grab the top of his stall door, slam it shut, and walk to the back "to pout." This intelligent animal seemed to make a point of standing where he could not be seen. He also would not respond, no matter how hard someone tried to coax him to do so.

Regarding Allan in the environment surrounding Les Hilton's place, Lore said:

> *I knew Allan as a teenager would know an adult. I didn't know him really well; just saw him every so often. If he had a troublesome side, I did not see it. I liked him and don't have any bad memories of him, but then, my focus was horses. You have to know horse people to know what that means in depth, but on the surface, that means we share a common language and focus, so being together is easier than being with others in the movie industry. He was gentle and knowledgeable with the horses, which I admired. Had an easy way of being around them.*

She explained how Allan and Les would interact with each other in close quarters.

> *Allan couldn't have been all that difficult to get along with, or he wouldn't have been Les' friend. I doubt he would have acted badly at Les' because Les would not have tolerated it. Les was a shy man, quiet and laid back. He didn't like being around people who were hard to get along with, although he sometimes had to tolerate them at work. When that happened, he'd usually just walk away and find something important he had to do. He wouldn't have had anything to do with him [Allan] off the set [if Allan had been a problem for him].*

There was a qualifier, however.

> *Of course, nice guys aren't always nice. They can get in bad moods too, and their behavior would reflect that." She compared Allan with Les. "It seemed to me, Allan was the same. Comfortable talking horses, not so comfortable talking about things outside the horse world. Whatever happened on the set was never discussed in front of me though.... Les didn't talk shop at home, although he was glad to talk about horse training and work with horses while I was around. If Les didn't feel kinship with Allan, he would not have invited him to his home. He would have kept it strictly business so I doubt Allan was hard to get along with around Les.*

Lore summed up her perception of Allan Lane's public persona. "Perhaps that impression was given to those who didn't understand cowboys or who tried to push him into places he didn't want to be." Allan and Les were man-buddies. Both into horses, recreational beer, and coffee...a relationship made perfect in a horse stable.

Lore may have been a teenager but she spent a good deal of her spare time amongst these adult males, observing them in the world in which they lived — similar to hers when it came to horses. As a student of human nature, she found them interesting, but more simply, she just enjoyed their company. "Allan was friendly toward me," she explained, "but then being a girl in a 'man's world' often played a part in how I was treated. In those days, girls around horses were rare enough. Girls who were good around horses and intended to make a career out of the horse industry were even rarer."

She appreciated that she was accepted amongst this group. "I was fortunate my friends and I were welcome in their stables and were able to learn a whole lot just hanging around, picking up tips by watching and listening, and counting ourselves especially blessed when we were asked to help with the horses."

Lore offered insight into what could have been part of Allan's issues amongst the general population. She observed:

> *I'm an introvert. Most people think that means I'm shy, but what it really means is my brain processes things different than the brain of an extrovert. I do better alone and without a lot of people to interact with. I love the silence of nature. I get cranky and some would say hard to get along with if I have too much noise and too many people making*

demands on my time and attention. Perhaps Allan was the same. Just
something to think about.

Most in the industry were aware the idea for the *Mister Ed* TV show
for the most part arose out of the popularity and ingenuity that had been
the basis for the *Francis the Talking Mule* movie — an animal Les Hilton
also trained. Parts of Ed's persona were patterned after him. Francis was
sassy and impudent — similar, and not-so-childlike, attributes Mister Ed
also claimed.

There was, however, a more mature foundation for this improbable
show. Walter R. Brooks is best-known as author of the *Freddy The Pig*
books for children. His prolific career spanned from 1915 to the late 1940s.
In addition to his children's output, he wrote nearly 200 adult short stories
for popular magazines.

One of those storylines, in a series of twenty-three installments, told
of the bawdy antics of a talking horse named Mister Ed and his usually
drunk owner, Wilbur Pope. Stories centered on Wilbur's proclivity for
spirits and his friendship with a horse who spoke only to him. They drank
and man-talked in ways not used in polite company, but that mattered
little since they were best buddies. Without Mister Ed's unique qualities,
Wilbur was simply an over-imbibing architect with an odd proclivity for
his horse. Since no one else would believe Mister Ed could talk, nonetheless swear and drink like a sailor, his part in their naughty behavior was
seen only from Wilbur's point of view.

His somewhat unusual output, which combined children's literature
and adult material, gave Brooks a solid foot in both doors, ultimately
proving to be the cornerstone of *Mister Ed*'s success. Brooks's ability to
write equally well for both kids and adults gave his adult work a sassy twist
which appealed to a mixed audience. He died in 1958, and just before his
passing, Arthur Lubin became enamored of his *Mister Ed* stories, licens-
ing the rights as his first foray into television. He had made a success of
Francis the Talking Mule and hoped to take a similar concept farther with
an expanded audience.

There is still confused mystery surrounding how Allan Lane became
the voice, and the persona, of TV's talking horse, *Mister Ed*. The most
often circulated story to date was told by Alan Young, the show's human
star. Alan has always said he was part of a group who went to Les Hilton's
"little tiny wee house" to check out a horse Les owned and trained. Alan
claimed during the visit a voice was heard coming out of Les's home. The

booming tone got their attention with the simple words, "Hey Les, where do ya keep yer coffee?" So, as Alan's story went, executive Al Simon immediately announced, "That's Ed's voice."

Great tale but with problems. First, the horse that would have been the subject of such a visit wasn't named Mister Ed. When the *Mister Ed* horse was purchased, he was called Bamboo Harvester and details of the show's final storyline were still being worked out. Even if Al Simon had spoken of the horse as "Mister Ed" in a figurative manner, Filmways, the studio, purchased Bamboo Harvester from a private owner. They paid $1,500 to secure him precisely for the role of Mister Ed. Why would these men have gone to see if Les's horse fit the bill if the studio had already put out good money with no purpose other than to use him for this TV show?

Issues with this particular story are further confused by the timing of when Alan Young came into the picture. This reveals the biggest complication with his version. The original pilot was filmed in 1958 over about a four-day period. This was during, or right after, Allan Lane was agented by Danny Winkler who is believed to have secured the *Mister Ed* role for him. The pilot did not star Alan Young. Scott McKay had the part.

According to Scott's son, Peter, now an attorney in New York, his father was delighted to be cast as Wilbur Pope in *The Wonderful World of Wilbur Pope*. His agent with William Morris got him the part and everything had gone well, or so he thought. He was so excited, in fact, he called his son at his boarding school soon after he completed the job. None other than Jack Benny had complimented him on his performance, saying he'd been "terrific" in the role.

Yet in as little time as it took to get the pilot in the can, everything about the original effort changed. While it took years to go from the initial efforts to the final success story, cast changes came early on. The title and storyline were tweaked — names and professions for the main character were dumped for updated versions and the starring role was given to the horse rather than the man. Now the show was called simply *Mister Ed*.

Scott McKay and Sandra White were out. Alan Young and barely-known actress Connie Hines were in. Peter McKay said his father received little warning and less explanation for the change. Scott was disappointed. He had been looking forward to adding a solid comedic television role to his resumé. The assumed reason he lost the part, according to Peter, was his dad's image as more of a "leading man." He didn't come off well as a "goofy" type. One review said Alan Young's "bumbling demeanor as Wilbur" fit the character perfectly. Scott would soon marry glamorous movie actress Ann Sheridan, and he had an extensive history on Broadway and dramatic television as well as in movies. The family was led to believe Scott's professional image simply was not right for the part.

Not only were the human actors changed for a new cast but the animal in the initial Scott McKay effort was not the horse who became the famous *Mister Ed*. That first horse had belonged to Les Hilton. Even though Alan Young wasn't yet part of the project, over the years he has

been quoted as giving the official reason why the first horse was not used. He recalled that the first horse was darker and didn't photograph as well on television as Bamboo Harvester, who became Mister Ed. Ed was already eleven years old when he was set on a path to become one of the most famous horses in entertainment history.

No matter which horse they used and the horse's name, if the pilot was shot with a horse, and it was, and if it was shot with a horse who talked, which it was, there had to be a human being behind that horse's voice. Comparing Mister Ed's voice in the Scott McKay pilot with Mister Ed's voice in the Alan Young series, clearly the same individual personified both.

Scott McKay during the same period as the new Mister Ed was being readied for TV...with another actor, Alan Young.

This begs the question: how could the often-circulated story about Alan Young as part of the moment when Allan Lane was "discovered" be true? Alan Young came on the scene after Allan Lane. The book *The Famous Mister Ed, the Unbridled Truth About America's Favorite Talking Horse*, written by Nancy Nalven and published by Warner Books, states, "The voice of the horse in the McCadden pilot [the original] is played by Allan 'Rocky' Lane, the same man who played Ed's voice for Filmways TV." Another source said, "...the only actor who carried over from the pilot to the eventual series was the individual who provided the speaking tones for Mister Ed — former B-Western cowboy star Allan 'Rocky' Lane."

The origination of Allan Lane's roots with *Mister Ed* remained mired in conflict until recently. One person who truly knows how Allan came to be Mister Ed's alter ego is Les Hilton's nephew, Larry Hilton. Through

Lore Kemsley, Larry explained Allan had been living with Les for a year or more in 1958 before *The Wonderful World of Wilbur Pope* went into production. Larry remembered Allan would sit for long periods of time on Les's couch and watch reruns of his old Westerns. He wasn't doing well financially, and Les's kindness offered him a place to hang his hat until he figured out his next move. Larry remembered how Allan would swing "his right leg over the arm of the couch" and it "was completely worn through." Larry thought that was "kind of strange but kind of funny, also."

He explained how Allan got the job as Mister Ed's mouthpiece. "…they didn't have a voice for [the horse.]" One day as a studio boss spoke with Les on the phone, Allan called across the room to Les to put on a pot of coffee. The executive wanted to know whose voice he had just heard in the background. In answer, Les simply put Allan on the phone. As Larry put it, "The rest was history."

This closely resembles Alan Young's tale, though this version puts the facts in a logical timeline with the most logical people involved. As soon as Allan Lane's voice was heard, everyone was sure he was the one for the job. Al Simon approved the selection, saying, "I was looking for a deep voice. Rocky's was right." He commented, "Rocky truly thought he knew how a horse would react."

Allan's innate sense of horsemanship was proven. He did know horses, and the history of his interactions with people proved he knew how a horse would act far better than he had ever been able to pinpoint how a human would behave. His current work status was also right for what was needed on the *Mister Ed* set.

Filmways, supported by their sponsor, Studebaker, required Mister Ed's voiceover actor not be involved in any other full-time project. They wanted the actor to be available to work late hours several days per week. Allan fit that bill. The part didn't ask for much insofar as how well the actor did or did not get along with the other human stars. Allan was, after all, playing the part of the horse, and Mister Ed interacted with no one but Wilbur. Allan had that down also, since he didn't communicate well with most humans. Allan Lane and Alan Young got along well enough. Allan and Les Hilton, the horse trainer, were good friends, so he proved to be the right man for the job.

Lore Kemsley explained how some of the on-set scripting worked.

When they filmed Ed's talking, Allan was on the set. They filmed the scenes with the people first and saved the talking scenes for the last part of the day. That allowed the actors to go home. So the crew, Ed, Les and

Allan were on the set at that time working to get the talking scenes down. Since Les had to time Ed's lip movements, he had to learn the words Allan was going to say. Because that was a time focused on talking, Ed learned that when Allan was there and talking, he'd have to move his lips. Ed was a very smart horse and loved being the center of attention, so this was a natural for him.

When Alan Young was on set, Allan Lane often was not, unless there was a specific reason to have them do the scene together. Lore said, "Not sure if that was by design or just because he wasn't needed. The two were very different. Alan chattered, especially when nervous. Allan Lane didn't."

So it was that only Allan's voice was needed for the end product, not his physical person. By this time, Allan was no longer the movie idol he had once been. As he put it he was "fat and bald." This was more than an exaggeration. Lore Kemsley clarified. "He had thinning hair, not completely bald all the way back but bald on top back from his face. No comb over. Tall man, still trim. No double chin. Wore glasses if I remember right but not around the horses." She thought he might occasionally have worn a hairpiece.

Allan was fully able to fulfill the requirements for this gig — he was between jobs, he would be heard and not seen, he didn't have to deal with many people. And he needed the paycheck.

He did have one peculiar condition before he signed on the dotted line. One might say he couldn't be choosy at this point, but Allan continued to demand that his name not be associated with the voice coming out of the horse's mouth. He didn't explain his reasons publicly but told people close to him that after his long career as a leading man in Westerns, he was embarrassed to become known as the voice of a talking horse. This has been verified as fact. His mother told the family Allan initially refused to have his name listed in the credits.

After all he had done over the years in Hollywood, all the effort he expended honing his craft to be seen as a talented actor — and having more than one starring series to his name — Allan Lane felt it was beneath him to be known as nothing more than a horse's mouthpiece. In a role that did not require his presence on camera, no less. Not only was he embarrassed but he was also sad over the direction his career had taken. Little did he know what the role would do for his legacy.

The Powers That Be granted him his wish without argument. They did so to the point, in fact, that after time had passed and the show gained an eager audience, Allan changed his tune. He asked to have his name added as "voice of Mister Ed." He wanted to receive credit for his work.

By then, Mister Ed had become a personality unto himself. He was real in the eyes of the most important viewers. Executives felt that to unmask the horse and admit a man was behind the horse's voice would ruin the mystique which had enveloped the show to everyone's absolute amazement. Including, and espe-cially, Allan. The most important viewers were children, the pre-dominant consumers of the show as well as the target audience. They saw Mister Ed as larger-than-life and very real. To do anything to endanger that success was not an option.

Allan's request was flatly denied. He was told at this stage it was not possible to give him his public due. He was told to keep his part in the show a secret, and if he did, he would get a sizeable raise as a reward for his compromise. This was the next-best-thing and, for his wallet, probably a better choice. So Allan Lane remained the never-revealed comedic straight man to a horse, and Alan Young's top-of-

Allan Lane in a mid-1960s headshot. PHOTO COURTESY RICK FREUDENTHAL

the-line funny, bumbling human star. Allan was true to his word. He never breathed a public world to anyone, and the show went merrily on.

A magical quality enveloped every aspect of this unique horse. Adults enjoyed the show almost as much as kids, though not for the same reasons. As popularity grew, not only were kids delighted to know there was at least one talking horse in the world — and producers were not about to disap-point them — but there was much chatter around *how* the horse talked.

This may have been discussed mostly between adults when the kids weren't around. Interest in how the horse's mouth moved in the right pattern, and at the exact moment to respond to Wilbur's conversation, made for excellent public relations fodder. Filmways executives knew they had a goldmine in the guise of this amazing horse. That there was a human attached, standing invisibly on the sidelines, would never be revealed. Never. Neither would the manner in which the horse's mouth moved be explained. End of discussion.

During the show's tenure and for so many years afterward, the trick was steeped in controversy. Alan Young was often asked in interviews, and he would always sidestep the question, until one day he decided to play with the press. Finally, he would tell the world the truth. Or the truth as he wanted to tell it. Mister Ed could talk because of…peanut butter placed strategically under his lips. The peanut butter supposedly forced the horse to move his lips, and, in turn, corresponded with scripted conversation. This revelation received so much traction it became the accepted truth.

Peanut butter, however, never had a single thing to do with these mechanics. Lore Kemsley, in recent years, finally spilled the beans. She explained, "Alan Young was the source of a lot of misinformation about Ed…Alan claimed they used peanut butter…which entirely negated Les' ingenuity and hard work as a trainer. That was believed until a few years ago when I told the world how it was really done…I figured neither Les nor the studio would care at this late date."

Lore detailed how a light fishing line situated inside Ed's mouth in just the needed spots would get the horse's lips to open and shut at the right time. That was connected to a tether and Les Hilton was off screen holding the end of the tether. Ed learned quickly how Allan Lane's presence on the set, though out of Ed's line of vision, meant he was expected to respond when he heard Allan's voice. This translated into the conversations between Ed and Wilbur.

Allan wasn't often physically on the set and Mister Ed was a talented and intuitive horse. When Allan arrived late in the afternoon to do his bit after all the other in-person work had been completed for the day, the process operated seamlessly to create the illusion of a talking horse. Les trained Mister Ed, and they both trusted Allan, one of the key points in making the process work so well.

Mister Ed knew Allan's voice — his cadences and inflections — and understood if he heard that voice, they were expected to act as a team. Ed was ready to do his job at the same time Allan did his job. Ed and Allan had known each other informally for some time as well as during their time together on the set. Ed would have heard and come to recognize Allan, and his voice, from the time Allan had spent at Les's home. Their familiarity allowed them to play well together.

In Thornton and Rothel's book, David Rothel offered parts of an interview he did with Ron Honthaner, a sound effects editor during the last year of the show's production. Honthaner explained how he "split off Lane's sound tracks because we always did some fussing with the horse's dialogue to make it a little different." He went on to acknowledge how Allan's voice was modified in the final product to "make it a little deeper." They used filters on the sound as the program was being shot.

Honthaner explained that "the trainer," Les Hilton, and Allan were "so in sync on the dialogue" that little had to be done with sound effects. "Lane's voice," he went on, "and the trainer's manipulation of the horse's mouth were right on target."

CHAPTER TWENTY-ONE

A Horse is a Horse...
Or is He a Man?

As time went on and Allan became more comfortable with his role, he sometimes ad-libbed if he felt the dialogue warranted added creativity. If Mister Ed was in a precarious physical position, Allan might groan along with his conversation. Or if Mister Ed was supposed to have a cold, Allan made his voice sound more nasal to accommodate the ailment.

This brought about an interesting point in how "health reports" were listed for each week of work. Nancy Nalven's book explained how having a man behind that voice created the need for the dual situations: Mister Ed's scripted health, and Allan's actual health. There were episodes, if one listened closely, where Mister Ed's voice may have sounded under the weather. This wasn't because Mister Ed, the horse, was ill but because Allan had been. If Mister Ed was supposed to be sick in the script, the problem was nonexistent since Allan could easily exaggerate his voice to sound as if he had a cold.

A humorous summation of how man and horse fit so well together was found in Nalven's book in the section titled, "Typical Mister Ed Dynamics." A bit of dialogue during the episode, "Be Kind to Humans," had Ed stating, "It was such a nice day, I thought I'd go down to the stables, rent me a man and go riding." The book continued, "This is whimsical outrageous stuff! Yet Rocky Lane's delivery of Ed's voice is so convincing that we don't doubt the palomino for a second."

This was the root of success behind the show's bottom line. No one ever doubted the infusion of humanity into this horse. Allan Lane was born to play Mister Ed. Alan Young and, to a lesser degree, Connie Hines have been credited over the years for the show's success, yet there would have been no Mister Ed, as he became known, without that deep and gravelly, laconic voice breathing Mister Ed into life on the screen. Other actors had tried out for the part but none fit. Show executives thought of replacing Allan between the pilot and the series. He was never replaced, though, because no one else could replicate the sound of Allan's voice.

This horse's voice, Allan Lane as Mister Ed, was much the same voice that had brought to life a version of Red Ryder, and Rocky Lane himself. These characters became synonymous with, and more often than not over-

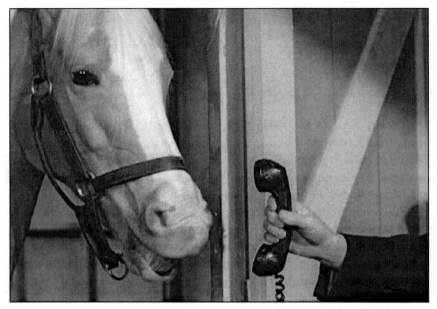

Mister Ed uses the telephone with the help of his good friend, Wilbur.

rode, Allan's stage name, and certainly his birth name. They also in many ways overrode him as an actor and as a man.

What is rarely discussed in this odd marriage of horse, man, and man, is the relationship that had to develop between Alan Young and Allan Lane for the persona of *Mister Ed* to be even remotely believable. These two actors needed to be simpatico as they related to their shared horse, and they absolutely had to anticipate each other's cues.

Alan Young verified this. He said he got along well with Allan. "He was very quiet," Alan Young remembered. "A good guy. Les Hilton respected him." This seemed important to Alan Young. He also recalled how Allan helped him learn to ride a horse. Allan told him to "keep heels down and relax." The advice served him well in his work as Mister Ed's best friend.

David Rothel's interview with Ron Honthaner gave insight into how Alan Young and Allan worked together. Honthaner told David, "It wasn't just Alan Young doing his dialogue and then cutting to the horse...Allan Lane was giving a performance with Alan Young. They were doing scenes together with the horse. These were two performers going at it..."

They were involved in a complicated process. One of them, Alan Young, was on the screen the entire time, visible, and literally responding to a camera.

The other, Allan Lane, was never seen on screen at any point in the history of the show. As far as the show was concerned, he didn't exist. Still, he was unquestionably there, responding to how the horse followed Alan Young's cue, and Les Hilton's direction behind the scenes and the scripts' comedic and emotional overtones. Allan Lane had to follow a script and play the part of the horse — vocally and psychologically — but he had to play off Alan Young with his every vocal move to achieve that over-riding goal.

Not an easy task. A heavy dose of talent was required on Allan's part to simultaneously be in synchronization with both man and beast, to seemingly move effortlessly between the two well enough to create the believability which became the show's, and the animal's, hallmark. Alan Young commented once, "I never thought of Rocky Lane off camera." Alan Young always felt as if he played off another actor, but he admitted he often forgot that other actor was a man, not a horse.

It is important to again note how Allan knew Mister Ed off screen as well as when the cameras rolled. Their relationship did not end when the director yelled, "Cut!" Allan loved being around his co-worker, and horse and man developed an oddly intimate interaction. His ability to under-stand Ed would have been hard to replicate with any other actor. Les Hilton owned Mister Ed's double, Pumpkin, and he kept Mister Ed in his stables. Allan would often visit not only the owner but also the horses, even after he had gotten back on his feet financially...thanks to the suc-cess of *Mister Ed*.

Lore explained that while Mister Ed's double was at times credited as "Punkin," the correct spelling was most likely the formal version. Les, who had a heavy Oklahoma drawl, had purchased Pumpkin from Audie Murphy when Pumpkin was only three years old. The horse had never been trained. Whenever Les spoke of or to Pumpkin, it came out sound-ing like the second "p" wasn't there.

"Pumpkin was a quarter horse but looked remarkably like Ed, with the lone exception of a palomino spot in the middle of his white blaze on the forehead," Lore wrote. "This spot was covered with white makeup made especially for horses when he worked as Ed's replacement." He was often used instead of Mister Ed for personal appearances — the Hollywood Christmas Parade, for example. Lore surmised, "This may have been per the orders of the insurance company. Les used to marvel that a horse had more insurance than he did, a million dollars if I remember right."

She also mentioned that the horse representing Mister Ed's mother in the show was a palomino gelding named Nicker. She and her family owned Nicker who was quite old, but Les thought he was perfect for the role. Les's horse sense obviously won out yet again. No one ever suspected Mister Ed's mom wasn't a "mom" after all.

While cast and crew of course knew Allan was on the set when it was his time to work, and they were aware of what role he played in the show's success, the dynamics which had been created to get the show to the point where it was a ratings winner gave way to an almost forgotten status for the man Allan Lane. The old adage, "Out of sight, out of mind" might have been his personal tagline while he was a part of the *Mister Ed* show. He became so totally invisible to many in the *Mister Ed* executive offices that he was literally often forgotten when it came time to hand out benefits.

While the other actors had dressing rooms, Allan did not. While the other actors had parking spaces, Allan did not. While the other actors received the visible perks of being stars of the show, Allan did not. Some of this may have been his own doing, as a result of his loner personality, and as time went on, his agitation over not being able to publicly claim his success. Yet a good deal of his non-entity status evolved as a by-product of Allan doing his job so well that he made himself invisible. When he was finally remembered, say, for a cast get-together, the "mistake" would be rectified. Yet if there was any press involved, Allan was intentionally left out so the secret would not be revealed. His contract specified he must remain anonymous whenever media might get wind of his part in the show.

Years later, according to Nalven's book, Connie Hines was awed over Allan's performance. She said, "His character merged so much with the horse…. He was so great at his job. He became one with that horse." She was the one who spoke of the lack of amenities Allan received. Ultimately, Allan did at least get a parking space but it was across the street from the Filmways studio in the Eastman Kodak parking lot. Not exactly the best way to make him feel like part of the crew.

Over the many years of Allan's career and interactions with his co-stars and producing executives, much was made of his lackluster sense of humor. This is ironic when compared against his stint as Mister Ed's voice. The show would have not had the ratings it did if the horse's conversation hadn't had such a humorous delivery. The show would not have enjoyed the tenure it had if the horse was not himself a true comedian.

While Allan didn't write his lines, he knew he had to infuse those lines with every inch of humanity and funniness. Though few people, if any, ever discussed Allan's comedic ability, his family knew he had that in him. When he was comfortable with the people around him, he was more than capable of letting loose and being genuinely amusing. "He joked around a lot," Tom Costello remembered.

Allan had done well in his earlier years in comedic roles, in the days when he was young and handsome and seen onscreen as an up-and-coming leading man. That he could turn around all these years later and go behind the scenes to recreate his ability as a funnyman should not have surprised anyone who knew of his quiet off-beat sense of humor. As the voice of Mister Ed, Allan interacted only with a horse, a rather funny situation unto itself.

Most of the conversational content of what the show, *Mister Ed*, delivered over the years was in the guise of a talking horse interacting with just one man. The chatter was, for those who knew Allan well in his personal life, at times comparable to events which occurred in his own life. As the voice of Mister Ed, some of the lines Allan delivered were infused with quirky words and phrases from his personal world.

Allan's additions to the script became accepted more and more as time went on and producers grew to believe in his ability to *be* Mister Ed. Ultimately, executives realized how good a match the Mister Ed characterization was with the man who voiced him. Allan was able to offer a distinctive angle from which the writers could elaborate with every episode.

Some of the horse's dialogue delivery was even recognized by his nephew Tom Costello. Vocal inflections Allan used in conversation with his mother often found their way into Mister Ed's jargon, to the delight of his family. There were instances of modified dialogue always recognized by family members, and delivered in the same way Allan would speak them when he was at home. He used his part in *Mister Ed* as a salute to his dear mother.

CHAPTER TWENTY-TWO

Allan Lane's Well-Kept Secret — He Wanted To Be Liked

Rumors of Allan's generosity and kindness away from the cameras, particularly where children were involved, could not have been better illustrated than with a story told by Tad Dunn. Allan's undercover charity work didn't stop after he was no longer seen regularly on the screen. In fact, such instances may have increased. Tad's father, T. W. "Wally" Dunn, was a well-known and respected thoroughbred racehorse breeder as well as a good friend of Allan's. Tad was about ten years old when *Mister Ed* came to the small screen, and he remembered well Allan's visits to his home. As with many of Allan's other friends in his later years, he and Wally became acquainted at the track.

During one visit to his home, Allan brought Tad a present: a *Mister Ed* talking puppet made by the Mattel Corporation. These toys were generally sold for $6.88 and loved by young children. They were also the latest in the line of Allan's never-public product endorsements. Though the public in general didn't know Allan "Rocky" Lane was the voice of *Mister Ed*, most of those close to him were aware and they kept his secret. Allan had access to the many products that arose from the show's success. He also received royalties.

As Tad related, "He showed up at our house one Christmas Day in his huge royal blue Cadillac, with the trunk and back seat loaded with puppets. He told me, 'C'mon Tad. Let's go find some poor kids around town and give 'em a surprise they won't forget.' He didn't have to ask me twice… That's the kind of guy he was."

There are historical accounts which indicate that Allan was a destitute recluse in what would become his final years. Those who knew him well argue this point. He did live alone in a small apartment on a modest income.

269

Yet the idea he had no money at all was not true. Endorsement deals made in his name or, more accurately, his names over the years, continued to bring in income. There had been comic books and products from *Red Ryder* as well as from *Rocky Lane*. Not to mention the *Mister Ed* products from which he continued to make money. The comics had been a particularly big seller. His movies still played and any time one of his pictures hit the air, he received small residuals.

Left: *The* Mister Ed *puppet loved by many children.* Right: *Allan "Rocky" Lane iron-on posse decal.*

Much had been made over Rocky's horse, Black Jack, during the heyday of the serial itself, particularly the insurance Allan kept on the horse as well as how much money he spent on him. The horse worked hard and earned all the perks afforded him. Black Jack even had his own comic series in the mid-1950s, under his name and a smaller-type banner which read: "Rocky Lane's Black Jack." This was a working animal in every sense of the term, and even Black Jack added additional money to Allan's pocket in his retirement years.

Under the "Rocky Lane" moniker, Allan had endorsed and received enumeration for any number of products. For example, in the back of comic books in 1949 — Carnation Company's fiftieth anniversary — and in 1950, were ads for the "Rocky Lane Posse." Kids could wear a Posse shoulder patch as they happily drank Rocky's "official" Carnation chocolate-flavored malted milk. His picture was emblazoned across the middle of these full-page ads.

"It's a beauty!" he reportedly told kids who couldn't wait to wear that patch on their clothes, applied by Mom with a "magic new hot iron method." Rocky's image announced, "It tells at a glance you're a pal of mine." The milk endorsement came at the end, with his hearty words, "And, say, pardner, we hard-ridin' posse members got to have plenty of energy. So fuel up regularly with my favorite…Carnation Malted Milk…"

At the same time, kids could get six comic books for only ten cents or a *Rocky Lane* bandana for a quarter if they sent along one Carnation Malted Milk label. The kids would get their moms to send this to "Rocky Lane, c/o Carnation Malted Milk" at a post office box address

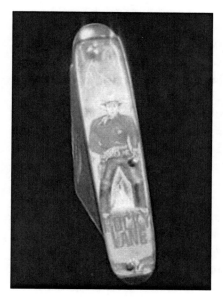 

Left: *Rocky Lane pocket knife.* Right: *"Member Allan 'Rocky' Lane Posse" emblazoned at the bottom of a full-pin picture of Rocky and his gun.*

in Hollywood. The children would undoubtedly believe Rocky dutifully picked up those envelopes each day and in return, personally sent them their comic books or bandanas. In truth, Allan's accountant ensured he got his cut from these smartly created advertising packages put together by savvy promotional folks.

Pocket knives, a favorite of adolescent boys of the mid-century, were created with Rocky's image on them — as well as many other cowboy and action stars of the period. Made in full color, these knives were mass produced and marketed, created for large audiences of young males who would find the western genre just their cup of tea for a full Saturday afternoon's entertainment. Believing they could be as brave as Rocky Lane or Lash LaRue or any of their other heroes, they would badger their parents mercilessly until Mom or Dad bought them their own pocket knife with their heroes' image on the front. In turn, Allan and all the others would get a cut from each sale.

In the early 1950s, not long before the *Rocky Lane* series ended, Allan's face was put on ice cream Dixie cup lids that announced, "Save any 12 Dixie picture lids for a color picture of me." These treats were served up around the country in many family run ice cream parlors, with the ice cream packed at the same plant and the advertisement standard no matter where it was sold. Kids enjoyed both the treat and color pictures of their favorite stars, which they wrote in for after they were sugared-up and well-satiated.

All of these items, along with cigarette and gum cards, small metal pins with images, postcards, trading cards, and even gambling chips as well as assorted other promotional pieces, were part of Allan's sideline business efforts in the 1940s. This was after his rise to visibility truly began with his jump into *Red Ryder*, through his time as *Rocky Lane,* and well into the 1950s. A period just shy of about ten years accounted for his major stardom, and during that time he accrued a considerable amount of wealth and visibility. His audience was predominantly the adolescent male, and some young girls who found Rocky exciting. All of them were junior consumers who would besiege their parents until they got exactly what they wanted. In turn, the residuals helped support Allan and his family, as well as Allan's overwhelming passion for the horses.

Once *Mister Ed* had moved into Allan's rear view mirror, he effectively retired for good from the entertainment industry. He was nowhere near wealthy anymore but he was comfortable, and he'd had enough of movies and television. His surprisingly successful stint as a talking horse had been a solid gig which gave him a brand new, decent source of income. Most of that money was poured almost exclusively into his addiction: horses.

Detractors made disparaging comments about how irresponsible he was with his money once it started to come in again during and after his work on *Mister Ed.* Allan no longer owned a home, and he had little in the way of personal property. Almost everything he had earned as the voice of *Mister Ed* went, right off the bat, into a horse he purchased soon after he felt secure in his new position. During the show's tenure, whenever Allan wasn't working, he was tending to that horse, named King Blenheim.

He spent nearly all his free time preparing Blenheim for the track, and with people involved in and around the horse racing industry. By the mid-to-late 1960s, Allan was consumed by the racing world, and would spend most of his days at the track betting on the horses, or at home preparing betting sheets for the next time he went to the track. When he wasn't doing that, he worked with King Blenheim in anticipation of his next race.

Allan wasn't seen much in family situations anymore. His nieces and nephews were by this time young adults. They were older and building their own homes. He dedicated his family time most often to his mother rather than to extended relatives.

A good bit was written about how Allan was zealous about the races and betting in his later years, while in reality he had been doing this for years. Owning, training, and racing horses had been part of his life for no less than ten years, and likely many more. Allan had owned horses in the 1940s. He trained his own race horses from the early to mid-fifties under the business name of Allan Lane, and he likely placed bets as a sport starting in the late 1930s. In the mid-1960s, Allan was a partner in the Longlane Stable along with Howard Long, about ten years Allan's senior and the officially recognized trainer of King Blenheim. Allan had known Howard as far back as 1956.

An interesting aside…Howard Long's first stakes winner came in 1955 with a horse named Trigonometry, a word quite similar to *Trigger-Nometry*, the title of the book Allan was so enamored with just six or seven years before while he still did time in the saddles in front of a camera. How many years Allan had known Long isn't certain. Whether this was a coincidence or not…again unknown.

King Blenheim, a horse with an extensive pedigree going back no less than five generations of regal racehorses, was the one known horse in the spotlight for Allan during this period. From 1963 to 1966, at least, he was ridden for Allan by various jockeys.

On Saturday October 23, 1965, Blenheim won a race almost by default. One newspaper article declared, "Tanforan Meet Ends On Unforgettable Note." The race was held at Bay Meadows in San Mateo but was named after the race track. The Tanforan Race Track had burned to the ground the year before. King Blenheim's jockey was Roy Yaka and this race may have been the most memorable of Yaka's entire career.

He was said to be "in the right place at the right time." He wasn't the original jockey intended for that horse and that race. The job had been given to James Cassity who broke a collarbone as he worked another horse the day before. The horse dropped dead of a heart attack and threw Cassity, making him no longer available for the race.

Yaka was brought in at the last minute as a substitute. As the gates swung open, one of the other horses, Switchback, was expected to take the win, and he easily had the lead. He'd already won two straight stakes and was "accorded much public support." Unexpectedly, he pitched forward and his feet buckled under him. His jockey sprawled head first into the turf. Now without a rider, Switchback got up and took off down the field on his own steam.

The other jockeys, including Roy Yaka, continued around the track with no way of knowing what might happen next. Switchback was a wild card and had the potential to cause catastrophic results as he ran out of control. He moved without direction between the other horses. Their jockeys tried to keep their attention on the race while looking from side to side to determine where Switchback might be at any moment.

Once on the homestretch, Switchback came up in line with the two leading horses, one of which was King Blenheim. Switchback bumped Blenheim and Roy Yaka was forced to bring Blenheim to the outside, battling with Switchback, the riderless horse, all the way to the finish line.

When the chaos was finally all said and done, photos indicated Switchback technically won the race, three quarters of a length in the lead. King Blenheim came in second. However, Switchback was disqualified due to the circumstances and Allan's horse was declared the winner, going home with over $19,000 of the $34,050 purse. Allan had won a race in 1956 at the original Tanforan, during a time when he actively trained and raced multiple horses. This event was much more dramatic from start to finish, and his win was hard won.

King Blenheim proved to be an ongoing moneymaker for Allan, not always a clear-cut winner but regularly bringing in a decent purse. In March of the following year, a race at Golden Gate Fields in Berkeley had the horse closing in on the finish line just before another, Sir Bolco, "prevailed by a neck," edging out Allan's chance at a win. Still, he went home with a piece of the pie and a second place standing.

King Blenheim raced again at the same track the following month. Hawaiian-born Roy Yaka was usually the jockey when Allan's horse was on the track. Yaka revealed in a later interview that since he was a young boy he'd had "a burning desire to be a cowboy." Thirty or so years younger than Allan, maybe he lived his cowboy dreams vicariously through the years he rode Allan's horse.

Allan knew most everyone in the close-knit racing industry, socializing at restaurants such as Talk o' The Town in Pasadena, owned by ex-jockey Ralph Neves and Monty Levine, and Monty's Steak House in Encino. Another favorite place was Jerry Wilson's El Gordo on Las Tunas in San Gabriel. El Gordo advertised with a large colorful neon sign atop the restaurant, enticing patrons with their "beeg theek steaks" and Mexican food.

Allan and Wilson were "real friendly." Wilson was a horse owner himself who catered to the race track crowd.

In these later years Allan had an active social calendar, though not with the insider Hollywood crowd. Instead, he kept company with people in the horse world, those who shared similar interests and understood his intense connection with racing and the animals themselves. He had been in the midst of this horse-related environment most of his adult life, with a close circle of compatriots before, during, and after his Les Hilton cowboy ranch days. Allan had always been able to pick up with folks who worked and played in different factions of the horse industry.

One of his best friends in his post-*Mister Ed* days was a man named Bill "Pete" Peterson. Pete was a friend of Allan's recent business partner, Howard Long, and met Allan through him. Pete, who trained horses, and Allan, "Rocky" to him, regularly enjoyed each other's company, and Pete was there for Allan in his last days. He said the racing community was a tight-knit group and many of them ran around together during and after the races.

Another good friend was Allan's step-brother, Justin. Their close association had held strong for over ten years. Nephew Tom Costello stated plainly Uncle Harry "fed horses lots of his money." So did Uncle Justin and the two men would often satisfy their habit together, hanging out at Santa Anita, socializing and enjoying the races. Tom said Allan was a "riding high in April, shot down in May" sort of man. When he had it, he enjoyed it. When he didn't, he hibernated.

Pete added insight into Allan's love of the track and the stables. "Training horses wasn't cheap," Pete flatly stated. He knew Allan had already gone through a great deal of the money he made during his movie heyday. Despite the expense of Allan's horse habit, Pete avowed his friend always paid his bills. He was never late on payments and was generous with those around him. Pete recalled how kind Allan had been to other owners, trainers, and even the groomsmen. He would come out to the stables in the mornings and greet everyone with whom he came in contact. There were in-depth conversations every day, and Pete never knew him to be rude or unkind.

Yet others in the same community said Allan could be short-tempered, and he would, at times, easily misunderstand what was said to him. When he finally picked up on the gist of the conversation, he backed down and all was well.

Despite Allan's close friendship with Pete, Pete was never invited to his buddy's home. In fact, Pete had no idea where Rocky lived. This was the late 1960s, and Allan had a small, nondescript apartment. He wasn't proud of his residence. He hung his hat there, and that was about all. Occasionally he ate a tasteless meal there. At night he would figure out his bets for his visit to the track the next day. The apartment was a place to keep his clothes and his racing sheets — nothing more. He left in the mornings and, when he had to, he went back there at night.

Brother Justin Costello's gravesite.

Allan still had a small amount of entertainment money coming in. In 1966, an edited-for-TV version of 1944's *Tiger Woman* — cut down to 100 minutes to fit a television schedule — was released in syndication as *Jungle Gold* (1966) through an entity known as Century 66. They were a result of the now-defunct Republic Pictures and existed almost exclusively to release a series of twenty-six made-for-TV versions of old Republic serials. The intent was to cash in on the popularity of the *Batman* (1966) series, which had proven to be a hot commodity.

Though there was no fanfare or notable promotion of Allan "Rocky" Lane's name and movie history as part of this release, at this point in his life Allan was more than happy with the money added to his pocket and the opportunity that afforded him to spend more time, and more money, at the tracks.

*Allan's California Horse Racing Board ID card, stamped 1972,
the year before he died.* PHOTO COURTESY THE COSTELLO
FAMILY COLLECTION

CHAPTER TWENTY-THREE

The End

Allan found out he was seriously ill late in September of 1973. He had just turned sixty-four. He hadn't been feeling well for some time and finally took himself off to the doctor. His malady could have assaulted him with any number of symptoms including pain in his abdomen — his spleen would have been enlarged. Fatigue likely disrupted his regular daily schedule as a result of anemia, shortness of breath, and an overall increasing bone pain. He might have had infections initially not appearing as life-threatening but would become exactly that. After a series of tests, predominantly blood tests, the terrible news was delivered to him: Allan had cancer of the bone marrow. Myelofibrosis was the official ugly diagnosis.

His mother was distraught and could not be consoled. Cancer had already killed her daughter. Now her only living child, her beloved son, was in the throes of a related monster. She had not known Allan was as sick as he was. No one had known. Tom Costello said he and the rest of the kids learned of the severity of Allan's illness only as it related to their grandmother's increasing grief. They visited her every week or so, and it wasn't until they saw her in such emotional turmoil, and were told the reason behind her anguish that they understood the gravity of Uncle Harry's condition. He had chosen to keep everything to himself until he was no longer able to do so.

Due to the nature of his illness, considered to be a chronic leukemia, he had been able to live with the symptoms for a time. Even then, Myelofibrosis was known to usually develop slowly and was for the most part treatable, for awhile at least. After a period of time, as his normal blood cells were no longer being properly produced and his bone marrow grew more and more involved, his symptoms became pronounced, and he could not ignore or hide his condition.

Allan lived alone in his rented modest apartment at 941 Osage Avenue — a less-than-ten-year-old complex. Allan fast got to the point where he was completely unable to take care of himself. About the second week in October he was forced to give up his apartment and go into the Motion Picture & Television Hospital. Having years before done a good amount of charity work for the Motion Picture Fund, Allan Lane never had a clue he would one day benefit from the efforts he and his co-workers had expended.

A current-day view of Allan's last apartment.

Pete Peterson and his wife visited Allan in the hospital. They found him hallucinating, ranting about all the people who were in his room, even though there was no one there but the three of them. Allan was certain, Pete said, these people wanted to listen in on their conversation, and Allan was wildly against that. The brief time Pete and his wife spent with Allan deeply upset him, and he couldn't bring himself to go back. He was sad to see his friend in such a condition. He wasn't sure Allan recognized him even though Pete had seen Allan only about a month earlier. He seemed fine then, though he probably had already begun to show minimal signs of his ailment — signs Allan chose to not share.

Allan's attending doctor was Morris B. Daitch, who took care of him for his few-weeks hospital stay. Dr. Daitch was in to see him on Friday, October 26. While Allan was not in good condition, he was minimally responsive. There was no indication his physician expected imminent danger.

No more than eighteen hours lapsed between the time the doctor last saw Allan and when he passed away at 8:45 p.m. on Saturday, October 27, 1973.

Allan probably had known from the point his diagnosis was received that he didn't have a lot of time left on the earth. His personal affairs were suspiciously well-organized, to the point of being lined up and

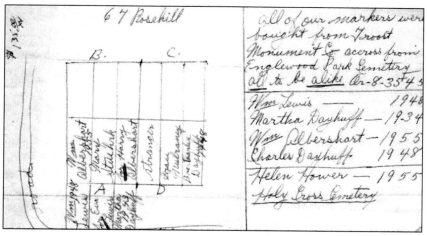

Anne Costello's handwritten burial instructions for the family. PHOTO COURTESY THE COSTELLO FAMILY COLLECTION

ready to be put into play at the time of his death. Information about his passing was soon thereafter reported to the state of California, not by his mother or any other family member but by his personal accountant, Charles Franklin. Franklin had every last little detail of Allan's life, and death, fully in order. When the time arrived, Franklin took care of the business side of the post-mortem arrangements, per Allan's instructions. His mother organized his funeral. Everything except for one major detail.

Franklin called Pete Peterson and asked him to do Allan's eulogy. Pete was honored. He worked hard to ensure his words expressed how he felt about his friend, and what he believed Allan "Rocky" Lane had thought of the world around him.

Allan Lane, known to his family as Harry Leonard Albershart, and to close friends simply as Rocky, was dead. He was put to rest on Halloween in a well-groomed, peaceful family plot in Inglewood Park Cemetery, not far from the racetrack he had so often frequented. Buried nearby was his sister; his in-life estranged father; his grandmother, Martha Dayhuff; his uncle, Charles Dayhuff; Uncle Billy Lewis and Aunt Eva; and two family friends — Mary Stuehrk and Grace Mulraney.

The two lady friends had been close to Allan's mother and she had personally made Mary Stuehrk's arrangements. The last people to be buried in that location were Bill Albershart and Helen, both in 1955. An early rendition of who belonged in which plot was painstakingly written out longhand by Anne. Her son's spot was designated "for Harry Albershart."

Pete Peterson understood Allan in ways most others never had. Despite the age difference between them, they shared a close association for nearly a decade. When Charles Franklin asked him to speak at Allan's memorial, Pete was surprised but willing to take on the task. He spent the days between Allan's death and the burial working on exactly what he wanted to say about his friend.

Pete arrived shortly before the ceremony was set to start. He found a number of Allan's friends there, as well as his mother, all surrounding the casket next to the newly prepared upended ground. This debunks the story previously told, and widely circulated, claiming there were only a few people in attendance. Franklin pulled Pete aside and told him it was time for him to speak his part. Considering Anne's staunch faith, it was surprising there was no minister or priest — no religious service whatsoever. Pete suddenly realized he was meant to speak in place of the minister. This added more weight to his self-written eulogy and he was informed that once he said his piece, the burial would take place.

Pete's tribute was a touching, heartfelt insight into a complicated man who had been hard to know — an honest ending to the life of a difficult individual. Pete choked up more than once as he spoke his tribute, finding it hard to continue each time. But after a few moments, he cleared his throat and went on.

Allan "Rocky" Lane was properly sent riding off into the sunset with the words of his friend, Bill "Pete" Peterson, ringing in the ears of all who stood at the gravesite that day.

*Final resting place for Harry L. Albershart, aka Allan Lane, with a most
fitting tribute from his best friend, his mother, who called him her "beloved son."*

Afterword

Dear Heavenly Father:
Someone's on their way to see you
He'll be walking tall and straight,
But if no one's there to meet him
He might pass up Heaven's gate.
He will probably have a sweater on
And he'll have on a hat,
Please step out and bid him welcome
With a handshake — he'd like that.
You'll find his grip is firm and sure,
The pressure of his hand
Will tell you of the warmth within —
He was that kind of man,
He believed in people — loved them
But he held back, with reserve
And put up a shield to Life, itself,
If it should throw a curve.
If there ever was a self-made man
It had to be this one.
Wealth or praise meant little —
Wanted more — a job well done.
He worked hard — knew lean and meager times
Had tightened up his belt.
Had compassion for less fortunates,
He knew, Lord, how it felt.
But when fortune took him by the hand
And lights began to glow,
It didn't make much difference
To this man — he seemed to know

285

That tinsel dulls and tarnishes
And glitter fades away —
But the light that shines within a man
Is always there to stay.
He had his fame and fortune,
But he never missed his stride.
He kept himself intact
It never reached the man inside.
Loved his country with a passion
He was loyal and was true.
He felt that he should have respect
And see his homeland through
Good and bad times — even if he felt
There might have been a wrong.
"It's men like him, with faith,
Who've kept our Nation free and strong."
He had no time for fol-de-rols
Frivolities and such —
But tradition, beauty, tenderness
Were things he treasured much.
He was a loner, Father —
Was afraid of grips and ties
But he was a family man at heart —
I've seen it in his eyes.
And on very rare occasions
When his guard slipped down a minute
You knew he longed for family life
And all the love that's in it.
He loved his Mother as a Mother,
The same as other men
But he felt a special privilege
That she also was his friend.
He was quite opinionated
I have heard him argue long
But I've heard him too, apologize —
When he found he was wrong.
That's about all, Heavenly Father —
Just be sure you're there to meet him —
I'm sure he'll be so pleased to know
You took the time to greet him.

There's something that he's going to miss though
Father — from down here —
Could you maybe part the white clouds
In the springtime of the year
And let him see the mares and foals
All running with abandon —
His horses were a part of him —
He didn't choose at random,
But loved to study bloodlines,
Conformation — watch them grown.
With his sixth sense, he often knew
Who'd Win — and Place — and Show.
Please let him watch the races —
He'd deny it from the start
But when he watched them running —
He was watching with his heart.
And I'm sure there's folks who'll hear
"THE FLAG IS UP" — and look on high —
To see if "Rocky's" watching —
From his box — up in the sky.

WILLIAM "BILL" OR "PETE" PETERSON, OCTOBER 31, 1973,
IN HONOR OF ALLAN "ROCKY" LANE
(transcribed exactly as originally written)

Film, Television, and Theater Credits

Film

1961: *Posse from Hell*...Burl Hogan
1960: *Hell Bent for Leather*...Kelsey
1958: *The Saga of Hemp Brown*...Sheriff
1953: *El Paso Stampede*...Rocky Lane *(starring role)*
1953: *Bandits of the West*...Marshal Rocky Lane *(starring role)*
1953: *Savage Frontier*...U.S. Marshal Rocky Lane *(starring role)*
1953: *Marshal of Cedar Rock*...Marshal Rocky Lane *(starring role)*
1952: *Desperadoes' Outpost*...Rocky Lane *(starring role)*
1952: *Thundering Caravans*...U.S. Marshal Rocky Lane *(starring role)*
1952: *Black Hills Ambush*...Rocky Lane *(starring role)*
1952: *Leadville Gunslinger*...U. S. Marshal Rocky Lane *(starring role)*
1952: *Captive of Billy the Kid*...Marshal Rocky Lane *(starring role)*
1951: *Desert of Lost Men*...Rocky Lane *(starring role)*
1951:*Fort Dodge Stampede*...Deputy Sheriff Rocky Lane *(starring role)*
1951:*Wells Fargo Gunmaster*...Rocky Lane *(starring role)*
1951: *Night Riders of Montana*...Rocky Lane *(starring role)*
1951: *Rough Riders of Durango*...Rocky Lane *(starring role)*
1950: *Trail of Robin Hood*...Rocky Lane *(starring role)*
1950: *Rustlers on Horseback*...Marshal Rocky Lane *(starring role)*
1950: *Frisco Tornado*...Marshal Rocky Lane *(starring role)*
1950: *Vigilante Hideout*...Rocky Lane *(starring role)*
1950: *Covered Wagon Raid*...Rocky Lane *(starring role)*
1950: *Salt Lake Raiders*...Marshal Rocky Lane *(starring role)*
1950: *Code of the Silver Sage*...Lieutenant Rocky Lane *(starring role)*
1950: *Gunmen of Abilene*...Rocky Lane *(starring role)*

1949: *Powder River Rustlers*...Rocky Lane *(starring role)*

1949: *Navajo Trail Raiders*...Rocky Lane *(starring role)*

1949: *Bandit King of Texas*...Rocky Lane *(starring role)*

1949: *The Wyoming Bandit*...Rocky Lane *(starring role)*

1949: *Frontier Investigator*...Rocky Lane *(starring role)*

1949: *Death Valley Gunfighter*...Rocky Lane *(starring role)*

1949: *Sheriff of Wichita*...Sheriff 'Rocky' Lane *(starring role)*

1949: *Land of Opportunity: The American Rodeo* (Documentary short)...
    Narrator (as Allan "Rocky" Lane)

1948: *Renegades of Sonora*...Rocky Lane *(starring role)*

1948: *Sundown in Santa Fe*...Rocky Lane *(starring role)*

1948: *The Denver Kid*...Rocky Lane Posing as the Denver Kid *(starring role)*

1948: *Desperadoes of Dodge City*...Rocky Lane *(starring role)*

1948: *Marshal of Amarillo*...Marshal 'Rocky' Lane *(starring role)*

1948: *Carson City Raiders*...Rocky Lane *(starring role)*

1948: *The Bold Frontiersman*...Rocky Lane *(starring role)*

1948: *Oklahoma Badlands*...Rocky Lane *(starring role)*

1947: *Bandits of Dark Canyon*...Rocky Lane *(starring role)*

1947: *The Wild Frontier*...Rocky Lane *(starring role)*

1947: *Marshal of Cripple Creek*...Red Ryder *(starring role)*

1947: *Rustlers of Devil's Canyon*...Red Ryder *(starring role)*

1947: *Oregon Trail Scouts*...Red Ryder *(starring role)*

1947: *Homesteaders of Paradise Valley*...Red Ryder *(starring role)*

1947: *Vigilantes of Boomtown*...Red Ryder *(starring role)*

1946: *Stagecoach to Denver*...Red Ryder *(starring role)*

1946: *Out California Way*...Allan Lane *(starring role)*

1946: *Santa Fe Uprising*...Red Ryder *(starring role)*

1946: *Night Train to Memphis*...Dan Acuff

1946: *A Guy Could Change*...Michael 'Mike' Hogan

1946: *Gay Blades*...Andy Buell

1945: *Trail of Kit Carson*...Bill Harmon

1945: *Bells of Rosarita*...Allan Lane

1945: *Corpus Christi Bandits*...Captain James Christi/Corpus Christi Jim

1945: *The Topeka Terror*...Chad Stevens

1944: *Sheriff of Sundown*...Tex Jordan

1944: *Stagecoach to Monterey*...Bruce Redmond as Chick Weaver

1944: *Silver City Kid*...Jack Adams

1944: *The Tiger Woman* (a serial)...Allen Saunders

1944: *Call of the South Seas*...Kendall Gaige

1943: *The Dancing Masters*...George Worthing

1943: *Daredevils of the West* (a serial)...Duke Cameron

1943: *Air Force*...Marine (uncredited)

1942: *King of the Mounties* (a serial)...Sgt. Dave King *(starring role)*

1942: *The Yukon Patrol*...Sgt. Dave King (compiled footage) *(starring role)*

1941: *Military Training* (Short)...Lieutenant Instructor, Bayonet Drill (uncredited)

1941: *All-American Co-Ed*...Second Senior

1941: *Coffins on Wheels* (Short)...Police Lieutenant

1940: *King of the Royal Mounted*...Sergeant Dave King *(starring role)*

1940: *Grand Ole Opry*...Fred Barnes

1939: *Conspiracy*...Steve Kendall

1939: *The Spellbinder*...Steve Kendall

1939: *Panama Lady*...McTeague

1939: *They Made Her a Spy*...Huntley

1939: *Twelve Crowded Hours*...Dave Sanders

1939: *Pacific Liner*...Bilson

1938: *The Law West of Tombstone*...Danny Sanders

1938: *Fugitives for a Night*...John Nelson

1938: *Crime Ring*...Joe Ryan

1938: *Having Wonderful Time*...Mac

1938: *This Marriage Business*...Bill Bennett

1938: *Maid's Night Out*...Bill Norman

1938: *Night Spot*...Pete Cooper

1937: *The Duke Comes Back*...Duke Foster

1937: *Sing and Be Happy*...Hamilton Howe

1937: *Fifty Roads to Town*...Leroy Smedley

1937: *Big Business*...Ted Hewett

1937: *Charlie Chan at the Olympics*...Richard Masters

1937: *Step Lively, Jeeves!*...Party Guest (uncredited)

1936: *Stowaway*...Richard Hope

1936: *Laughing at Trouble*...John Campbell

1932: *One Way Passage*...Joan's Friend (uncredited)

1932: *The Crash*...Geoffrey's Associate (uncredited)

1932: *A Successful Calamity*...Polo Player (uncredited)

1932: *Crooner*...Dance Floor Heckler (uncredited)

1932: *Miss Pinkerton*...Herbert Wynn (scenes deleted)

1932: *Winner Take All*...Monty (uncredited)

1932: *Week-End Marriage*...Clerk (uncredited)

1932: *The Tenderfoot*...Actor (uncredited)

1932: *The Famous Ferguson Case*...Reporter (uncredited)
1932: *It's Tough To Be Famous*...(uncredited)...reported bit part
1932: *Heavens! My Husband!* (Short)...Jimmy Benson
1932: *Any Old Port*...love interest (potentially cut — uncredited)
1931: *Smart Money*...(uncredited and cut part)
1931: *How I Play Golf,* by Bobby Jones No. 8: "The Brassie" (Short)...
   Allan (uncredited)
1931: *Local Boy Makes Good*...Runner (uncredited)
1931: *War Mamas* (Short)...Doughboy
1931: *Expensive Women*...Party Boy (uncredited)
1931: *Honor of the Family*...Joseph
1931: *The Star Witness*...Deputy at Leeds Home (uncredited)
1931: *Night Nurse*...Intern (uncredited)
1930: *Madam Satan*...Zeppelin Majordomo (uncredited)
1930: *Love in the Rough*...Johnson
1929: *Words and Music*...(uncredited as Harry Albers)
1929: *The Forward Pass*...Ed Kirby
1929: *Detectives Wanted* or *Two Detectives Wanted* (Short)...(uncredited)
1929: *Knights Out* (Short)
1929: *Pleasure Craze* (or *Crazed*)...bit part
1929: *Nighty Nighties* (Short)...starring role (unreleased)
1929: *Not Quite Decent*...Jerry Connor
1929: *William Fox Movietone Follies of 1929*...bit part (uncredited)
1928: *Dreams of Love*...bit part (uncredited)

Television

1966: *Jungle Gold*...Allen Saunders (edited-for-TV from *The Tiger
   Woman*)

Mister Ed:
1958: Pilot, *The Wonderful World of Wilbur Pope*...Mister Ed (voice
   uncredited)
1961-1966: Complete Series...Mister Ed (voice uncredited)

Cheyenne (TV Series)
1961: "Massacre at Gunsight Pass"...Sheriff Milton

Bonanza (TV Series)
1961: "Long Hours, Short Pay"...Capt. Graves
1960: "The Blood Line"...Luke Grayson

1960: "The Badge"...Mac
1958: "Texas Cowboys"...Kin Talley

Lawman (TV Series)
1960: "The Payment"...Joe Hoyt

Colt .45 (TV Series)
1960: "Trial by Rope"...Mayor
1960: "Arizona Anderson"...Gilby

Bronco (TV Series)
1960: "Death of an Outlaw"...Sheriff Brady

Walt Disney's Wonderful World of Color (TV Series)
1960: "Texas John Slaughter: Geronimo's Revenge"...Johnny Ringo
1960: "Texas John Slaughter: Kentucky Gunslick"...Johnny Ringo

Tales of Wells Fargo (TV Series)
1958: "The Reward"...Chuck Latimer

Wagon Train (TV Series)
1958: "The Daniel Barrister Story"...Mr. Sam Miller

Alfred Hitchcock Presents (TV Series)
1958: "Lamb to the Slaughter"...Patrick Maloney

Mike Hammer (TV Series)
1959: "Husbands Are Bad Luck"...Lefty Jones

Red Ryder (TV Series)
1955: "Gun Trouble Valley"...Red Ryder

Theater

1925: *The Patsy*...bit part
1927: *If I Were King* (previously *The Patsy*)...bit part
1927: *Young Woodley*...bit part
1928: *Hit The Deck*...bit part
1928: *Murder With Music*...bit part
1930: *Life Is Like That*...bit part
1931: *Zero Hour*...unknown (potentially male lead)

Sources

Interviews/Correspondence

Ahern, S.J, Fr. Denis P. E-mail correspondence with the author. 2012.

Anderson, Chuck. E-mail correspondence with the author. 2012–2013.

Bergeron, John. E-mail correspondence with the author. 2012.

Cappello, Bill. E-mail correspondence with the author. 2013.

Cline, Mike. E-mail correspondence with the author. 2012.

Copeland, Bobby. E-mail correspondence with the author. 2012.

Costello, John. Interview with the author. 2011.

Costello, Judi. Interview with the author. 2011.

Costello, Tom. Interview, e-mail correspondence and phone conversation with the author. 2011–2013.

Curtis, Candice. E-mail correspondence with the author. 2013.

Daitch, Carolyn. E-mail correspondence and phone conversation with the author. 2012.

D'Arc, James. E-mail correspondence with the author. 2012.

DeCleene, Rob. E-mail correspondence with the author. 2012.

DeJong, Hal. E-mail correspondence with the author. 2014.

Doyle, Pat. E-mail correspondence with the author. 2012.

Ewing, Gary. Phone conversation with the author. 2012.

Francis, Joan R. E-mail correspondence with the author. 2012.

Fraser, Sally. US mail correspondence and phone interview with the author. 2013.

Freudenthal, Rick. Phone and mail correspondence with the author. 2013.

Garcia-Myers, Ph.D, Sandra. E-mail correspondence with the author. 2012.

Grace, Roger M. E-mail correspondence with the author. 2012.

Grayson-DeJong, Pat. Interview, e-mail correspondence and phone conversation with the author. 2011–2014.

Green, Babbie. E-mail correspondence with the author. 2013.

Guzman, Tony. E-mail correspondence with the author. 2012.

Hegar, Doug. E-mail correspondence with the author. 2013.

Heike, Mark G. E-mail correspondence with the author. 2012.

Hill, Kathi. E-mail correspondence with the author. 2012.

Hutchings, Linda A. E-mail correspondence with the author. 2012.

Jackson, Lori. Interview with the author. 2012.

Kemsley, Loretta. E-mail correspondence with the author. 2012–2014.

Krueger, Kristine. E-mail correspondence with the author. 2012.

Lampert, Zohra. E-mail correspondence with the author. 2012.

Langford, Wil. E-mail correspondence with the author. 2013.

Lertzman, Rick. E-mail correspondence and phone conversation with the author. 2013.

Lettieri, Louis. E-mail correspondence and phone interview with the author. 2013.

Lieberson, Dennis. E-mail correspondence with the author. 2012.

Lockett, Annette. E-mail correspondence with the author. 2011–2014.

Lodge, Stephen. E-mail correspondence with the author. 2012.

Lowery, Susan. E-mail correspondence with the author. 2012.

Luther, Claudia. E-mail correspondence with the author. 2012.

MacBride, Mac. E-mail correspondence with the author. 2013.

Maese, Carlton. E-mail correspondence with the author. 2013.

Maher, Tod. E-mail correspondence with the author. 2012.

McKay, Peter. E-mail correspondence and phone conversation with the author. 2013.

McKay, Tony. E-mail correspondence with the author. 2013.

Montoya, Vivian. E-mail correspondence with the author. 2013.

Morenberg, Steve. E-mail correspondence with the author. 2012–2013.

Nalven, Nancy. E-mail correspondence with the author. 2012.

Ng, Yvonne. E-mail correspondence with the author. 2013.

Nistal, Cyndi. E-mail correspondence with the author. 2013.

Ojea, Joeline. Phone conversation with the author. 2011.

Olson, Gordon. E-mail correspondence with the author. 2012.

Powell, Chandra. E-mail correspondence with the author. 2012.

Peterson, Bill. E-mail correspondence and phone conversation with the author. 2013.

Rothel, David. E-mail correspondence and phone conversation with the author. 2012.

Scharff, Gerri. Interview and e-mail correspondence with the author. 2011–2012.

Schmitt, Kathleen. E-mail correspondence with the author. 2012.

Schneider, Frederick. E-mail correspondence with the author. 2012–2013.

Senior, Doug. E-mail correspondence with the author. 2012.

Smith, Daniel G. E-mail correspondence with the author. 2013.

Soriano, Camille. E-mail correspondence with the author. 2012.

Stidham, Anita. E-mail correspondence and phone conversation with the author. 2013.

Summers, Carol. E-mail correspondence and phone conversation with the author. 2013.

Thornton, Chuck. E-mail correspondence and phone conversation with the author. 2012–2013.

Trueblood, Fred. E-mail correspondence with the author. 2012.

Vander Mark, Barbara. E-mail correspondence with the author. 2012.

Turner, Richard. E-mail correspondence and phone conversation with the author. 2013–2014.

Walkov, Cindy. E-mail correspondence and phone conversation with the author. 2014.

Young, Alan. Phone interview with the author. 2014.

Young, Mary Buttram. Correspondence with the author. 2013.

Zigler, Denise. E-mail correspondence with the author. 2012.

Books

Boggs, Johnny D. *Billy the Kid on Film, 1911-2012*. McFarland. 2013.

Barbour, Alan G. *Days of Thrills and Adventure*. Collier Macmillan Ltd. 1974.

Nalven, Nancy. *The Famous Mister Ed, The Unbridled Truth About America's Favorite Talking Horse*. Warner Books. 1991.

Miller, Don. *Hollywood Corral*. Popular Library. 1976.

Johnson, Dorris and Leventhal, Ellen, Selected and edited by. *The Letters of Nunnally Johnson*. Knopf. 1981.

Young, Alan with Burt, Bill. *Mister Ed and Me*. St. Martin's Press. 1994.

Mathis, Jack. *Republic Confidential, Volume 2, The Players*. Jack Mathis Advertising. 1992.

Lahue, Kalton C. *Riders of the Range, The Sagebrush Heroes of the Sound Screen*. Castle Books. 1973.

Weiss, Ed and Goodgold, Ken. *To Be Continued...A Complete Guide To Motion Picture Serials*. Crown. 1973.

Columns and Syndicated Columnists

Anonymous. "Screen Siftings"
Carroll, Harrison. "Behind the Scenes in Hollywood" and "Hollywood"
Coons, Robbin. "Hollywood Highlights"
Graham, Sheilah.
Hahn, Chester B. "This, that, and t'other...."
Harker, Milton. "In Hollywood"
Harrison, Paul. "Hollywood Closeups by Paul Harrison" and "Paul Harrison in Hollywood"
Keavy, Hubbard. "Screen Life in Hollywood"
Johnson, Erskine. "Behind the Make-Up," "In Hollywood," and "Overheard in Hollywood"
Kendall, Read."Around And About In Hollywood"
Kingsley, Grace. "Gossip"
Klingensmith, Betty. "Studios, Stars, and Stooges"
Mann, May. "Going Hollywood"
Morgan, Ken. "Hollywood Keyhole"
Neville, Lucie. "Hollywood"
Nikkel, Harold.
Parsons, Louella O. "Snapshots of Hollywood Collected at Random" and "Hollywood"
Sampas, Charles G. "Hollywood"
Scott, Vernon.
Sutherland, Henry.
Vernon, Terry. "Tele-vues"
Winchell, Walter. "Hollywood Heartbeat"
Woodbury, Mitch. "Mitch Woodbury Reports"

Magazines

All Movie Guide
Film Daily
Indianapolis Star Magazine
Motion Picture Almanac
Motion Picture Herald
Motion Picture Magazine
Picture Play

Newspapers

Abilene Morning Reporter News [TX]
Acton Concord Enterprise [MA]
Alton Evening Telegraph [IL]
Altoona Mirror [PA]
Annapolis Capitol [MD]
Associated Press [AP]
Augusta Chronicle [GA]
Bakersfield Californian [CA]
Big Spring Daily Herald [TX]
The Blair Press [WI]
Bradford Era [PA]
Brownsville Herald [TX]
Burlington Daily Times News [NC]
The Calgary Herald [Canada]
Carbondale Free Press [IL]
Carroll Daily Herald [IA]
The Charleroi Mail [PA]
Charleston Gazette [WV]
The Chicago Tribune [IL]
Christian Science Monitor
Clearfield Progress [PA]
Coshocton Tribune [OH]

Connellsville Daily Courier [PA]
Corpus Christi Caller Times [TX]
Decatur Herald [IN]
The Dothan Eagle [AL]
Edwardsville Intelligencer [IL]
Emporia Gazette [KS]
Estherville Enterprise [IA]
Evening Independent [OH]
Evening Post [New Zealand]
Evening State Journal [NE]
Hagerstown Daily Mail [MD]
Hamilton Daily News [OH]
Hammond Times [IN]
Hattiesburg American [MS]
Havre Daily News [MT]
The Hutchinson News [KS]
Iowa City Press Citizen [IA]
Joplin Globe [MO]
Kentucky New Era [KY]
Kingsport Times [TN]
Kokomo Daily Tribune [IN]
La Crosse Tribune and Leader Press [WI]
Laredo Times [TX]
Lethbridge Herald [Canada]
Lima News [OH]
Lincoln Star [NE]
Logansport Pharos Tribune [IN]
Long Beach Independent [CA]
Los Angeles Times [CA]
Lowell Sun [MA]
Ludington Daily News [MI]
Manitowoc Herald Times [WI]
Miami Herald [FL]
Middlebury Independent [IN]
Milwaukee Sentinel [WI]
Monessen Daily Independent [PA]
Montana Standard [MO]
Nashua Telegraph [NH]
Nevada State Journal [NV]

New York Times [NY]
Oakland Tribune [CA]
Ogden Standard Examiner [UT]
Panama City News Herald [FL]
The Piqua Daily Call [OH]
The Pittsburgh Press [PA]
Port Arthur News [TX]
Portsmouth Herald [NH]
Portsmouth Times [OH]
Provo Daily Herald [UT]
Reno Evening Gazette [NV]
Salt Lake Tribune [UT]
San Antonio Express [TX]
San Antonio Light [TX]
San Mateo Times [CA]
San Saba News & Star [TX]
Sandusky Register [OH]
St. Petersburg Times [FL]
South Bend Weekly Tribune [IN]
Syracuse Herald Journal [NY]
The Telegraph Herald [IA]
The Times Recorder [OH]
Tipton Tribune [IN]
Titusville Herald [PA]
Toledo Blade [OH]
Traverse City Record Eagle [MI]
Tuscaloosa News [AL]
Uniontown Evening Standard [PA]
Uniontown Morning Herald [PA]
Universal Service
Valley Morning Star [TX]
Van Nuys News [CA]
Wabash Daily Plain Dealer [IN]
Waterloo Daily Courier [IA]
Winnipeg Free Press [Manitoba Canada]
Youngstown Vindicator [OH]
Yuma Daily Sun [AZ]
Zanesville Signal [OH]

News Services

International News Service [INS]
King Features Syndicate.
United Press [UP]
United Press International [UPI]

Organizations/Businesses

The Academy of Motion Picture Arts and Sciences (including National Film Information Service of The Margaret Herrick Library and The Margaret Herrick Library).

Arcadia Public Library, California.

Brigham Young University's Arts & Communications Archives.

California Thoroughbred Breeders Association.

Christ Hospital, Cincinnati, Ohio.

Horse Racing Nation.

Inglewood Park Cemetery.

Los Angeles, CA City Directory (multiple years)

Los Angeles Public Libraries Special Collections

Mack Sennett Studios.

Mishawaka Public Library, Heritage Center; Indiana.

RKO Studios.

The Sandpipers Organization.

San Fernando Valley Issues Digital Library

St. Mary's Catholic Church, Grand Rapids, Michigan.

St. Xavier High School, Cincinnati, Ohio.

Texas Christian University.

Thoroughbred Racing Protective Bureau (TRPB).

UCLA.

USC Cinematic Arts Library.

United States Government Census

Westchester, NY County government.

Websites

http://www.ancestry.com

http://www.baseball-almanac.com

http://www.bonanza.com/booths/Yesterdayswhisper

http://www.boomerhead.com

http://www.b-westerns.com

http://digital-library.csun.edu

http://www.findagrave.com

http://www.glamourgirlsofthesilverscreen.com

http://ibdb.com

http://www.imdb.com

http://www.members.tripod.com/~horsefame/puppet.htm

http://www.mphpl.org

http://mygrandrapids.info

http://www.profootballarchives.com

http://www.redlandsdailyfacts.com

http://www.rrauction.com

http://www.southbendtribune.com

http://www.thestate.com

http://usmarriagelaws.com/search/united_states/divorce_laws/divorce_and_remarriage/index.shtml

http://www.visitsouthbend.com

About The Author

LINDA ALEXANDER started writing about well-known movie and TV stars in the 1970s. Since the early '80s, she has written books and for magazines, newspapers, and websites. Credits include *Soap Opera Update, Spotlight, Baton Rouge Advocate, Washington Times*, and she has appeared on *The Oprah Show, Sally Jesse Raphael*, and various cable shows. Known as the "Spirit Biographer" and sometimes called a social archaeologist, she has seven published books — five biographies and two dark, sexy suspense novels — and characters live large in her head 24/7, forever talking to her. She *always* talks back, and conversations are *always* entertaining and enlightening. She has worked as an adjunct faculty member at a local community college, teaching a popular course, "Getting Into Character: How To Develop Your People."

Linda has made her biggest mark writing about classic Hollywood stars. In 2008, a small publishing house brought out her book about Golden Era movie star, Robert Taylor, *Reluctant Witness: Robert Taylor, Hollywood, & Communism*. In 2011, BearManor Media published *A Maverick Life: The Jack Kelly Story*. She plans to republish *Reluctant Witness: Robert Taylor, Hollywood, & Communism* with BearManor Media in the near future. Her newest Hollywood biography is *I Am Mister Ed...Allan "Rocky" Lane Revealed*, the exhaustive biography of the well-established "B" movie cowboy actor with nearly forty years of credits in the entertainment industry. Lane ended his career as the voice of TV's popular talking horse, *Mister Ed.*

Index

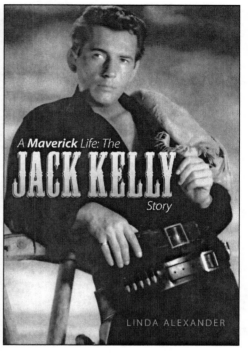
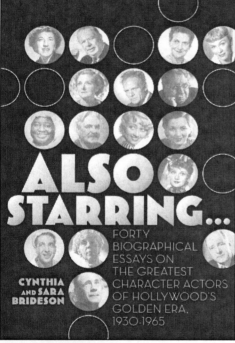
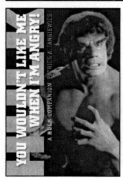
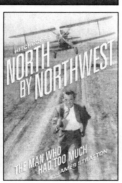

9/15 4

CPSIA information can be obtained at www.ICGtesting.com
Printed in the USA
LVOW07s2052190914

404932LV00020BA/717/P